Praise for *Always on Ca*

"Caring, kind, and funny, the indomitable Marion McKinnon Crook returns with a heartfelt memoir, reminding us that we all need comfort, understanding, and the courage to rip the bandaids off old fears and prejudices."

—KATHRYN WILLCOCK, author of *Up the Coast: One Family's Wild Life in the Forests of British Columbia*

"What do mischievous runaway piglets have to do with nursing? Read Marion Crook's brilliant memoir on life as a community nurse, wife, mother, and rancher to find out. With her fascinating stories and poetic descriptions of the BC Interior's landscape and seasons are meaningful glimpses into a wholesome, yet relevant past."

—CATHALYNN LABONTÉ-SMITH, author of *Rescue Me: Behind the Scenes of Search and Rescue*

"A thoughtful and engaging tribute to the intrepid women who delivered rural healthcare. The demanding geography and bureaucracy, over-stuffed schedules and under-stuffed pay packets, as well as the racism, misogyny and intolerance they faced is conveyed with humour and empathy. Thank goodness for public health nurses like Marion McKinnon Crook."

—JENNIFER L. BUTLER, author of *Boom & Bust: The Resilient Women of Historic Telegraph Cove*

"*Always on Call* chronicles the heartwarming, extraordinary care of rural home care nurses while balancing the demands of raising families, managing rural ranches, and being part of their community. Marion McKinnon Crook draws the reader into her world: bumping down isolated roads to visit young mothers, chasing down infectious disease contacts where everyone knows everyone's business, finding ways to encourage a recluse man to shower, and managing two bickering elderly women with dementia in their own apartment—giving insight into this important aspect of healthcare."

—HEATHER PATTERSON MD, emergency physician, award-winning photographer, and author of *Shadows and Light: A Physician's Lens on COVID*

"Clear, compelling prose shines with compassion and intelligence that inform the author's life as a young mother and public health nurse. Set in a beautiful and challenging part of rural British Columbia, *Always on Call* reads like a thoughtful, honest conversation with a trusted friend whose rich experiences educate, amuse, and inspire."

—LESLIE A. DAVIDSON, author of *Dancing in Small Spaces: One Couple's Journey with Parkinson's Disease and Lewy Body Dementia*

"Always, indeed! Nursing adventures at their best, stories of fierce independence, bravery, skill, and dedication. This book will make you wish you were a nurse or, if you are one, grateful for what we are able to offer individuals and communities."

—TILDA SHALOF, author of *A Nurse's Story: Life, Death, and In Between in an Intensive Care Unit*

"As a nurse whose career was mainly in an enormous tertiary hospital in a major city, this book is a window into an unfamiliar field of nursing. Marion McKinnon Crook's stories are an inspiring and fascinating look into a community nurse's professional and personal life in a remote Canadian community. For anyone who is interested in how health care was delivered in small northern communities, this is a great read."

—CAROL YOUNGSON, retired nurse and author of *Take your Baby and Run: How Nurses Blew the Whistle on Canada's Biggest Cardiac Disaster*

ALWAYS
ON CALL

MARION McKINNON CROOK

ALWAYS ON CALL

ADVENTURES IN NURSING, RANCHING, AND RURAL LIFE

Heritage House Publishing Company Ltd.
heritagehouse.ca

Cataloguing information available from Library and Archives Canada
978-1-77203-469-1 (paperback)
978-1-77203-470-7 (e-book)

Edited by Renée Layberry
Proofread by Nandini Thaker
Cover design by Jacqui Thomas
Interior design and typesetting by Rafael Chimicatti
Cover images by Mumemories/iStockphoto (*background*) and Dia Metodieva/
    BalkanHangar (*bag*)

The interior of this book was produced on 100% post-consumer recycled paper,
processed chlorine free, and printed with vegetable-based inks.

Heritage House gratefully acknowledges that the land on which
we live and work is within the traditional territories of the Lkwungen
(Esquimalt and Songhees), Malahat, Pacheedaht, Scia'new, T'Sou-ke, and
W̱SÁNEĆ (Pauquachin, Tsartlip, Tsawout, Tseycum) Peoples.

We acknowledge the financial support of the Government of Canada through
the Canada Book Fund (CBF) and the Canada Council for the Arts, and the
Province of British Columbia through the British Columbia Arts Council and
the Book Publishing Tax Credit.

28 27 26 25 24   1 2 3 4 5

Printed in Canada

To Janice, Glen, and the memory of David,
who were my joyous teachers,
and to the many people of the Cariboo
who remember those days of energy and productivity
—and who write to me and share their memories.

CONTENTS

AUTHOR'S
NOTE

I CAME TO THE CARIBOO in 1963 with a Bachelor of Science in Nursing from Seattle University. Although a Canadian from the Fraser Valley, I chose Seattle U for its comprehensive and rigorous education, which they emphasized would only give me a good *start* to nursing. My teachers expected me to keep learning. I left the Cariboo in 1986, obtained a master's degree in liberal arts from Simon Fraser University and then a PhD in Education from UBC. I taught nursing at Kwantlen Polytechnic University in the Fraser Valley, so I ended my career where I began. Retired now from nursing, I live and write in Gibsons, BC, on the beautiful Sunshine Coast.

This story is an account of my life in the Cariboo between 1975 and 1976. As I did in my last book, I changed the names of many of the characters, sometimes putting two characters into one, and often trying to make them totally unrecognizable. Occasionally, just occasionally, I moved events from one year to another—the events did happen, but not in that year. For example, the flight to Pan Phillips's ranch took place some years before, and the medical health officer who appears in the book worked there in a different year. Occasionally, I put two incidents together that didn't originally happen together. Because I was a nurse in the community, I dealt with people whose problems included disease, mental illness, and suicide. I also met people who showed me kindness, love, and humour.

The names we used in those days reflected the times, such as *fireman* instead of *firefighter.*

The terminology around Indigenous Peoples in this book is as it was in the 1970s. We do not use the same words today. I applaud the changes in the language, which, presently, is much more respectful than it was in the past. The term "native" could be respectful in the seventies, as it implied that the person was connected to the land and Indigenous, or it could be used derogatorily. "Indian" was a misnomer and had pejorative connotations in those days, but it was used officially and extensively. The language was part of the prejudice of those times. Now we use "Indigenous" to try to eliminate as much culturally oppressive language as possible. When I worked in the Cariboo, I used the most respectful language I knew and, for this text, have not editorialized or inputted modern terms.

Some place names have changed since the seventies. Alkali Lake Reserve is now Esk'etemc; Sugar Cane is now T'exelc. I used the names commonly used at the time, but I recognize that they have changed.

I raised a son who was a member of the Gitxsan Nation and experienced prejudice as I stood behind him. I have done what I could to fight it. I had naively thought that prejudice would disappear as he got older and the general public became more educated, but that didn't happen to the extent it should have. Racism is still strong, offensive, and debilitating. There are no more residential schools to abuse and brainwash children; Indigenous people are better educated and more able to use the law to their advantage. Governments are now aware that they must negotiate with Indigenous Peoples for equity and peace in the country, but combatting prejudice is an excruciatingly slow process.

The Cariboo encompasses Indigenous and non-Indigenous people who have a spirit of independence and hard work. Many still feel that the rest of the world is far away and that those who live in the Cariboo must look after themselves and one another. I loved living and working there.

History is written through the understanding of the writer and so contains the knowledge and limits of that writer. I relay here my experiences as I remember them, entirely from my point of view. I hope you enjoy this glimpse into those days.

CHAPTER ONE

LIVING IN
THE CARIBOO

I T WAS A BEAUTIFUL CARIBOO DAY. Cold, of course, but with none of the wind, hail, or snow that March could bring. The window in the clinic room looked over the town of Williams Lake and beyond it to the hills covered in fir trees standing in snow. From this distance, the snow was bright white, reflecting the sunshine. I imagined it radiating a vibrant energy into the air. The stark, white smoke from the cabins across the ravine at the lower end of town rose straight into the cobalt blue sky. I absorbed the beauty of the scene, but I couldn't get outside to enjoy it. I was taking the Friday afternoon well-baby clinic for Marlene, the regularly scheduled nurse, who was off work today. I had interviewed eight mothers and immunized eight infants, all of whom had cried. Three-year-old Marco was my last patient of the day.

"You'll feel a tiny pinch," I told him, "if you feel it at all."

He nodded solemnly and waited.

"Take a deep breath now." I demonstrated. "And count to five. Can you do that?"

He nodded again and took in the breath. "One, two . . ."

I used the syringe like a dart and had that immunization completed in seconds.

Marco looked at me and back at his arm. "It didn't hurt."

It didn't hurt because he was expecting a pinch and was not surprised. "It doesn't usually, but it does sometimes. Would you like me to draw a cat on your arm?"

He nodded and watched as I dipped a cotton swab into the copper-coloured betadine, an iodine substitute, and drew a cat at the site of the injection.

Marco smiled.

I returned the smile and turned to his father, who had brought Marco to the clinic.

"He's good now until kindergarten."

"Thanks, Nurse. That was better than we thought, eh, Marco?"

I was glad, as injections didn't always go that well. I saw the necessity of immunizing children, but I wished there was a less painful way to do it. Marco had been still and relaxed, and I'd been quick. It's a different story when the child is squirming, tense, and vocal—and I can't always be quick.

"Anything else?" I asked Mr. Biagi.

"Well, yes." He spoke over Marco's head. "We're a little worried about his . . ." He indicated height by holding his hand above Marco.

Marco *was* small for is age. "Marco, let me check your height and weight. Just step on the scale here."

An upright scale stood against the wall in the clinic room with the height scale on the vertical column. Marco hopped onto it, sending the weight indicator swinging. He grinned.

"Just hold still for a moment, my man." He did. I recorded the height and weight on Marco's chart and checked them against the bell curve for his age. He was in the bottom two percent.

I asked about Marco's diet and activity. They seemed normal.

"I don't have any idea, Mr. Biagi, but you can come and check it out here every six months or so. Also, please talk to your doctor." We were both choosing our words carefully so Marco didn't think he was sick. If there was a problem after a doctor investigated, then his parents could talk to him.

I stood to indicate the end of the interview. Mr. Biagi stood. His head came up to my nose. I looked at Marco and back to Mr. Biagi. When he'd been sitting, I hadn't noticed how short he was. Here was the answer to the problem. "Uh . . . we might be looking at heredity here," I said. *Obviously,* we were looking at heredity. Why wouldn't such a short man expect a short son?

"I'm afraid of that. What about growth hormones?"

"You could talk to the doctor, but those are usually given to treat an unusual condition, not for normal growth."

"It's not fair for him." He shook his head. Marco wrapped his arm around his dad's knee. Mr. Biagi put his hand on Marco's head and patted him.

I suppose Mr. Biagi was trying find a way to give his son all the advantages he could. Height *was* an advantage.

"Well, Napoleon was short," I said. That wasn't a helpful comment, but there wasn't much to be done to change heredity. Doctors wouldn't use growth hormones—which came with side effects—on a normal, healthy boy just to combat the prejudices of the culture. Who knew if, by the time Marco grew up, society might prefer short people.

"Can you think about instilling confidence and a sense of being in charge of his own life?" I asked.

"That's what my wife says."

"She's a wise woman."

"So she is. I should listen to her. Let's go, Marco."

"Ice cream?" Marco asked.

"You bet." He turned to me "I promised."

I smiled—they were charming together—and escorted them to the door as they were my last patients for the day. Well-baby clinics (officially called Child Health Conferences) drained my energy. I was tired and it was time to go home. It was March, and this far north, the sky was starting to darken. The forecast called for snow flurries and a further dip in temperature. It might be the weather—hot in the summer, bitterly cold in the winter—that made those of us who lived here feel like we were constantly engaging with an annoying, fierce, and sometimes dangerous Mother Nature.

In spite of that, I loved the Cariboo with its sparkling, bright daylight and cold nights. Twelve and a half years ago, when I'd first arrived as a newly graduated nurse, I found the vastness of the country overwhelming. It was still overwhelming at times—miles of grasslands in one direction and miles of conifers in the other—but I was more accustomed to it now and embraced it as *my* country, with its beauty and extreme weather challenges.

It was different country from the mild Fraser Valley where I had grown up. From there, I'd moved and taken my nursing degree at Seattle University, where it was even milder and wetter, before striking out on my adventure to the Cariboo. I'd planned to move north as far as the Arctic, but I had fallen in love with the country and the people and stayed in the Cariboo. I still felt intrepid, shovelling snow to get my car moving and packing chains, food, and a candle as I drove into remote areas. But I wasn't special; everyone here had to battle the elements. Perhaps that's why the people seemed a hardy breed—independent, eccentric, and, occasionally, challenging and confrontational. We had to confront wild weather.

I started work as a public health nurse at the Cariboo Health Unit when I was twenty-one, full of ambition and eager to experience life in this magnificent country. I was now thirty-four and still a public health nurse, still ambitious and enthusiastic about the people and the way of life here. Married with three children—ages ten, eight, and three—I was no longer encouraging the mad pursuit of the local bachelors.

"You're finally settling down," my mother had said.

I wouldn't count on it, Mom. I was still full of plans and ideas, shepherding my children, jousting and dancing with my husband, Carl, and reacting to the unpredictable patients on my case load. I loved the adventure of it all. I refused to think of my life as "settling down," although my mother had a point. I wasn't free to leave to work in the Arctic, but family life still allowed for adventure. Carl and I'd had a small wedding eleven years earlier here in Williams Lake, in the middle of a snowstorm. Carl's parents had helped us, and my cousin had made it up from the coast. Our friends gathered in spite of the weather, which cleared after the ceremony, and all managed to get home safely. Even weddings were complicated by weather, as was my nursing practice.

The country was a vast expanse of wilderness with pockets of villages and towns, remote ranches, and logging camps. The ranching, lumber, and mining industries attracted more and more workers and their families. With the increased number of families came the increased need for more public health nurses.

I appreciated the additional nurses. Marlene and Cathy joined the health unit as recent university graduates, so I was no longer the only one with a degree. Sophie, my intrepid, long-time colleague in the health unit, gave me wise advice and hilarious comments on life. Sylvia joined our staff as a public health nurse after years of working in the hospital. We exchanged information, helped, and supported each other. It was a tight nursing community.

My last supervisor, the redoubtable Rita, had retired. Her replacement was Angela Buckley, an experienced public health nurse from Ontario. She was slim and short, with dark curly hair and a businesslike attitude. She understood statistics, scheduling, government rules, and the myriad forms that accompanied those rules. I was happy someone else dealt with those irritating details, like the pesky time-management surveys government administrators found necessary. She also worked with the medical health officer, Dr. Paul Parker, who was new to the health unit and no doubt needed her guidance. She took on all administrative duties as hers alone and allowed us to manage our district as we saw fit. I missed Rita, but I could work with Angela.

My public health district was the same as it had been when I first started: Williams Lake, 150 Mile House, Horsefly, Likely, and south down the highway to Lac la Hache. It encompassed about 3,600 square miles—as big as a small country like Puerto Rico. A huge, wild country. Overpowering, if I thought about it for long. To the east of Williams Lake, it was heavily forested. Around the town and south to Lac la Hache, the country was rolling grasslands with forested hills and wide valleys. To the west, where I went only occasionally, lay the vast Chilcotin Plateau.

Although I had the same district east to the Cariboo Mountains as I'd had before, I no longer had to schedule overnight trips. I didn't want to be away from home now that I had three children who relied on me. That was a hard decision as I missed those trips into the heart of the logging country and the immersion into the small communities that came with the overnight stay. I did day trips now and didn't visit as often as I used to. More people had vehicles and were able to come to town, so my visits weren't as necessary. The roads weren't much better, though, and I still had to dodge logging trucks, wandering cattle, and the occasional moose.

Angela endeared herself to me the first day I was back to work, after I'd been home for a few years looking after my babies, by telling me I would not be asked to give immunizations at the weekly Williams Lake Friday clinic. I could have kissed her but didn't. Giving shots for four hours to crying babies required strong nerves and discipline. I was happy to avoid it—most of the time. I still had to conduct my own clinics out of town and fill in occasionally if someone was off sick.

"You are working point-six of a full load: Monday, Tuesday, Thursday, and Friday from nine to three. Correct?"

"Yes." That was what I wanted. I could be home when the bus dropped off my older children, Janice and Glen, and it would give me one day a week exclusively with little David, who was only eighteen months at that time. He needed my focused attention, and I needed to enjoy him without the distraction of the older children.

"I prefer you don't work the Friday clinic, and instead spend that time nursing in your district and supervising the nurses in the home care program. We have five nurses working in that program now."

"NICE TO HAVE you back," Sally, the senior home care nurse, had said when I returned to work. "We won't have to hide so much now."

I wondered what she'd been doing but I didn't ask. Sally was the oldest nurse in the health unit and had nursed in Williams Lake for twenty years. She was a knowledgeable, decisive nurse who was often unorthodox. She had creative ideas about how to care for patients, and I knew she was going to keep me alert. Supervising the home care nurses would be lively.

CHAPTER TWO

HELPING BABIES, HUMAN AND ANIMAL

WHEN WE WERE first married eleven years ago, Carl had built me a new house. He'd lived in a small cabin, but we chose to build on a site on the ranch where we had a view down the valley. With the help of his crew, he constructed a house with five bedrooms and a fabulous kitchen. I designed that kitchen and loved it. It had a huge pantry, a central island, a wall oven, and a refrigerator with shelves that rolled out for easy cleaning and a lower freezer. The burnt-orange Formica counters created a feeling of warmth, and the house, although big, felt cozy. We filled the house with furniture, paintings, musical instruments, and three children: Janice by the usual biological method and Glen and David by adoption and the generosity of their birth mothers. My mother's comment that three children were six times the work of one turned out to be true. Three were enough.

Carl had changed his life. He'd wanted a new challenge and, by selling off a few plots on our ranch, we financed three years of study for him to get his law degree at the University of British Columbia in Vancouver. I'd thought about getting my master's degree at the same time, but the children were small then and needed my attention. I managed one advanced English course and a short refresher course in nursing. Motherhood complicated my ambitions. We came home to the ranch for four months in the summers between his law school classes and moved back permanently two years ago.

Living on the university campus had been active and busy with growing children and city living, so different from life in the Cariboo. On our return, Carl cut back on the ranch work, and we now kept only eighty head of cattle and sold the calves at the end of the summer. I loved my family, but I had been almost desperate to get back to nursing. I'd been back at the job almost two years and I was happy. The children were older and, in some ways, easier to work around. Janice was now ten, Glen eight, and David three.

I wanted my master's degree but I couldn't see any way of accomplishing that. I was busy with ranch life, parenting, helping the kids with their 4-H projects, and, of course, cooking for all. Getting my master's degree would mean moving to the coast and leaving all this for months at a time. It wasn't an option. Even if I couldn't get my master's degree, I was determined to stay nursing. I needed to work. I loved the challenges, the social contacts, and the constant learning the job provided.

One evening, I sat in an easy chair in the living room, catching up on some reading. It was quiet; everyone was somewhere else. David was in his room playing with his toys, Glen was in his room building a model of a Second World War Spitfire airplane, Carl was in the barn fixing something—there was always something to repair—and Janice was in the pigpen talking to her pig. I had a new mystery, Agatha Christie's *Curtain,* the last book she wrote before she died earlier that year, and I was anxious to read it. My dream was to have enough time to read a complete book in one sitting, but ranch life seldom allowed for that.

"Mom. Mom! Cleo's in trouble. You have to come." My ten-year-old daughter Janice was insistent. Cleo was her five-hundred-pound sow, who was farrowing. I was out of my depth with veterinary medicine. Yes, I was a competent labour coach for women. Obstetrics for pigs, though? Not so much. I hoped Cleo wasn't going to have a crisis. I should have been used to it. Family life lurched from one drama to another.

"What's happening?"

"She has nine piglets. She did that really well, but she's straining and it's been a long time since she had the last one. I think it's stuck."

I glanced at Carl. Sows had a long uterus. A piglet might have to travel four to six feet to successfully deliver. I'd read up on it, determined to be of some help to my daughter, but I didn't have any practice pulling piglets.

"One of us might have to reach into that pig and help ease the birth," I told him. "You have the longest arms."

"You're the nurse," he said, "and *so* good at the bedside." He grinned.

I snorted. Such calculated flattery was not convincing. "I hope I don't kill one," I mumbled. I grabbed some cream and rubbed it into my hands, trying to combat the dry air. My hands chapped and the kids sometimes had cracks on the skin of their knuckles. It was a constant battle to keep our skin protected.

I shrugged into my quilted jacket and followed Janice out to the pigpen, a small hut Carl had built to accommodate Cleo. It gave her some protection from the cold and snow. The March winds kept the temperature just above freezing, but it could drop suddenly to a frosty ten below. It was dark by eight o'clock and the wind drove the chill into your bones.

I hurried after Janice as she flew along the boardwalk to the pigpen. She was tall for her age, slim and quick in her movements. I increased my pace.

"Is the heat lamp working?" I asked.

"It's working," she called back to me.

The pen wasn't wired for electricity but Janice had run an extension cord from the barn, which *was* wired, to the pigpen. Janice knew when Cleo was due to farrow—three months, three weeks and three days after service by the boar. She kept faithful records both because she liked order and predictability and because she was a member of the Soda Creek 4-H Club, part of an international club that fostered resilience in children, care of animals, entrepreneurial spirit, and accurate records. Janice took responsibility for her pig. She'd made the pen comfortable with fresh straw, plenty of water, and a full trough of pig pellets. Cleo had started farrowing precisely on time and Janice had been attending her for hours.

Cleo wasn't just a business proposition for Janice, although she did plan to sell the piglets when they reached about twenty pounds. Cleo's most important function was as Janice's best friend. If Janice had an argument with me or her brother, she'd run out to Cleo and tell her all about it. I assumed Cleo always took her side. She fed Cleo before she left for school every morning and when she came home in the afternoon. She groomed her, cleaned her feet and her ears, and kept the pen clean. I worried about Janice a little because pigs can be ferocious. I saw one of the chickens flutter into Cleo's pen last fall. In seconds, all that was left of the chicken was two yellow feet. I'd stared at those feet, then at Cleo. Rapacious. Voracious. An efficient predator. I was cautious around her.

"Cleo'd never hurt me, Mom," Janice insisted, and so far, she hadn't. She seemed tolerant of the rest of the family as well.

Janice had faithfully stayed with Cleo all afternoon. I'd peeked into the pen occasionally and had found Janice reading stories to the sow. I wondered what Cleo made of *The Lion, the Witch and the Wardrobe*. Carl thought everything was proceeding normally and Cleo would birth the piglets without help.

Whether Cleo needed help or didn't need it, Janice wanted me with her.

Janice had arranged the heat lamp about three feet away from the piglets to keep them warm. The sow was stretched out on her straw bed.

"She made a nest," Janice said.

"I see that." All the straw in the pen was gathered around Cleo. The piglets were squirming and jostling each other searching for Cleo's teats. They were definitely cute. Janice picked up one who was at the outside of the group.

"She had this one while I went to get you, Mom. Good girl, Cleo." She looked at me. "I guess she didn't need any help. Sorry."

"It's okay."

"Good girl, Cleo," I echoed. I was relieved she had managed without me.

"Will you stay?" Janice asked.

"Yes, I'll stay," I reassured her.

"I'll call this one Alvin," Jan said, studying the little pig. "He might be a bit slow." She gently placed the piglet beside Cleo and guided his mouth to the teat. "I'm going to have to watch out for him."

She would. She sat down by Cleo's head, leaned over her and started to talk to her. "Mom's here and she's going to check you. Okay?"

I took that as a directive to me as well as reassurance for Cleo. Obediently, I went to the lower end.

"I don't see a head, Jan. She's not going to deliver right now."

"I know, but she has more."

"Maybe."

We sat in the rosy glow from the heat lamp, waiting on Cleo. It was warmer here than outside, almost cozy. I watched my daughter, her thick, light brown hair with its slight curl that framed her face. I envied her that curl and the thickness. We both had blue eyes and one thumb wider than the other, but Janice was almost terrifyingly smart. She was logical and had firm ideas about what she needed. I learned it was my job to help clear the paths she chose, not direct her. That wasn't how I'd expected to parent, but it suited us.

She was murmuring words to Cleo, patting the sow's face and communicating comfort. Cleo snuffed, snorted, and panted.

We waited. Time went on.

Finally, I said, "That may be it."

"No," Jan said. "She's going to deliver the next one."

"How do you know?"

"She told me."

I stared at Jan then at Cleo's vulva. There was a head. "Yes," I said. "Here it comes."

"There's another one after this. Then, that's all."

I nodded and waited, caught the piglet as it slid out and handed it to Jan. I paid attention and caught the second. "Here it is. Well done, Cleo."

Janice patted her pig. "She's a good girl. A really good girl."

"Are there any more?" I realized I was asking Janice to ask Cleo.

Janice murmured something to Cleo and I heard the pig grunt.

"No, that's it. She had twelve. Perfect."

How could she interpret that grunt with such confidence? But somehow, they were both convincing.

"School tomorrow," I said as I stood and brushed the straw from my jeans. "Don't stay here too late."

"I want to make sure every piglet is drinking. They all need colostrum." Janice had read the books the 4-H club provided. She knew more about pigs than I did. She would stay until she was satisfied and, no doubt, be up early to check Cleo in the morning.

"I'll wait until the afterbirth comes," she told me.

"Good idea." I hoped it would come naturally. I didn't want to fish around inside Cleo trying to pull it out. "Let me know if there's any trouble."

There wasn't, and Jan came into the house a half-hour later.

I liked the farm animals, although pigs were Janice's choice, not mine. Flip, our stocky pony, was a perfect ride for the kids, even-tempered and willing. The hens were less engaging, and Sylvester the rooster had a mean personality. I liked sheep and had a flock of twenty-six ewes plus Archie, the ram. They challenged me, though; in spite of my experience looking after my dad's small flock when I was a teenager, I couldn't manage to keep weight on my ewes. The grass must have had a much lower level of protein in the Cariboo than it did at the coast. I resorted to buying alfalfa hay from a neighbouring rancher that winter, which meant, at the high cost of alfalfa, my sheep were indulged pets rather than a commercial success. I wasn't a particularly competent farmer.

Marriage made me happy. There was much that was joyous and much that required work. As Sophie told me once, "Sex is simple, but love is more complicated." I found that loving someone required time and attention, compromise and hours of talking. It didn't always go smoothly, but, for the most part, it worked. But when I had to deal with a husband, children, my career, and ranch life, there were moments when I felt that some of the moving parts of my carefully balanced life were decidedly clunky.

BEFORE BREAKFAST, Janice was up and out to check on Cleo.

"Can I see the piglets?" Glen asked her. Talking didn't slow his rapid ingestion of cornflakes.

"You can, but you have to be quiet." That was a big request as Glen was rarely quiet.

He thought it over. "I can do that."

We all stayed at the door of the pigpen while Janice entered. The sun streamed in and we could see the pack of piglets squirming at Cleo's side. Janice picked up one and brought it to the door. Cleo grunted. Janice said. "I'll bring her back, Cleo."

Cleo flopped her head back and grunted again. I swear she understood.

"It's cool," Glen said.

Janice squatted down and held it out to David. His eyes widened. "Can I pet it?"

"Yes." Janice guided his hand. "But you can't go into the pigpen and pick them up if I'm not there. Cleo will bite you."

Cleo could not only bite him—she could kill him.

"That's important," I said.

David looked at me solemnly. "Okay."

"That means you too," I said to Glen.

He promised, and he and Janice dashed off to catch the school bus. Carl went to his law office and I put Ben, Glen's dog, a golden cocker spaniel, back in the house, where he and Missy, our calico cat, would reign until I got home. I fed the sheep, loaded David into the Suburban, and drove to the sitter who lived in the centre of Williams Lake, only two blocks from the health unit. The road was clear. We hadn't had any serious snow for weeks, just sudden flurries then sun. The land was brown and grey with snow in the meadows and open areas waiting for the warmth of spring. Willows poked new shoots through the snow drifts. Ah, a sign of spring! Even though their roots and lower stems were in freezing snow, the top boughs were giving new life. I stopped the vehicle and dashed to the side of the road. One of the joys of the Cariboo was very little traffic. I broke off several branches and returned quickly.

"Look, David. Pussy willows. They're soft."

He reached over and petted the fuzzy buds. "Are they kitties?" He stared at me, puzzled.

"Kittens? Oh. Pussy willows. No, they are just called that because they are as soft as a kitten."

He stared at the pussy willows. "They are flowers. Not kitties." He looked at me with some disapproval.

I couldn't argue with that. "You're right."

I took David to Edith's house, where she looked after him while I worked. She was a retired registered nurse who had raised four talented and admirable children. That didn't prevent me from dissolving in tears the first time I left David with her.

"He looked at me with those huge brown eyes," I'd told Sophie when I walked into the health unit that day. "I feel like a monster for leaving him. And I'm going to miss him," I'd almost wailed.

Sophie had looked at me for a moment, then pronounced, "Be strong. It's worth it." It sounded like a command. Since she had two school-aged kids, I listened to her and didn't hand in my resignation. Work was a distraction and I managed to ignore my feelings. It got easier to take him to Edith's as he was obviously happy there.

Today, my morning at the health unit was not going according to my plan.

"Can you adjust your day to take someone out to a meeting at Alkali?" Angela stood at the door of my office with some papers in her hand.

I gestured toward a chair. She sat and put the papers on my desk. "Can you?"

I glanced at my diary. I had two baby visits in the afternoon.

"What time?"

"Noon."

"I'll see if I can shift the first baby visit to this morning."

Angela waited while I called Mrs. Dickson. She was agreeable to my visiting at ten o'clock. She sounded upset, though, so perhaps she wasn't happy with this change. I'd find out when I got there.

"What's the meeting about?" I asked Angela when I hung up the phone. "Do I need to prepare for it?"

"No. You just have to drive this Ms. Saunders out to a meeting with the Band. She wants to present a smoking prevention program she hopes they'll adopt for their grade five classes."

"Why didn't they ask us to present the program?" We were actively doing that in our schools.

"Alkali is a federal reserve," she reminded me.

I knew that, but I also knew the Band was good at juggling bureaucracy to their advantage—at least that's what I'd heard. They understood the politics of health care and applied for programs and support when they needed it. They had lobbied for their own school, which they, and not a religious sect, controlled—and got it. I shouldn't have been surprised that they had looked at our programs, petitioned the federal government, and got a provincial organization to supply it.

"Why didn't they ask the federal nurse?"

"He's scheduled on holiday today."

"Hmm."

The inefficiency of having two health care systems in the province—one for Indigenous Peoples, which was managed federally, and one for everyone else, which was managed provincially—was ridiculous. Most of us weren't as adept as the Alkali Lake Band at juggling the various components of care.

Innate prejudice was another difficult challenge. When I first arrived in Williams Lake, I was unaware of the prejudice against Indigenous people. It hadn't taken long before I saw it in the health care system and in the general society. Individuals tried to combat it and subvert it over the years, yet now in the mid-seventies, not much had changed. I had a heightened sensitivity to it as both my sons were adopted. Glen was blond with brown eyes. David was Indigenous—Tsimshian, the social workers told us, with brown skin, brown eyes, and almost-black hair. I hadn't seen any prejudice against him as a charming child. That didn't mean he wasn't going to encounter it.

"Basically, I'm supposed to meet Ms. Saunders and drive her out there?"

Angela gave instructions. "Just make sure she gets there on time, doesn't get lost, and stays out of trouble."

"When does her plane get in?"

"Ten-thirty."

"I'll meet it."

"Thank you." Angela smiled and left me to reorganize my day. I would have to hurry to fit in the well-baby visit before I drove to the airport.

MRS. DICKSON LET ME into her three-bedroom rancher in the subdivision near the hospital. I could hear the baby crying before she opened the door.

"Come in, please," she said, stepping back to allow me and the cumbersome metal baby scale I carried to manoeuvre through the doorway.

She was a tall, thin, red-headed woman, dressed in a tweed skirt and wool sweater. I wondered if she dressed that formally all the time or had dressed up for my visit. The baby continued to cry. I followed her to the living room, where the bassinet with the complaining infant resided.

She indicated the coffee table and I placed the scale on it. I put my black bag beside it and went over to look at the baby.

"Does he cry like this often?" I asked and turned to look at her.

Her blue eyes were huge. I could see the purple smudges below them and the pallor—signs of fatigue. "All the time."

"Why don't you pick him up while I wash my hands?"

She sighed. "All right. The bathroom is just down the hall."

I returned to take the baby from her. He had stopped crying and continued to stay quiet while I held him. He was rooting into my hand, though—a sign of hunger.

"What are you feeding him?"

"Formula."

"How often, how much, and what kind?"

She told me. I nodded without giving her any advice. "Let's get this little man weighed. What's his name?"

"Henry."

I undressed Henry, which he didn't like as he began to cry again. I weighed him and compared the results to his birth weight.

"That's just fine," I told Mrs. Dickson.

She seemed relieved. If Henry had been crying because he was constantly hungry, she may have been worried he wasn't gaining weight. That was most mothers' primary concern, which was why they wanted me to bring a scale. I sometimes thought I was only valued by the mothers as the keeper of the scale.

I measured Henry's length, chest circumference, and head circumference. I checked his reflexes and his eye movements. It was difficult to check hearing on a baby this young, so I asked Mrs. Dickson whether she noticed if he could hear.

"Oh, he can hear all right. The least little noise wakes him up."

I put a new diaper on Henry and re-clothed him, then wrapped him in a small blanket. "If you warm the formula, I'll feed him while we talk."

"I'll get it."

While she was in the kitchen I looked around. Everything was tidy. Mrs. Dickson might be working too hard trying to keep the house up to her usual standards as well as looking after Henry.

Henry latched onto the nipple as if he hadn't been fed in a day.

"When was his last feeding?"

"Just two hours ago."

"He's a good little eater," I said.

She smiled and sat back on the sofa and watched him. "That's for sure."

We talked about the formula. I told her babies needed fat and she might find a different formula, which I named, would suit him better. "He might be eating so often trying to get enough fat."

"No kidding?" She got up to retrieve a pen and paper and wrote down my suggestion. Since she seemed open to that, I asked her about relatives or friends and found she had no relatives nearby and only a few friends.

"I see your house is immaculate. Do you do it all yourself or do you have a house cleaner?"

"I do it myself. Mike said he'd pay for a diaper service or a cleaner but not both."

We were silent. Most men in this area didn't pay for either and most mothers let the housework slide because they couldn't do it all.

"I was thinking of getting the diaper service," she said.

"That would help relieve you of some of the work Henry creates, but you might think about the fact that the diaper service won't be needed in two years, while the cleaner could stay on forever."

She stared straight at me, her interest caught. "True. I hadn't thought of that."

"And while we are dealing with the fact that you are overworked, does your husband wear dress shirts to work?"

"Yes. He works in the bank."

"And does he iron them himself?"

"Are you kidding?"

I grinned. "Try to persuade him to take his shirts to the dry-cleaners. It isn't very expensive and that's another thing which might become a habit."

She laughed.

I didn't learn those tips at university. A neighbour visited me when Janice was an infant and told me how to save my energy. I still had Eileen, my treasured cleaner, who came once a week and saved me from hours of tedious housework.

By this time, I'd burped Henry and put him back into his bassinet. He drifted off to sleep.

I stayed another half-hour while Mrs. Dickson told me about her worries. She was so conscientious that she felt she had to do everything perfectly. She'd been a teacher before her marriage and was used to planning her day and being responsible. I expect she made charts with goals listed in priority and Henry's expected dates of accomplishment set in neat columns. That over-conscientiousness was driving her into exhaustion. She seemed to accept my advice, so I ventured more.

"Does Henry have a pram?"

"He does."

"Take him out every afternoon. The sidewalks are clear of snow now and you could walk to the shops. Today you could pick up that new formula, but a regular afternoon walk is good for you both." She'd probably be more motivated if she had a goal for those walks. "You can stop in at the health unit and weigh him any time."

I left her looking more cheerful than when I'd first arrived, but that could have been because Henry was momentarily and blessedly quiet. I'd come back in a week to see how she was getting on. Just because I'd done hundreds of baby visits and could assess infants quite well didn't mean I got it right every time. Mrs. Dickson could have been experiencing postpartum depression and I might have missed it on this visit. The new formula might not agree with Henry and he'd still scream. A constantly screaming baby is hard for anyone to cope with, especially a young mother with no relatives to help her. Mothers have resorted to leaving the baby crying and walking around the block—fine if there was someone else in the house but not wise if the baby was alone. Some have been driven to suffocating the baby in an effort stop the crying. I didn't think Mrs. Dickson would do that; she was more likely to drive herself mad or collapse from exhaustion. Many people don't realize how difficult it is to be alone with a baby, particularly in the cold months when it isn't possible to go for a walk or take children to a park. It's amazing to me that more mothers don't simply walk out of the house and catch the first bus out of town.

I glanced at my watch and saw that I'd have to hurry if I was going to meet Ms. Saunders at the airport on time.

CHAPTER THREE

ACCOMPANYING A CITY NURSE

I HAD JUST ENOUGH TIME to stop at my office, read my messages, and answer questions from Ellie, one of the two office clerks, before I headed for the airport.

Ellie had worked at the health unit before I arrived years ago, and she knew everything there was to know about government forms. She was consistently pleasant and helpful, although clear on what was her responsibility and what was not. She still typed my letters and kept my paperwork flowing. She wasn't my private assistant; she looked after the other four nurses in our office as well. I appreciated her because my handwriting was not always legible and my spelling was definitely creative.

Drama didn't usually take place at the health unit, but this morning was an exception. I was standing at my office door when a young man climbed the stairs to the office and leaned drunkenly on the counter.

"I want my money," he said in a low voice.

Ellie and Ann looked up.

"I want my money," the man repeated in a louder voice.

"I beg your pardon?" Ann said.

"I want my money!" the man shouted.

I froze for a second. Was he violent?

Ann, who had started toward the counter, faded back to the side. Ellie looked up from where she was seated at her desk.

"Yes?" she said, polite as usual.

I waited. Should I call the police? It would take them at least ten minutes to get here. Should I intervene? I didn't want to approach him and get a fist in my face. I dithered, unsure.

"My money," the man yelled and, with one hand on the counter, vaulted over it to stand in front of Ellie. He shoved his face at her. "Give it to me."

I started toward them, with no idea what I could do.

"Do you want your Welfare cheque?" she asked.

"Yes," the man snapped, glaring at her.

"You have the wrong office," Ellie said calmly. "You want the Welfare office."

He stood straight and cocked his head. "I do?"

"Yes. Next block. The grey building."

"Oh. Sorry." He shuffled around the counter, nodded at me as he passed, and stumbled down the stairs and out the door.

My heart rate went back to normal. I leaned on the counter. "Ellie, how did you know what he wanted?"

"It's Welfare Wednesday."

Of course. It was the once-a-month payday for those who needed government help.

"Are you all right?" I watched her for a moment.

She straightened some files on her desk and stood. "I believe I need a cup of tea," she said. She brushed past me, dignified and composed. I took a calming breath. If she could take that in stride, I could as well.

I RETURNED TO MY OFFICE, settled into my chair and concentrated on a bulletin on preventing smoking while I sipped a quick coffee. The evidence about the hazards of smoking was mounting, although tobacco companies were still trying to discount it. We'd been trying to establish such a program in the grade five classes. Public health nurses taught it, but we were hoping it would soon become part of the school curriculum and the teachers would be confident enough to teach it themselves. Preliminary studies showed that if elementary school children were convinced smoking was harmful, they not only were less likely to smoke than those who had not partaken in the program but were also more likely to influence the adults in their lives to either stop or curtail their habit. I had smoked myself for years—most of my friends smoked when I was young—but stopped when I started to teach the program in schools. I should have stopped when I had children, but it took the school program to convince me. The kids would know if I taught them a class then went into the staff room to smoke. That would make me a hypocrite, and I really couldn't live with that contradiction. I could just hear Janice and Glen:

"Ew, Mom. You're lying to those kids!" Or "You're sneaky!"

Far too embarrassing. Luckily, it wasn't as hard for me to stop as it was for most people. It had been a habit, not a need. My body just didn't crave it.

So my conscience was clear when I waited to greet Ms. Philippa Saunders. She was easy to spot. Most of the passengers had shopping bags, spoils of their trip to the city. Ms. Saunders had an over-the-shoulder leather satchel. She was tall, slim, with long, dark hair clipped at the back of her neck. Her eyes were a light brown and she was beautiful. I was conscious of my glasses slipping down my nose, my flyaway hair, and the spit baby Henry had left on my shirt. I'd tried to wipe it off but hadn't been entirely successful. Ms. Saunders looked polished in her short, dark fur coat, tailored slacks, and small-heeled black boots. She was stylish and cosmopolitan—and would look like a swan in a hen yard out at Alkali. Still, she had paid them the respect of dressing up. At least, it looked like it.

Public health nurses didn't wear uniforms anymore, but we tried to dress in conservative clothes so we didn't appear so far removed from our clients that they saw a huge void between us. I missed my uniform because it had flattered me and meant that I didn't have to choose what to wear every day. Now, my fellow nurses and I had closets filled with clothes mostly in dark blue to replace the previous uniform. "Menopause blue" Sophie had called it one morning at coffee break. I don't know why she labelled it that as no one was of menopause age except Sally in the home care unit. I was sure we had red, green, pink, and yellow in our off-duty wardrobes, but at work we did look drab, and now I felt like a dull wren beside Ms. Saunders, the best-dressed nurse I'd ever seen.

"Mrs. Crook?" Ms. Saunders asked.

"Marion," I said.

"Pippa. I have a suitcase of material on the baggage carousel."

Luggage didn't take long to arrive in our airport. The plane was parked right outside the building, and we could watch the cargo being unloaded and trundled into the terminal.

"Have you eaten?" I asked her as we drove down the broad, curving airport road to the highway. The health department no longer supplied cars to nurses, so we used our own and billed monthly for the maintenance. I drove a big Suburban SUV, which I needed to haul kids, grain, and sometimes animals. My Suburban was less likely to skid than the Chevy II I used to drive, and it had more power in its V8 engine. The seat was as high as in a pickup truck, giving me a better view of the country. It was basically a truck that looked like a van with three rows of bench seats and room for cargo: children, several bags of feed, and a couple of dogs.

Pippa turned to look at me. "I ate at the airport before we left."

That was good as Alkali Reserve was an hour's drive south down the Dog Creek Road, and we didn't have time to stop. There was still snow on the sides of the road and in the fields, but because the temperature was above freezing, the snow would recede day by day. It was too cold at night for new growth, so the fields revealed by the vanishing winter blanket were barren. The sunflowers on the south-facing hillsides, which were one of our first signs of spring here, would be weeks yet.

"Tell me about your program, Pippa," I said as I manoeuvred around the potholes in the road—another sign of Cariboo spring.

The thaw of the daytime and the freezing at night caused the roads to buckle and crumple.

She filled me in on the studies behind the program, the probable statistical results of five years of implementation, and the estimated reduced cost to the health care system. I tentatively suggested she add some anecdotes into her presentation about how the program could make a difference to individuals.

"People seem to find stories motivating," I said.

"I know how to make a presentation. I do this all the time."

"Sorry," I said and ceased to advise. *You may do it all the time*, I thought, *but, if what you're telling me is what you're going to tell the Alkali Lake Band Education Committee, they're going to be bored.*

I pulled into the parking space in front of the Band office with five minutes to spare.

I approached the receptionist. "I'm Marion Crook, a nurse from the health unit in Williams Lake." I didn't work on this reserve and wasn't a familiar face here. I'd met Phyllis Chelsea and her husband Andy, prominent members of the community, at a meeting in town. I knew no one else. "This is Ms. Pippa Saunders from the Lung Society, here for the meeting of the Education Committee."

"Martha." The slim, young woman behind the desk announced her name and looked sideways at Pippa, taking in the fur, the leather purse, and the boots. She probably compared Pippa's boots to mine. I wore my winter snow boots, waterproof on the outside with felt liners inside for warmth. Besides mud from the barnyard, I'd likely picked up some manure when I dashed in among the sheep to pour some oats into the trough. I'd have avoided dirt if I'd stayed at the edge of the yard, but there was one neurotic ewe I was worried about who was almost ready to lamb, so I had walked over to check her. She was fine. I'd wiped my boots on the snow before I got into the car but, just now, I suspected I'd missed some spots. I hoped the rich scent of manure didn't rise up from my boots in the warm meeting room.

"You are five minutes early. Have a seat."

"I love your earrings," Pippa said, attracted to the beaded circles dangling from Martha's ears.

"Thanks," she said. "I made them."

"Can I buy them?"

My jaw dropped. That was rude. Martha sent me a quick glance. I recovered.

"They aren't for sale, Pippa," I said.

Martha rose and gestured us to follow her. Just before I entered the room, Martha put her hand on my arm. "I have a pair for sale."

"Sorry," I said. "She surprised me. I shouldn't have said anything. She didn't mean to be offensive. She just admires them."

"Got that. No problem. I'll give her the tourist price." Pippa should have spent more time getting to know Martha before she almost demanded to buy her earrings.

There were about twelve men and women in the room. Phyllis wasn't there but her husband Andy was. He nodded at me, and I returned the nod.

Andy said, "Marion, we are ready to hear the proposal. You can start."

I looked around at everyone, nodded and smiled, then introduced Pippa.

She barely gave me time to finish before she burst into her presentation. She didn't acknowledge anyone, just started talking.

I caught Andy's eye and raised an eyebrow. A slight smile came and went in a moment. Apology accepted. I didn't know much about this reserve except it was a dry reserve, and the Band members headed by Andy and Phyllis were determined to keep alcohol away from everyone. As far as I could tell, they were succeeding. I remembered the reserve had also taken control of their school and ran it themselves, with some Indigenous teachers, one of whom was the principal. Their health system was federal, which was why no one from my provincial health unit was nursing in this school. They were aware of our programs and found ways to get the programs they wanted into their community. They were well on their way to creating a more traditional, hopeful society. By reputation, this was a competent committee.

Pippa finished up her presentation after twenty minutes of steady talking. No one took notes. No one asked a question. There was silence. I watched as Andy looked around the table. Each person he looked at gave an almost imperceptible nod.

Pippa rushed into speech. "I can answer any questions you might have. It's a really important program, and I can provide literature if you'd like to discuss it."

Andy looked at me. I waited. He nodded.

I turned to Pippa. "They have decided to accept it. They will teach it here." I thanked the committee for their time.

"Give Martha the particulars and all the contact information," Andy said to me.

I stood. Pippa stood a little reluctantly and seemed confused, but she followed me to the reception area.

I gave her directions. "Please give Martha your business card, a copy of the program if you have it, and get the mailing address for this office and the name of the person who will be responsible for the program. Martha will have all that."

Pippa stared at me, then fished a business card from her satchel and passed it to Martha. She pulled out a bundle of papers from the satchel, which she also placed on the desk. Martha handed Pippa a business card. "That's your contact person."

"Thank you," Pippa said. She stowed the card safely in her wallet.

"I have a pair of earrings here if you want them." Martha reached into her desk drawer. She set a pair of beautifully beaded earrings on the desk.

"Oh, those are pretty. How much?"

Martha named a sum at least double what they usually would have sold for. Pippa was delighted to get them. Both buyer and seller were pleased.

"Thanks, Martha," I said and left.

"Have a good drive. Mind the potholes."

"Will do."

Pippa remained quiet until we were in the car and heading back down the Dog Creek Road to Williams Lake.

"That's it?" she said. "No questions. No discussion. They didn't even vote."

"Yes, they did." I said, slowing to let two teens saunter across the road. I waved. They returned my wave.

"How do you know?"

I realized it was almost impossible to explain to her that not every discussion was verbal. The young man at the end of the table was probably the principal of the school. He'd rolled his eyes. An older woman across from him, perhaps a parent, had raised her eyebrows, smiled, and given a quick nod. If that had been verbal it might have sounded like: "This is going to be a lot of work." And the response: "We'll help." This took place before the silent roll call Andy did. Some of it went on while Pippa was speaking. She hadn't seen it.

"Will they do it, or were they just fobbing me off?" She sounded worried.

She wasn't deliberately insulting the committee; she was just concerned that the program would go ahead, and she didn't understand how the committee worked.

"Yes, they will do it."

She watched the country on either side of the road. Compared to the bright yellow daffodils and pink cherry blossoms of Vancouver, it must have looked drab to her. At times it looked that way to me, as if the country was a brooding, powerful entity that could overcome the people who tried to live in it, including me. At other times, that sense of presence seemed awe-inspiring, as if I was living in a vital, energizing landscape that held me and sustained me. I suppose, after all these years, I'd made peace with it.

I took her to the Lakeside Hotel for tea, listened to her talk about the scope of the Lungs for Life program. I agreed with her— it was important and was going to make a difference.

I deposited her at the air terminal in time for her flight and wished her a good trip. I watched her for a moment before I drove away. She really was an exotic bird in the Cariboo.

I RUSHED TO THE BABY I'd scheduled and found a happy, healthy infant who was gaining weight. Then I picked up David from Edith's and proceeded straight home, driving into the ranch yard just as Janice and Glen were walking up the stairs. They'd hiked the quarter of a mile from the school bus stop.

Janice threw her books onto the counter and dashed out the door to Cleo.

I gave the boys an apple each to hold them until supper.

"Here are two more apples," I said to Glen. "Take one to Janice and one to Cleo."

"Will Jan let me see the piglets?"

"She will if you bring apples and are quiet."

The quiet challenge again. "I will be."

I pulled a step-stool to the counter, stood David on it, and gave him eggs to beat for the apple cobbler I was making. I hauled the frozen stew from the downstairs freezer. We had three freezers. The one in the barn held both the beef from a steer and the pork from a pig. Everything else was in the fridge freezer in the kitchen or the huge chest freezer in the basement.

I put the stew in the microwave then the oven and sliced apples while David told me about his day. I was too busy to miss him while I was working but, at times like this, I realized I'd missed what he had experienced in the day. Thankfully, now that he was speaking fairly well and had opinions, I got to hear snippets of his life away from me.

I spread the apples in the cake pan, added sugar, vanilla, and butter to the eggs, and encouraged David to stir. He passed me the bowl and I added the flour, baking powder, salt, and milk. I whipped it together, spread it over the apples, and popped it into the oven, setting the timer for thirty-five minutes. Without the timer, I burned many a cake.

"Do you want to come with me to feed the sheep?"

David shook his head. "Play in my room."

He had many toys there, so I shrugged on my jacket, slipped into my snow boots, and headed out to the barn alone.

I stopped at the pigpen.

"All okay here?" I asked.

"Mom, look at this one—it has a black patch on its ear." Janice held up a tiny piglet.

I duly admired it. "Glen, would you go to the house and stay there until I get back from feeding the sheep? I left David alone." David was reliable, but he was only three.

"Do I have to?"

"Yep."

"Can I come back later?"

"If Janice agrees."

"Can I?" he asked her.

"Okay."

I turned on the barn lights and repeated the morning feed. This time I walked through the flock, checking to make sure no ewes were lambing; they should be dropping them soon. I liked to separate the new mothers and lambs and feed them away from the rest of the flock.

We'd built this barn after we built the house. We wanted everything convenient, and it was. The hay was stacked in the loft. A chute allowed me to break the bales and drop them through into the manger below. The oats were in a big oak barrel on the lower level, but it wasn't difficult to dip into the barrel and spread the oats in the trough attached to the manger. I sometimes had to push sheep out of the way, but they were easy to move—except for Archie, the ram. He was heavy and occasionally obstructive. Today, he was too busy trying to eat as many oats as possible to pay me any attention.

Carl drove in as I was walking back to the house. He climbed out of his vehicle, a Buick sedan, carrying a briefcase. He'd always had a briefcase to hold his papers, but now that he was a lawyer it seemed a symbol of his profession.

He reached to encompass me in his long arms and kissed me thoroughly.

"Stolen moments," I said.

"No kids."

That wouldn't last.

"Dad," Janice called from the pigpen. "Come and see Cleo."

"I'll take your briefcase in." I reached for it and headed for the house. The timer was beeping as I arrived at the kitchen door.

I took the cake out of the oven as Glen came running up the stairs from the lower floor, where he and Janice had bedrooms. He'd heard the timer. Ben bounced around his feet, a golden ball of spaniel enthusiasm.

"It's okay. I've got it, thanks" I said.

Carl and Janice were talking as they came in.

"Dad!" Glen interrupted and threw himself at Carl.

"How's it going, buddy?" He gave Glen a big hug.

"Me too, Daddy." David hurried around the corner from his room.

Carl picked him up. "How did it go today?"

"I didn't like the snack."

"Is that so? Did you tell Mrs. Fawcett?"

"I did."

He put David down. "I have to get changed, guys."

The kids headed for their rooms.

"Dinner in half an hour. Practice time," I warned. Janice went to her room to practice her violin, Glen went to the far end of the house to do his piano exercises, and David headed to his room to play.

I set the table, took a beer from the fridge, and poured it into two glasses. When he was comfortable in jeans and a work shirt, Carl joined me. Those clothes were what he wore every day when we were first married, and they suited him. Back then, he spent his working life outdoors. His curly hair was receding now, but he still had bright, sometimes mischievous hazel eyes. We sat at a small table in a corner of the kitchen, where we could see down the valley to distant tree-covered hills. This was our time to catch up on what had happened in each other's day. He told me about clients. Sometimes they came with strange stories and sometimes with difficult problems. I told him about the aggressive man at the health unit.

"Did you recognize him?"

"No, I didn't, but Ellie was right—he had the wrong office."

"Nothing personal, then."

"No." Carl worried that someone who didn't like the public health directives I gave would threaten me. It had happened, but only once or twice. I remembered the man who had trained his rifle on me while we discussed my taking his six-year-old son to his mother, and the woman who was sure I was the social worker and her worst enemy; I'd narrowly escaped a beating that time. I shivered a little. Those incidents were in the past. I didn't expect any danger now.

CHAPTER FOUR

LEARNING FROM THE HOCKEY TEAM

"WE HAVE TO DEAL with the Stampeders, Marion," Angela told me one Monday morning as she popped her head into my office.

The local hockey team took their game seriously. There was a snarling rivalry between the Williams Lake Stampeders and the Quesnel Kangaroos. I didn't expect to be involved in any capacity other than as an onlooker from a seat in the arena.

"One of them has mono," she continued.

I waited, knowing there would be a task for me in her announcement. I'd been sitting at my desk conscientiously reading one of the many reports that appeared in the wooden in-box on my desk every morning. The central office in Victoria expected every public health nurse to have current knowledge of many diseases, as well as the updated and changing policies. I was much more interested in the hockey team, so I happily put down the directive on how to tabulate nursing statistics.

"We don't see that often," I said.

"The players are at a vulnerable age. Dr. Anderson is concerned and the manager is worried the whole team will get it."

I conjured up the page on mononucleosis in my *Communicable Diseases in Man* text. I'd memorized large portions of that book as a student. Mono was contagious, but not highly contagious.

"It's transferred in saliva," I remembered. It's sometimes called the kissing disease. I'd have to forget that term when dealing with the hockey team.

"They probably share water bottles," Angela said. "Or towels."

I could see how the team might be more vulnerable to infection than most people. "What do they want us to do?"

"Take blood from the whole team. You've taken blood before. You should be competent."

Nurses knew how to withdraw blood but usually left that chore to the lab technicians. But I took blood every Monday from inmates at the jail, where everyone had to have a test for syphilis. Usually, the prisoners were young men with big, accessible veins. The hockey players were a similar age group. It shouldn't be hard. The challenge would be in setting up a special clinic and getting everyone to arrive on time.

"You can deliver the samples to this lab at the hospital, where they'll test for antibodies." Angela gave me instructions.

"I'll call the lab so they can block off some time to deal with it. How many people will there be?" I asked.

Angela looked at her notes. "Twenty-two players, two referees, and four management staff. I'll get Ellie to type up these notes. The manager is Robin Ferris. You can tee it all up with him."

Within the hour, Ellie had typed up the notes and placed them on my desk.

I reached for the phone and contacted Robin Ferris. He wasn't a full-time manager—no one was full time, neither management nor players; they all had other jobs. Robin Ferris owned a garage and auto repair shop.

"Hell of a thing," he said on the phone. "Big strapping lad. Weak as a kitten."

"It hits some people like that. I hope he's getting rest. That's the treatment."

"Yeah. He boards with my sister and she's looking after him. I'm worried that more guys are going to come down with it. I don't want them playing when they're sick, but I need to field a team to meet Quesnel this weekend. Hate to forfeit that game. Quesnel's at the top of the league. Lose this Friday and we won't have a snowball's hope in hell at the trophy."

"The lab results usually come back in a day or two," I reassured him. "If we could hold a clinic here tomorrow at the health unit, it will give the lab time to get the results back to me then to you, before Friday."

"Sounds good. What time?"

We arranged for an after-hours clinic at 6:00 PM the next day. That was as quick I could manage to get it organized. I asked him for two volunteers to help with the clinic and gave Robin some advice. "You need to make sure the players and staff don't share towels, water bottles, or anything that might come in contact with their mouths."

There was silence for a moment, then he said, "I can do that."

The next night, the waiting room was filled with young men of every size and shape: tall and broad, short and chunky, wiry, thin, and even chubby. The first volunteer, Thelma Parks, the wife of the assistant manager, helped by keeping order and demanding everyone fill out their requisition slip. The second, designated to help me in the much quieter treatment room, was Peggy Ferris, Robin's wife. I knew Peggy as she was the receptionist at the elementary school and would be used to handling everything from playground accidents to truants to hallway fights. She'd be efficient.

I had my syringes, needles, sample tubes, rubber tourniquet, and alcohol swabs on my desk. Peggy had a table beside me with a pen and tape. She would take the requisition from the patient, write his name and requisition number on the tube, and hand it to me. When I had taken the sample, I'd pass the filled tube over to her. She'd tape the requisition to it and place it in the insulated container beside her. It was important *not* to mix up any of the samples or end up with unlabelled samples. It was an orderly process, and I expected it would go smoothly.

All went well until Wayne Abbot shuffled in. He was about six foot two, bulky, and cheerful.

"Hi, Wayne." He worked for Robin at the garage; I often saw him when I got gas and had my car serviced.

"Hiya, Mrs. Crook. How's it goin'?"

I smiled. "Pretty good. Just give Peggy your requisition."

He did that.

"You can sit here." I waved toward the chair.

"Nah. I'd rather stand. Seems easier, somehow."

He seemed relaxed, so there wasn't any reason not to accommodate him. I stood as well.

"Just rest your arm on the gurney here." I indicated the padded stretcher against the wall.

Peggy handed me the sample tube with Wayne's name written on it. I picked up an alcohol swab and the tourniquet. I wrapped the rubber tourniquet around his arm and picked up a syringe with an attached needle.

"Just open and close your fist a couple of times. That's right. Lovely veins." I slipped the needle into the vein. Easy.

"Watch out!" Peggy called.

I looked up just in time to see Wayne's eyes roll back and his body start to slide sideways. I grabbed him by the shoulder with my left hand and eased him to the floor—very quickly as he was so heavy he could pull me down with him. The needle was still in my right hand but no longer in Wayne's arm.

"What happened?" Peggy asked

"He fainted." I dropped the syringe into the basin on my desk, then checked Wayne's colour, his breathing, and his heart rate. "Hand me another syringe, please, Peggy."

She plucked a prepared syringe from my desk and passed it to me. I found Wayne's vein again, released the tourniquet and withdrew the blood. I shot the blood into the sample tube and handed it to Peggy. I was wiping Wayne's arm with alcohol when he blinked.

"All done," I said in case he was worried he'd have to face a needle again.

"Ah, shit," he said. "I hate blood. You won't tell the guys, will you, Marion?" If he'd told me that at the beginning, I'd have insisted he stay seated. He could have injured himself or given me some bruises. But I wasn't about to make his day worse.

I glanced at Peggy. She was supressing a grin.

"I won't tell a soul," I said.

He sat up and got to his feet. We eyed him warily, but he had good colour and was intent on leaving.

"Uh, thanks," he said.

"He's such a baby," Peggy said with affection after he'd gone.

"He'd hate to know we thought about him that way."

"I won't tell him."

I took a couple of deep breaths. There were about twenty more in the waiting room. This was going to take some time.

I thought about where I usually was at this time of the day— home. Carl was with the kids. He was on Cleo duty but had assured me when I'd called earlier that the pig and piglets were fine. None of my sheep had started to lamb, and he'd manage supper. I ceased to think about home.

We worked until eight. I thanked Peggy and Thelma, loaded the samples into my car, and drove in the dark, cold evening. It was only a six-minute drive to the hospital lab. When I got there, I delivered the samples to the night orderly who was expecting me.

"Andrea told me where to put them. She said thanks for collecting the blood. It saved her all kinds of time." Andrea, the lab technician, had probably gone home at five.

"No problem," I said. I was immensely satisfied with the work I'd done that day. I liked doing practical tasks that made a difference in the community.

"She'll call you."

I drove home along our gravel road. The headlights picked up the white of the snow still in patches by the roadside. I was the only driver on the road. It felt as though I was alone in the universe.

Andrea did call me early in the morning two days later.

"Can you come up here?" Her tone was serious. She didn't give me the results of the tests.

"Sure." I left the office and drove up the hill to the hospital. What had gone wrong? Were there many cases of mono in the team? Would I have to deliver bad news to Robin? The game was tomorrow.

Andrea was in her thirties and had been the lab technician at the hospital for years. While I knew how to get blood from patients, she knew everything about how to test it, preserve it, and report on it.

It wasn't the results that were bothering Andrea.

"You hemolyzed the whole lot," Andrea said.

I looked at her, stunned. I didn't even know I could do that.

"You must have shot the blood into the tube too fast. All the red cells clotted."

I sat down on a chair with a thud. I could see Robin Ferris's face as I explained I'd made a mistake and would have to arrange another clinic and take blood from every one of those young men again. I couldn't do that and get the results by tomorrow. They'd have to forfeit the game. Hard on them and hard on me. Robin would think I was incompetent. That information would fly around town like wildfire and *everyone* would think I was incompetent. Well, I had been. I hadn't known I *could* hemolyze the sample. Should I have known? Probably. But I hadn't. What about the samples I took every week at the jail? But I didn't shoot the blood into the sample vial at the jail because I never felt rushed there. I'd only done that with the hockey team. Wayne would have to go through it again. I was not going to be his favourite person, or anyone's favourite person. I thought about resigning.

"I have to do it all again," I whispered. What would Angela think of me? What would my colleagues think of me? I bit my lip and tried to concentrate.

"No," Andrea said. "Luckily, it didn't interfere with the test. We could still use the samples. The results were all negative."

"Oh, thank God!" The relief was incredible. My hands tingled. I took several deep breaths. I'd collected the samples incorrectly, but I wouldn't have to admit it to everyone.

Andrea nodded with understanding. She knew how difficult it would have been for me to admit my mistake and convene another clinic.

"Why don't you come here after work tomorrow? You can take blood from me and I'll show you how to put it into the sample tube without hemolyzing it. There are lots of tests it can affect."

"You're on," I said. "Thanks so much."

The next day, I drove up to the hospital after work. Andrea bravely bared her arm and I took blood from her. Then she showed me how to carefully let the blood flow into the tube. It was such a simple correction, and I'd managed to work in this field for years without knowing about it. It made me think there might be many other mistakes waiting for me.

"I hate making mistakes," I said to Andrea.

"Yeah. It's called being human. You can fix this one, though. Just don't use much pressure."

"No fear of that." I'd escaped public humiliation by pure luck. As a lesson in lab technique, it was unforgettable.

CHAPTER FIVE

NURSING AT LAC LA HACHE

APRIL ARRIVED with its cold nights and warm days—well, relatively warm days. The snow had disappeared from the trees and was slowly melting from the fields, but it was still deep under the thick fir groves. I admired the greening fields with their neat barbed-wire fences and the grazing Hereford cattle contained within. Fenced acreage was only a small portion of the ranch land here, usually used for growing hay. Cattle grazed in the miles of tree-covered wilderness surrounding the ranches. Hereford cattle were the most popular breed, but some ranchers had others. We had Hereford cows but a Black Angus bull called Thor. Carl thought we got better weight on the calves with the paternal Angus breed, but he wasn't willing to abandon the Hereford line completely. Occasionally, I saw a white Charolais. The fresh grass must have tasted wonderful to the cattle after dry hay all winter.

Daylight was lengthening and spring was on its way, and on this day, I drove on a clear highway toward Lac la Hache. I had two visits to make on my way to the school there. The first was to a ranch a little off the highway; the teenaged daughter of the family had given birth to a baby in Kamloops then had given it up for adoption. I was hoping to see her and check that she was getting postnatal care and some psychological counselling.

The large, weathered grey log ranch house loomed over a gar-den of what looked to be lilac bushes, still looking dead and bare of any green shoots. They would eventually come to life and the blossoms would give off a heavenly scent in June. Borland Street in Williams Lake used to have lilacs on either side of it. You could close your eyes and think you were in Paris with perfume all around you. I parked and then knocked on the door. A woman about ten years older than me—slim, brown curly hair, brown eyes—answered the door.

"Yes?"

"I'm Marion Crook, public health nurse. I came to see Hayley. Is she home?"

She stared at me. "She's at school."

"Already?" I was surprised. The baby had been born last week. I would have thought she'd need another week to recover.

"You'd better come in."

I followed her into the ranch kitchen, where she had been wash-ing breakfast dishes. We sat at the table. I pulled out the birth notice and the family chart.

"How is she doing?"

"Why do you want to know? There's no problem with the Wel-fare, is there?" Mrs. Brown stared at the chart in my hand. The Human Resources Department, known generally as "the Welfare," had placed the baby for adoption. Was she worried I was going to tell her the adoption had not gone through?

"No. No. I'm just doing a routine check."

She glared at me. I was beginning to feel that Mrs. Brown regret-ted letting me into the house. "How did you know about Hayley?"

I pointed to the file. "I get the birth notice."

"It's supposed to be secret."

Government forms are processed. Birth and death notices are filed. Officialdom is relentless. In any case, I wanted to tell her, the days of secrecy are numbered. Adopted children are not going to tolerate not knowing their past. Birth mothers are not going to suffer never knowing what had become of their children. She did not look ready for that information. She looked decidedly hostile.

"This is confidential information, Mrs. Brown. No one sees these files. How is Hayley? Did she see her doctor? Is she having any difficulty?"

"She's fine. She's back at school, and we are doing our best to put it behind us and make sure she can forget about it."

That wasn't going to happen. No sane person would have a child and simply forget about it, but I could see Mrs. Brown wouldn't believe me. She had decided she was going to cope with this by denying it ever happened. She didn't want to hear anything that would shake her stratagem. Recommending psychological counselling would be wasted breath.

"I see." I gathered my papers and stood to leave. I wanted to do that with dignity before she threw me out. She was close to anger.

"I am sure you have been a great support to your daughter through this time," I said as I was leaving.

"Yes. Yes," she said. I felt the rush of air on my back from the fast-closing door.

I drove back to the highway thinking I had done no good at all. I certainly hadn't helped Hayley and had only shaken Mrs. Brown's belief in the secrecy of government agencies. Hayley had had a baby and given it up. She was bound to feel many emotions complicated by heightened hormones. Denying the facts might make Mrs. Brown feel safer and more in control, but it wouldn't help Hayley. At sixteen, she was protected and overprotected by her parents. There wasn't much I could do for her. Perhaps I could talk to her at her school without alerting the teachers as that would really upset Mrs. Brown. Why hadn't I considered that the family might want to keep the birth a secret and my appearing at the door would shake them? Because I *hadn't* considered it. And failing to think this through had upset Mrs. Brown and not served Hayley. Perhaps because I had two adopted children, I didn't think it should be a secret. Obviously, not everyone felt that way.

Adoption had always been something Carl and I had considered. Janice's birth had been smooth in that I spent only six hours in the hospital in labour. The prenatal exercises I both taught and practised worked well. It was after her birth that I started to bleed. There were six units of blood in the hospital, the only blood supply for hundreds of miles. They used them all on me. Then people from the town, friends, and people I didn't know, thirty-five of them, lined up to offer their blood. I took six more units before the bleeding stopped. The nurses told me that Carl had gone into the lab on the night I was in deep trouble and had insisted the staff stay overtime and match the blood to be sure there was enough for me. We got through it, but Carl said he wasn't going through it again. I agreed with him. The birth of the boys was easy for me—their birth mothers did all the work—but I endured the anxiety of wondering if the agency would consider us good enough parents to ever give us a baby. There were secrets in that I didn't know much about the boys' birth mothers except what the social worker told us. There was no contact and no way of contacting them. Perhaps they were like Hayley's mother and determined not to have any contact—or perhaps they *did* want contact. I didn't know. The boys arrived. They were wonderful. Adoption seemed socially acceptable to me. But obviously not to Mrs. Brown.

I hoped to do better at my next stop. Mrs. Lawrence lived at the old mill site about five miles before Lac la Hache. She must have spotted my car turn off the highway as she was on her porch waiting when I pulled up. She stood in the sunshine and raised her head to let the warmth bathe her face. She looked calm and at peace with herself.

"Hello, Nurse."

"Hello, Mrs. Lawrence. How are you?"

"I'm doing well. Won't you come in?"

I followed her into the small house. It reminded me of my grandmother's house, although much smaller, because there was not one extraneous article in sight. Like my grandmother, Mrs. Lawrence bought only what was necessary. There were no knick-knacks or souvenirs scattered around. Living on the brink of poverty didn't allow for anything impractical. And like my grandmother's house, the floors, counter, and windows were scrupulously clean.

Mrs. Lawrence had two other children besides Charlie and a husband who worked periodically in the logging industry. She was educated, I think—her manner of speaking suggested as much— but she had not told me her background. Her dignity was such that I never asked.

"How's Charlie doing?"

Charlie was twelve, intelligent, studious, and determined. He had a heart condition for which there was no cure—yet. Mrs. Lawrence took Charlie to the specialists in Vancouver every three months for assessment and prescriptions in the hope that something would help him. I had recommended Mrs. Lawrence to Annie, the social worker, and she had arranged to subsidize the Vancouver trips.

We sat at the kitchen table.

"Coffee, Nurse?"

Mrs. Lawrence could not afford to give me coffee. "No, thank you. I've had my morning allotment."

"All right, then."

"When is Charlie due to go back to Vancouver?"

"We'll take the bus on Sunday night to be there for Monday morning." That would save them a hotel bill for one night.

"What are you expecting?"

"The usual." She smiled but her eyes looked sad. "They can't do anything to cure his condition, but the medication gives him more energy, so he enjoys life more."

"I see."

"We will love him as long as we have him," she said.

I reached over and held her hand. She squeezed my hand and patted it with her other hand. She was comforting me, recognizing my sadness at the inevitability of Charlie's death.

I stood. "If there is anything I can do, send word to me."

"I'll do that." The Lawrences didn't have a phone but had an arrangement with a neighbour. "I know you can't do anything for me, but thanks for stopping. I don't talk about it much. Fred doesn't want to hear it. Charlie doesn't want to think about it—well, he can't or it would weigh him down. So, thanks."

She accompanied me to the door.

I drove back down the highway feeling as if I hadn't accomplished anything this morning. Mrs. Lawrence had perhaps found some sustenance in my understanding of her situation, but it wasn't much help.

The ice on Lac la Hache looked dark at the edges. It was finally melting. I saw a deer, front feet splayed for support, drinking at the edge of the lake. There were many people with guns around here. It should disappear into the trees before it ended up in someone's freezer.

I pulled into the parking lot at Lac la Hache Elementary School at ten-thirty. The principal, June Striegler, was energetic, sharp, and ready for me.

"I expected you at nine."

I grinned at her. "Here I am! On the right day! That's all you can expect."

She snorted, then laughed. "Come to the staff room at lunch."

"Will do."

She handed me a paper. On it were the names of several students the teachers wanted me to check, most of them for visual acuity but one for hearing.

First, I had a whole class that needed vision checks. I routinely did grade two and grade five, so I'd call the additional students in when I finished. This was a small school, about 180 students in grades one to six. I completed the work by noon, sending home three recommendations for parents to take their child to an optometrist and five to take their child to a dentist.

I had coffee and my packed lunch in the staff room with the teachers. One teacher was out in the yard supervising the students at play. She came in at twelve-thirty and another took her place. The staff was full of community news, but I didn't know most of the people they talked about. It was relaxing to let the gossip and chatter wash over me.

I had a well-baby clinic at the community hall at one, so I left and drove the short distance. Enid Stone, a volunteer, had opened the hall for me.

"I've turned on the heat, but you won't notice it. It takes hours to warm up."

It was cold in spite of the sunshine outdoors. These old, wooden halls seemed to hold the cold all year.

I set Enid up at a table with the scale. It was my big scale with a concave tray that held the baby, a metal arm with the weights marked on it, and a sliding balance. I put a towel on the tray and balanced the scale to zero.

"Let's not shock the poor babes with the cold," I said, explaining the use of the towel.

"Good idea," Enid said. She put a tissue-thin paper mat on the towel. She'd change that for every baby. She'd weigh the babies, write the weight on a slip of paper, and give it to the mother who would bring the baby to me for immunization and assessment. Enid told me she liked the monthly clinic because it gave her a chance to catch up on the local news. It did sound like a party when the mothers, four of them, arrived and took turns having their babies weighed. They called out to one another and laughed. I expect it was a much-anticipated social outing for them as well. Soon the loud conversations, the cries of babies who objected to being immunized, and the clatter of the scale made this clinic a little raucous. I had to concentrate on what the mother who was sitting in front of me was saying and ignore what else was happening.

"I hear a beer is good for babies," a young mother, probably about eighteen, said to me. Her baby looked to be a healthy two-month-old.

"Sorry," I said. "Beer is not good for babies either given directly to them or indirectly through breast milk."

"I heard they sleep better if you have a beer while you're nursing," she persisted, clearly wanting approval.

"You mean they sleep better if you drug them?"

She looked at me. "Oh. I guess that's what beer is, isn't it?"

"Yeah. Sorry."

She sighed. "Oh well. I'll manage without it." She gathered her crying baby and rocked her. The baby quieted.

"You're doing a great job with her. She looks good, and she's gaining weight."

She beamed at me. "Yes. Something I've done right." There was immense satisfaction in her voice. I expected she had people in her life who doubted her.

I smiled my encouragement. "Keep at it."

I left the clinic at two-thirty. It was an hour's drive back to the health unit in Williams Lake, and I was supposed to join a three-thirty staff meeting; I'd just make it. Staying late at work meant making arrangements for the children. David would stay with Edith until I picked him up at four-thirty. Janice and Glen would take the bus and walk home the quarter mile from the bus stop. Janice would immediately head out to Cleo's pen and check on the piglets. They were getting close to twenty pounds each and would soon be going to other homes, except one weaner which Janice would keep for 4-H. Glen would do something constructive, I hoped, for the forty-five minutes before I arrived home. He was supposed to feed his 4-H calf, Pedro, but I expected he'd forget if I wasn't there to remind him. He was only eight and, since the world was full of wonderful things, easily distracted. He was also impulsive and given to trying new experiences—fine if he was taking apart a motor, but not fine if it was plugged in. He was exceptionally bright, though, and learned quickly. He was much wiser at eight than he had been at six. He should be safe enough for forty-five minutes. He could take Flip, our solid, safe, placid pony, for a ride. She was easy to catch. Or ramble with his dog Ben. There was lots to do.

I was looking forward to the staff meeting this afternoon. Angela had circulated the agenda a few days earlier, and it looked like our medical health officer, Paul Parker, was asking for our opinion on the primary health problems of the area. Traffic accidents were unreasonably high, but I didn't know what we could do about it. Dr. Parker was also going to give us some education in collecting samples for testing for gonorrhea. I found it interesting—I'd never had to do that before, but he wanted to start a clinic to treat venereal diseases one day a week here at the health unit and we needed to be educated and ready for it. I wondered how we would staff that clinic.

The meeting had just begun as I slipped into my seat beside Sophie. She passed me a printed agenda.

"Thanks."

She smiled. "I need you to support my imitative."

"Sure." *Initiative*, I mentally translated. Sophie liked to try new words and she sometimes only approximated the word she wanted. Whatever her initiative was, it would be practical, possible, and necessary. I scanned the agenda. The fifth item was immunization blitzes. That was probably Sophie's item. We tried to gather two or three nurses to go to one of the larger schools and do all the immunizations quickly. Sophie was going to organize that.

Dr. Parker conducted the meeting. We had been many years without a medical health officer, so we were pleased when Dr. Parker arrived last summer, appointed by the Ministry of Health in Victoria. He was young, perhaps in his late twenties, about six foot two, with dark hair. He combined good looks, energy, and enthusiasm. He had theoretical knowledge of public health, although I doubted he'd ever mingled in the streets. His wife, Tansey, was a bubbly young woman who rarely came to the health unit. They had arrived in a Winnebago, which they'd parked in the health unit parking lot. Other than connecting their van to the electrical plug on the outside wall of the health unit, they were not causing any problem, but there was some gossip and complaints until finally the town councillors said Dr. Parker and his wife needed to find another place to stay as the parking lot was not zoned for recreational vehicles. They moved to a rental house on North Lakeside, within walking distance so they didn't need a car. It was unwise and unnecessary to provoke controversy immediately when moving to a new town, but perhaps that was his style. We'd find out.

I knew Dr. Parker wanted to establish this venereal disease clinic at the health unit. We hadn't been able to do that previously because we needed a doctor to sign prescriptions and make referrals. Now that he was available, he was keen to get it in operation. Today, I expected to hear he had managed to get approval from Victoria. Every nurse had a VD caseload. Contact information came to our in-baskets regularly, and we actively searched for people who needed antibiotics. Often, the information was vague. I routinely walked through town on Friday afternoons, trailing through the bars looking for named contacts. I never said I was looking for people who were likely positive for gonorrhea; I could have been looking for tuberculosis contacts, but I expect most people knew. Bartenders passed on the word. Usually on a Monday, someone came to the health unit for treatment having heard I was looking for them. A dedicated clinic would be more efficient—and more private.

"We have the highest rate of sexually transmitted disease in the province," Paul told us.

"We probably do better reporting," Sophie said.

"Possibly," Paul agreed.

Paul—Dr. Parker—outlined the way the clinic should be organized. I assumed Angela had done most of the work, but Paul was eager to get it functioning.

"We'll start small, with one afternoon a week. We picked Tuesday afternoon. Will that suit?"

The nurses agreed. As I had suspected, there were no new nurses hired for this clinic. We could take turns staffing the clinic, so we only had to commit one afternoon every five weeks.

"If it gets busy and we need more time, we'll hire a dedicated RN for that clinic."

That was a relief, and it made sense. I thought people would use the clinic once they knew it was available.

While I listened to Paul describe how we would need to collect samples, I drifted into thoughts of what I would make for supper, until he grabbed my attention again.

"To collect a sample from men, they need to ejaculate." He proceeded to lower his hands and mime the jerking process. He seemed oblivious to what his hands were doing, but the five female nurses in the room didn't dare look at each other for fear we'd burst into laughter and jolt him into awareness. If he realized what he was doing, he would be profoundly embarrassed. The moment passed. Paul continued talking about forms and procedures.

Sophie caught me in the parking lot as I was getting ready to leave.

"Do you think you know how to direct a man to give a specimen?" she asked. I did laugh then. Paul might have been a bit too enthusiastic.

CHAPTER SIX

THWARTING THE SYSTEM AND CHASING PIGS

T HE NEXT MORNING, I made the rounds of the maternity ward at the hospital and elicited precise directions to the homes of those who lived in the country. Many of the homes didn't have addresses and the visiting nurses needed some direction. I was the liaison nurse at the hospital and made these rounds twice a week. I was gathering the names from the charts at the nurses' station when Helen stopped me. She was an efficient nurse, but I didn't find her empathetic. I'd have liked to have her at my bedside if I had a physical emergency—she'd know what to do—but not if I had an emotional crisis.

"Mrs. Waterton is going home tomorrow. I've called Social Welfare to apprehend that baby."

I stared at her. That was dramatic, maybe over-dramatic. "Why?"

"She's as stupid as a gnat. She can't understand any instructions, and that baby will die of starvation if someone doesn't intervene."

Helen couldn't apprehend a child, but she could recommend a social worker do so. Some social workers were quick to take a child. This was a distinct threat. I put Mrs. Waterton on my list of mothers to interview.

She was tall, thin, and young—eighteen, her chart had said. She was holding her baby when I walked into the ward, and she beamed at me.

"Hello. Isn't my baby beautiful?" She held up the baby for my approval.

I smiled back. It was impossible to resist her effusive good nature. "Lovely," I agreed. "What's her name?"

"Johnny will decide. Oh, here he is. What's the baby's name, Johnny?"

Johnny was about twenty, five foot eleven, broad-shouldered, and smiling.

"We'll call her Sandra after my mother and Amelia after yours. Sandra Amelia Waterton."

Mrs. Waterton blinked and looked at her daughter. "That's a long name for such a little baby."

"How about we call her Sandy?" Johnny suggested.

"Oh, that's better."

"I will come and visit you the day after tomorrow. Will you be home?" I spoke to Johnny. It was clear any discussion about the baby should include him.

Mrs. Waterton looked at her husband.

He smiled at her then turned to me. "I have the rest of the week off, so you can come any time."

I'd call Annie, the social worker, in the morning. This mother deserved a chance to raise that baby. She may not be very bright, but she had a heart full of love, and that baby had a right to it. I knew adoptive parents were waiting for newborn babies, but this one wasn't going to get scooped up if I could help it.

The next day was Wednesday and my day off, but I called Annie right at 9:00 AM.

My favourite social worker had left with his wife for Prince George a few years ago. His replacement, Annie Cavell, was older, probably close to sixty, experienced, and easy to work with.

"Can you hold off on the Waterton baby?" I asked her. "I'd like to try to guide the mother. She has a supportive husband, and I think she's teachable. I'll try to get to see her tomorrow."

"I sure can," Annie said. "Just keep me informed."

I promised to do that and hung up the phone, relieved the baby was safe for a while.

I forgot work for a time and headed out to the barn with David. We tossed hay down to the sheep—there wasn't enough fresh grass to sustain them yet—and dumped oats in their trough. David crouched on the manger above the milling sheep while I checked to see if any were ready to lamb. I didn't see any noticeable signs, so we left them and peeked in on Cleo, who was lying on her side while the piglets nursed.

"Can I pick one up?" David asked.

"Not unless Janice is here. Cleo might not like it."

Cleo grunted.

"Oh." David nodded. "She says no."

I glanced at him. *Could he understand pig language?*

"We'll take the truck to the far meadow. Mr. White says he's had to herd our cows back through a fence that's down. We need to fix that."

"Okay." David was agreeable and usually keen to go anywhere. I loaded the fencing pliers, wire cutters, staples, and hammer into the back of the old, red Dodge pickup. The dirt track to the far meadow was rough but flat and it took only fifteen minutes to get there. I looked for the saskatoon berry bushes, bearing in mind that saskatoon berry pie was a summer treat. Their white blossoms would be obvious soon, but I didn't see any yet. I'd have to walk in here next month and check farther back in the woods. Bright yellow dandelions hugged the sunny spots at the edge of the trail. It was still too early for the orange tiger lilies to be dotting the fields.

It was quiet in the meadow when I pulled up beside the fence and turned off the motor. I helped David get out as the truck was high off the ground. A spruce grouse drummed in the woods, trying to attract a mate; that was a reassuring sign of spring. A Steller's jay called its harsh song from a tree nearby. They were here all winter. I was hoping to hear the returning migratory birds like the Swainson's thrush or even a robin. I listened for a moment more but there was nothing. Suddenly, a sandhill crane rose from the eastern edge of the meadow where the ground was low and wet. We stood transfixed as it spread its huge wings and squawked a protest at our presence, rose into the air, and flapped slowly over the trees and out of sight.

"Sounds like a toy," David said. "Like a party."

It did sound like one of those New Year's Eve clackers.

David and I examined the fence. I liked these ranch jobs when I could do them, but it was frustrating when I either didn't know how or didn't have the strength. Fencing was possible for me. The top three wires sagged. The staples had loosened enough to allow the fence to droop and the cows to step over it. I looked down the fence line. This appeared to be the only problem. Thank goodness it wasn't completely down as that would have been more difficult to fix. As it was, pulling those wires tight would require strength.

I gave David a bag of staples.

"You stay beside me, and when I ask for a staple, you pick out one and hand it to me." David was used to helping with chores. Even a three-year-old can concentrate and be useful.

I used the fencing pliers to grab the wire. I pulled it tight, then leaned my shoulder onto the pliers, which were about a foot long, to hold the wire in place. David handed me a staple. I held it with my left hand while I hammered with my right, still holding the wire with my shoulder. It was awkward but effective. We worked along the fence posts until we had the wire in place. Then we did the same thing with the second wire, which was also loose. It took about an hour, much slower with a three-year-old assistant than a ten-year-old, but we finished it.

"Now," I said, "home for lunch, okay?"

"Macaroni and cheese, right?"

"All right."

I turned the key in the ignition and the truck roared to life. I put it in gear, put my foot on the accelerator—and nothing happened.

"What's wrong?" David said.

"It won't move."

David looked around. We were parked in a four-acre meadow with trees on every side. There were no houses close where we could get some help.

David started to cry. "I want macaroni."

"I'll fix it, David. Don't worry."

He looked at me, disbelieving. "*Daddy* fix it."

"Well, Daddy can fix it, but so can Mommy."

"Mommy fix owies. Daddy fix trucks."

Gender roles established so early. "Oh ye of little faith," I said and got out of the truck, taking the keys. I wasn't leaving a three-year-old in a truck with keys. I took a pair of small pliers and some wire from the back of the truck. I propped open the hood and dived head-first into the engine. Down at the bottom, the accelerator cable had disengaged. It'd happened before. I could do this. I reconnected it and put a piece of small wire through the connection to reinforce it.

"All fixed," I said to my doubting son. He didn't believe me until the truck moved forward. David liked his life to unfold as planned. He didn't like disruption. As long as he knew what to expect, he was cooperative. He hadn't expected me to fix a truck, so his worry made sense to him.

When we got home, he had his macaroni and cheese, some milk, and an apple. He didn't nap after lunch anymore, but we sat on the couch munching our apples while I read him a story. I tried to do this every night as well but didn't always manage it. Carl read to him occasionally, as did Janice.

About one-thirty, we headed to town, where I was going to meet my friend Cynthia for coffee at the Cariboo Friendship Centre and, after that, grocery shop. The Cariboo Friendship Centre on Third Avenue was a place where mostly Indigenous people gathered, but it was open to all.

Cynthia, mother of seven, had first come to me at the health unit when her daughter Charlotte was in hospital in Vancouver. I had helped her stay in touch with Charlotte, and we'd been friends since. All her children were in school now—public school, as she was non-status according to Indian Affairs and so the kids escaped the residential school. She was working part-time at the Friendship Centre. I bought a coffee for myself and a chocolate milk for David. I settled him with a bag of action figures and cars as well as the milk on a low table, then joined Cynthia. Neither of us was working today, and our coffee date felt like a luxury.

"How's it going?" I asked her.

"Good. And you?"

We talked about our lives—the balancing act of home, family, and work, school challenges, the irritating habits of husbands, the ways we could increase our kids' education.

"Do your kids speak the traditional Chilcotin language?" I asked her. Her husband grew up in the Chilcotin. I was pretty sure the language was still strong out there.

"Ron and I do, but the kids don't."

"Why not?"

"It doesn't do my kids any good to speak English with an accent."

I thought about that. Cynthia was convinced she was looking after her kids' best interests. Prejudice was still strong against Indigenous people. I looked over at my son happily playing, his brown skin and brown hair fitting in well here. He was going to meet the same prejudice Cynthia and her family did. I had thought things would be better for his generation, but I didn't see much improvement in Williams Lake. Cynthia felt she had to sacrifice the language to prejudice. She knew best what was important for her children, but I could see the disadvantages to them.

"My grandfather spoke Gaelic," I said. "He was born in Scotland. My grandmother was born in Saskatchewan and didn't speak Gaelic, so my dad never learned it. I never learned it. I feel cheated."

"Hmm."

"There are a lot of jokes in Gaelic that I miss," I said.

She grinned. "It's true you have to know the language to get the jokes."

We talked a while longer then both left. Cynthia wanted to be home for her kids, and I wanted to whip through the grocery store and be home when mine got off the bus. I was glad I'd managed an hour with Cynthia. I valued my friendship with her, but it was hard to keep a social life when I was working and looking after animals and kids.

My best friend Dorrie had moved with her husband to Kamloops, where he joined a large medical practice. They had two boys now. We talked on the phone but rarely met; we were both so busy. Most of my friends were occupied with the constant work around young children, although only a few of us worked outside the home. Carl and I still attended dances about once a month and made sure we connected with friends there, but it was difficult to find time to just socialize.

David and I were home before the older kids, and I was busy making supper when Janice flew in the door. "Pigs'r out!"

"Oh no!" That was an all-hands-on-deck emergency call. I slipped my feet into my gumboots, parked David on the porch, and told him not to move but to try to see where the piglets had gone. If he spotted one, he was to yell. It wouldn't be Cleo who had gotten out but those curious, busy piglets. There was wilderness around us; if they got far from the pen, we might never find them. Or we might just find their bones after the coyotes were finished with them.

"How many are out?" I yelled at Janice as she raced toward the trees.

"Five!" she yelled back.

Carl drove into the yard right then.

"Leave your briefcase and help us! Pigs are out!"

"Pigs are out!" David yelled from the porch.

Every minute counted.

"Got one," Glen yelled, and I went to help him with the squirming, pink piglet he'd pinned to the ground.

"Where did they get out?" I asked him as we carried the piglet to the pen and tipped it over the fence.

"There." He pointed to the bottom of the pen where I could see a piece of plywood acting as a temporary barricade.

"Did you and Janice fix that?" That was a good idea. There was no point in catching pigs and returning them to the pen only to have them escape again.

He nodded and hurried back to the trees. There was still some snow under the fir trees but the rest of the ground was clear.

I went to the east of the pen and spotted a flash of pink. I dived, sliding through a small pile of snow, and grabbed the leg. I stood holding it, triumphant but soaked on one side.

Carl had grabbed the other leg and we lifted that piglet into the air and started toward the pen. Then we stopped and looked at each other. We each had a leg and were on opposite sides of a small poplar. The pig, with one leg on one side and one on the other, was held fast by the tree. We weren't going anywhere. I started to laugh. "It's all yours," I said, dropping the leg I was holding.

He grinned, shook his head, and returned the piglet to the pen.

"How many have we caught?" I shouted to Janice, both to find out if we should still be looking and to locate her.

She answered me from near the barn. "Count them!" she directed me.

I went back to the pen and counted. "Eleven."

"There's one more!"

"It's over here!" Glen had spotted it hiding under the tractor. Carl went to assist him, and we got them all back. Carl and Janice stayed at the pigpen to make more substantial repairs on the fence. I washed and changed my muddy clothes.

"They chew the wood," Janice said as they arrived back at the house for supper.

"Maybe we can put rebar along there," Carl suggested. He looked at me. "I need a shower."

He had dirt along his arms and his face. "You do. I'll hold supper."

"That was fun," David said. From his position on the porch, our frantic search must have looked like a game to him. It was serious, though. Janice would have grieved over lost piglets.

ON THURSDAY MORNING, Ellie passed me a request from Dr. Anderson to take on a home care patient. Movan Whitey had a bad burn on his arm and needed a daily dressing change.

"The problem is," Ellie said when she handed me the newly made-up file, "he doesn't have a home, so you can't visit him. He's one of the Troopers."

The Troopers were a group of mostly Indigenous adult men and women who, although many of them had homes and relatives they could stay with in the surrounding country, preferred to band together in the downtown area. They drank together and also worked together: tree planting, doing odd jobs such as collecting and delivering firewood, and helping with the haying on ranches nearby.

I took the file. I didn't want the home care nurses to do a dressing change on the street. "We'll arrange for him to come to the health unit."

"Be careful," Ellie said.

I hadn't heard Movan was dangerous—at least not when he was sober.

Thursday was our regular staff meeting day for the home care team. I presented the file to the five nurses. Jane was on duty this weekend.

"There's no one here on the weekends but me, and I don't want to be alone with him," Jane said. "I've heard stories about him." Jane was my age, mother of two and wife of a busy forester. She was a confident nurse but was admitting to feeling out of her depth with this patient.

"I like Movan," Sally said. I swear she knew everyone in town. "Most of the time. But I'm off this weekend and I have plans."

"I'll come in and do his dressing change on Saturday and Sunday," I said. "You have a full weekend, Jane. You don't want to be waiting around for Movan." It behooved me to accommodate her, as she was usually willing to do most tasks.

"Thanks." Jane was relieved. She knew that, ethically, she should see every patient, but she was thankful not to be forced into caring for Movan.

I trusted Sally's judgement, especially when it aligned with mine. "I'll admit him this afternoon and set up the times. Sally, can you see him on Friday?"

"Yeah, I can do that. It will be nice to connect with him."

Jane sent her a sideways look.

"I'm on next week," Violet said. "I can see him." Violet was slim, quick in her movements, and willing to tackle almost anything.

"That's good, then. I'll ask the doctor to send him here."

I MADE A QUICK VISIT to Mrs. Waterton. She and her husband lived in town, in a small but scrupulously clean two-bedroom house. It was on the hill near Williams Lake. I took a moment to assess the lake. There was a competition in town, called "Guess the Date of Break-Up." You could buy a ticket and enter your best guess of when the ice would break up on the lake. Someone from the Rotary Club had placed a barrel in the lake, which had frozen in place. When the barrel moved to a certain point, break-up was officially announced. The Rotary Club had scheduled a dance for the middle of April, with a live band, lots of dancing, and a midnight buffet. Carl and I would dance until the last note of the band blasted a finale, to celebrate the beginning of spring. I had a ticket for the ice break-up to occur on April 8. It didn't look as though I was going to win. There was no darkening at the edges of this lake.

Johnny answered the door.

"They gave me two weeks off," he said.

"Where do you work?" I walked past him into the house, without my scale this time as babies often lose weight the first week and I didn't want Mrs. Waterton to notice that. The baby was a healthy weight at birth, so an ounce or two of weight loss was not important, at least this close to birth.

"At Mackenzie's," he said, referring to the local grocery store. That would be a reliable job as the Stevensons, who owned it, were good employers.

Mrs. Waterton was breastfeeding, which was the simplest strategy. We talked about how often she should feed her baby.

"My mom nursed my little sisters, and I saw her do it," Mrs. Waterton said. "She's coming over this afternoon to make sure Sandy is feeding all right."

Another support for the family.

Johnny showed me the diaper station and the way he had organized the laundry. Love and practical help. This child was going to be fine.

"I know the nurse at the hospital thought Amber was not going to manage," Johnny told me as he escorted me to my car. "But Amber is fine if you give her clear directions."

"I think she'll manage, but I'll come once a week for a while in case you have questions." That would give me a chance to gather enough evidence to defend her against the Welfare system, if necessary.

"Amber's wonderful, you know. She brings me so much happiness. And now she's given me a daughter. That's special."

"You are a lucky man."

"For sure," he said.

I wonder what Helen, the maternity nurse with her strict criteria for motherhood, would have made of this family if she could see them now.

AT TWO O'CLOCK, Movan arrived to see me. I brought him into my office and offered him a coffee.

"Two sugars," he said.

I fetched it and settled in my chair. Standing, Movan was intimidating—dark skin, dark eyes, dark hair worn long and shaggy. His clothes were dishevelled as if he had been sleeping rough. I expected he had been.

"Now, Mr. Whitey, could you come to the health unit at eleven every morning for," I glanced at the chart, "ten days?"

"Movan," he said.

"Movan," I repeated. "I'm Marion."

He nodded.

I read the chart for a few moments. "You have a pretty bad burn."

He nodded again.

"The reason for the daily changes of the bandages is to keep it clean and prevent infection."

"Right. Got that."

"So can you make eleven every morning?"

He thought about it. "One would be better."

"We can do that." I wrote on his chart. "Sally Chernoff will see you tomorrow."

"Sally? Good woman, that."

I smiled at him. "She's a gem."

He sipped his coffee and waited.

"I'll meet you here at one on Saturday and Sunday."

"Okay." He put his empty coffee cup on my desk.

I closed the file and stood.

He stood as well. I looked up.

"And Movan. Don't come if you're drinking."

"Why not?"

"Too scary," I said.

He thought about it. "Okay."

I walked him to the door then went back to my office to leave a message for Sally about the change of time. I also put a note on the outside of his chart so Sally would see it when she picked up her charts at the beginning of her day.

Marlene, whose public health district included several in-town schools, came to me late in the afternoon with her plans for a pre-school health screening fair. She was taller than me, a little heavier, with clear skin and a ready smile. She had an incisive mind that was able to relate policies and plans to practical situations. I thought she'd end up as a supervisor or even the head of public health in Victoria once her children had grown.

"I've got support from Paul and Angela, but I'm going to need a lot of help from the nurses," Marlene told me.

"Tell me all about it."

"I've got a date in mid-June. We can use all the offices and clinic spaces in the health unit. We'll set up stations all around the arena, like a trade fair, where we'll have testing for hearing and vision and a dental check station; we'll also check records for immunizations. The professionals will be there: the speech pathologist, the optometrist, the dental tech, and the nurses. People, probably mostly mothers, will bring their four- and five-year-olds to us, and we will screen them for impairments. We'll have a mental health screening questionnaire as well."

"Wow. That's ambitious." Marlene was impressive. I'd never even heard of a preschool screening fair, let alone had any experience organizing one.

"We can do it."

"I don't doubt it for a minute. What do you want me to do?"

She handed me a list. She had already worked out how to delegate some of the work. I had time to accomplish her directives and contribute to this. In terms of public health, it was an exciting idea. If we could catch impairments before kids went to school, we could prevent many problems. It was an ambitious project for five nurses. I hoped we could manage it.

I PICKED UP DAVID at Edith's house and turned onto the road to the house just as the bus deposited Janice and Glen at their stop. I picked them up and saved them the quarter-mile walk home. When we got home, I sniffed the welcome scent of pine and furniture polish. Our cleaner, Eileen, had come and gone, leaving my house sparkling. I appreciated her. Janice checked on Cleo then came into the house, grabbed an apple, draped Missy the cat around her neck, and went to her room; David went to his bedroom to sort out his toys; Glen took an apple from the fridge then sat at the counter with Ben at his feet, his brown eyes watching every move Glen made, waiting for a bit of apple to fall. I threw some potatoes in the oven to bake then pulled steak from the fridge, where it had been thawing all day. We paid by the pound to have a steer butchered and packaged, so it was the same price for hamburger as it was for steak. I was chopping vegetables for a salad when I realized Glen was staring at me.

The phone rang. It was my neighbour, Linda. She had three children: two teenaged girls and a nine-year-old boy.

"Marion, Andrea is a little upset with Glen."

I glanced at Glen. He must have been expecting this call.

"What's the problem, Linda?"

"Glen has been swearing at the bus stop and Andrea doesn't like it."

Andrea was basically a nice girl but going through her fifteen-year-old know-it-all stage. She could be condescending and sarcastic. I didn't say that, though.

"I'll speak to him, Linda." I didn't thank her for calling. I wasn't thankful.

"I knew I could count on you. Thank you."

"No problem."

I hung up.

There was silence. "That was Linda, Andrea's mother."

Glen looked glum. "She said she was going to tattle to her mother."

"You were swearing at the bus stop?"

His big brown eyes opened wide. "I was. But it's not fair!"

"What's not fair?"

"I can't swear at home. I can't swear at school. I can't swear on the bus. Now I can't swear at the bus stop! Where can I swear?" he almost wailed.

It was a legitimate question. Carl and I both swore occasionally. There were inappropriate and appropriate places to swear, at least as far as he had observed.

I reached over, hugged him, and whispered in his ear, "You can swear at the bus stop."

His eyes lit and he straightened. "I can? Thanks, Mom." And he was off, probably to see the piglets.

That was likely the wrong thing to say, but I'd be tempted to swear at Andrea myself.

CHAPTER SEVEN

WORKING IN THE SCHOOLS AND SUPPORTING THE 4-H

I WORKED MONDAYS at the elementary school. Hannah Harbinger was the energetic principal and usually had a list of what she wanted me to do. We had the lice conversation every year.

"I want you to check the students for lice," she always said.

"Lice are not a health hazard; they are a pest. I will instruct the teachers on how to look for them and what to recommend to parents, but I won't spend time checking heads."

"I can teach them that myself," she grumbled.

"Go ahead." I grinned at her. We were good friends now. She and her husband Jim acted as grandparents to my kids. Carl's parents went south for part of the year and my parents lived a day's drive away, so Hannah and Jim came to our home for holiday meals, birthdays, school concerts, and celebrations. I enjoyed their sharp-witted conversations, and I admired Hannah's efforts to manage the pupils, the staff—and me. I just didn't always do what she wanted.

"What's this I hear about you knocking on doors?" I asked. Sally had told me Hannah was actively counteracting the proselytizing message of a new religious sect.

"That group is highly organized," she said. "They're going door to door and trying to get the new immigrants, particularly those coming to work in the logging industry, to come to their church.

They're promising them a social life, food, and even financial help."
There were many immigrants from India in Williams Lake and the
nearby small community of Glendale.

"And you object?"

She snorted. "What they're *not* promising is education for girls
or even independence for girls, which go together."

I hadn't heard this. "Do you tell the new immigrants that?"

"No. I tell them they can't get their Canadian citizenship if they
join that group because one of the group's rules is they can't swear
allegiance to the Crown. That keeps them from joining, and the
girls are safe."

I pictured Hannah stumping up the path to the house, knocking
loudly on the door, her voice authoritative and insistent when she
explained her mission. Her argument might sway some, but it was
likely her presence that convinced them. She was trusted in the
community. If she said, "Don't join," no one would join.

I had three vision referrals at this school from teachers who suspected the children couldn't see well. Teachers were usually right
about this. They were seldom right about referrals for hearing loss,
though. I had one request to test a child for colour blindness and
had brought the Ishihara test book with me. There were coloured
numbers in the circles on the individual pages I presented to the
child. If they had difficulty with distinguishing colours, they saw
one number; if they didn't, they saw another. It was an easy test
to administer. After doing my assessment, I knew this little grade
two girl was not colour blind. Hannah wanted to know the results
before the teachers got them. She would make sure the teachers
followed up and talked to the parents.

In the afternoon, I met my long-time colleague Sophie at her
high school, which was up on the hill over Williams Lake but not
far from the health unit. We prepared to administer Rubella immunizations to the students who needed it. Sophie had sent out the
consent forms, collected them, and chased down the missing
forms by phoning the parents for verbal consent.

She was working in the staff room and had set up my work-station in the vice-principal's office. I was immunizing any grade ten girl who needed a shot. While Rubella or German measles is a mild disease, it could have drastic effects on a fetus, so we tried to make sure all the girls were protected.

A boy shuffled in and sat down.

"This immunization is just for girls today."

He looked up. "I *am* a girl."

I realized that, indeed, she was a girl, just hidden by shaggy hair, a heavy flannel shirt even though it was a warm day, jeans, and runners.

"I beg your pardon," I said, appalled I had made such a mistake. There wasn't any way I could negate my comment. Her consent form said *Leah*. I should have read it first.

While she was rolling up her sleeve I reflected on her clothes. Clothes defined gender in this school. Most girls wore jeans and shirts, but the jeans were flared at the bottom and the shirts were in pastel shades. She seemed to be deliberately and wordlessly stating *Don't notice I'm a girl*. What was behind that?

I knew her parents. I'd even been to her home once. Sophie had co-opted me to pick up donations for the school garage-sale drive, and when I'd gone into the house to collect a couple of boxes, I'd noticed there were no doors on the children's rooms. Those doorless bedrooms seemed ominous now. Was Leah hiding her femininity because she was being sexually abused at home? Was that far-fetched or reasonable?

I followed Sophie to her car as we were packing up to leave and told her what I'd seen and what worried me. "What do you think?"

"I think I'd better talk to her."

I didn't know what Sophie could do. If Leah didn't admit her father—or mother or uncle, but it was most likely her father—had sexually abused her, then Sophie couldn't pursue it. I didn't think the girl would admit the abuse if there was any. If she did, her dad would be arrested and her family home torn apart. She'd feel it was her fault. She might think no one would believe her, and they might not. Then her situation would be so bad she might have to leave home. She was only fifteen. She might feel her sole option was to remain silent.

If Sophie could get some time with Peggy MacFarlane, the psychologist, she might get some advice. Perhaps Paul, as medical health officer, might also have advice.

I asked Sophie the next week what she'd done. She said Leah did not admit to anything being wrong at home, but Sophie visited the mother with concerns that the girl's clothing choices indicated she was having trouble accepting her femininity, or perhaps she truly felt masculine. Sophie commented on the doorless bedrooms and said she thought Leah might feel more comfortable with herself if she had a door on her bedroom—a door that locked. The mother agreed to it.

"Will she do that?"

"I said I would be back to see if it helped."

"Do you think Leah would just prefer to be a boy?"

"Hard to tell, but if that's the case, then getting a locked door for her room won't do any harm."

I thought about that house. "There's another doorless bedroom."

"There's another daughter," she said grimly.

"They need two locked doors, then."

"You bet."

That was the best we could do. I trusted Sophie to follow up on this. If nothing was done by Leah's parents, I could see Sophie buying two doors and showing up with her six-foot-three husband to install them.

It probably wouldn't come to that. Sophie had signalled she was watching the family. That might be enough to protect Leah.

I finished up my charting for the day, but just before I was ready to leave, Sally, the senior home care nurse, arrived. Her grey hair was wet and plastered to her head.

"What happened?" I checked the window; it wasn't raining.

She threw her black bag onto my counter and flopped in a chair. I settled back down to listen.

"You know Jacob Ratenbury out on North Lakeside?"

I mentally reviewed this home care patient: Seventy-one, lived alone in a tiny cabin off the highway. We supervised his medications as he couldn't remember to take his pills. Kate had nursed him several times and, with the skill of her Irish grandmother, had sewn a packet with seven compartments and placed his pills into the separate compartments labelled with the days of the week, so he knew what to take every day. The nurses checked once a week and refilled the packet. So far, that system had been working; he was taking the meds.

"What happened?" I asked again.

"I was sick and tired of Jacob's dirty clothes, his filthy hair, and the squalor he lives in. I told him last week to clean up. He didn't."

"What did you do?" I eyed her still-damp hair.

"I pulled out all the beer bottles he'd stored in the shower—cases of them—and stacked them on the porch. All the time, he's fluttering around me like a nervous chicken saying, 'No. No. I need those.' I told him I'd take them to the liquor store and bring him the money they fetched. He still protested."

"Then what?"

"Then I took that skinny old man, stripped him, and shoved him in the shower."

I could see it. Jacob was only about five foot four, about Sally's height, and a lightweight. "You got wet?"

"Well, he didn't want to stay there. So I stripped down to my panties and bra and got in there with him. He was so astounded that he stood still and I got him cleaned—probably for the first time in years."

I burst into laughter. She probably transgressed many rules of professional behaviour, but she'd managed to get him clean.

"Was he still complaining when you left?" I might have to field an official complaint. I was wondering how I could get Sally out of any repercussions.

"No. I got dressed, found him some clean clothes, glory be, and dressed him. He's got a small washing machine on the back porch, so I put those dirty rags he wore in there and started it. I checked to make sure he wasn't stashing bottles in there before I turned it on. Then I fixed us both a cup of tea. He was drinking tea when I left. I promised I'd bring him a muffin next Friday."

"Do you think he'll be clean next week?"

She grunted. "I'm not expecting miracles."

I PHONED ANNIE AND REPORTED on the Waterton family. Amber and Johnny, with the help of Amber's mother, were managing very well. Annie said she'd create a report that used me as a reference and would close the file on the family. I was relieved and happy that neither Amber nor Johnny knew of the initial threat to their family, although Johnny had picked up on Helen's disapproval. I also was relieved that Annie was so practical and cooperative. Occasionally our paths crossed with mutual clients, and I appreciated how easy it was to cooperate with her. A year ago, I worked with her on the placement of the intellectually disabled in the area. Annie had managed to get enough funding to buy a home for group-living for five clients. It was a huge resource for the area and staffed by a married couple who watched over the house. Annie was a gem.

I WAS ABOUT TEN MINUTES LATE picking up David. Edith and her family lived only a few blocks from the health unit in the downtown residential area of Williams Lake. It was a tidy bungalow with a yard. Edith, who was as usual wearing a neat cotton dress, had David ready. I apologized for the delay.

"It doesn't happen often," she said, which told me she didn't *want* it to happen often.

On the drive home, David told me about a walk he'd gone on with Edith, and I admired the spring greening of the alder and birch along the road. It was a relief to see the last of the ice leave Williams Lake in the middle of April. Spring had to follow. The saskatoon berry blossoms showed white at the edge of the road. That was encouraging. I reviewed my menu for supper tonight: Stew was thawing in the fridge, and I'd make dumplings to go on top of it. Everyone liked that. No supper tomorrow as we were going to a 4-H competition and dance. I had a big tray of brownies and another of Nanaimo bars in the freezer I'd take out to thaw tonight. Kids couldn't seem to get enough chocolate. Other parents were bringing the main course, so there would be plenty to eat.

When David and I got home, Janice and Glen had just arrived. As usual, Janice changed her clothes then darted out to take care of Cleo. I encouraged Glen to go feed his calf, and I brought David with me to feed and check the sheep.

"Mom, look. Babies!"

Sure enough there were three new lambs. Singletons, each with a ewe. With David perched on the manger and out of the way, I managed to herd the three ewes and lambs into a separate pen, where I fed them extra oats and made sure they had water. I moved among the rest of the sheep looking for signs of impending birth while keeping an eye out for Archie, the ram, who wasn't above bunting me a solid whack when he thought of it. Luckily, he was preoccupied with getting food and not paying any attention to me. I found two ewes with bulging vulvas who were ready to lamb. I managed to get them into a second pen and feed them separately. Once the ewes started to lamb, they all did so within two weeks. I know estrus is governed by the hours of daylight and the moon, and probably some goddess of fertility somewhere, but I didn't yet understand it. The 4-H leader, Verna Dennis, wanted me to supervise the lamb projects of some of the members, so I'd have to learn.

When I emerged from the barn, I saw a black pickup truck in the yard. Jim Harbinger, Hannah's husband, was standing at the back of it talking to Janice. I walked closer.

"I was at a party last night at the Legion," he said. "See, it was a banquet. Good food and lots of it. So I persuaded the kitchen staff to load all the leftovers in this garbage can here, and I brought it up for Cleo."

He beamed at her. Jim and Janice had talked pigs for a year or so now. Jim and Hannah lived in town, where Jim could not keep pigs. Obviously, he wished he could.

I waited to hear what Janice would say.

"That's really nice of you, Jim. To think of Cleo like that."

"No problem." He opened the tailgate.

"But I can't feed that to Cleo."

He stopped, turned, and looked at her.

Janice spoke to him seriously. "First, because there may be tobacco mixed in with it. People are careless with their cigarettes, and tobacco is bad for Cleo. Second, it won't be nutritionally balanced the way the pig pellets are."

She was enumerating her reasons the way she did in a 4-H judging competition.

"And last, it hasn't been refrigerated, so it must be growing pathogens, and I don't want Cleo to eat them."

Jim looked at her. "Damned if those aren't good reasons. Sorry, I didn't think."

"That's okay," Janice said. She was friendly, but she was not going to let him feed that mess to Cleo.

I stepped forward. "Do you have time for coffee, Jim?"

He shut the tailgate. "Sure."

He settled at the kitchen table. Janice got her binder of pig accounts—the meticulous records all 4-H kids were required to keep, where all expenditures were listed. She took the binder and her glass of juice and sat beside him.

Jim looked over at the accounts. He had agreed to be a part owner of two piglets and took an active interest in the profits. He read Janice's numbers and reached into his pocket for his cigars. He absent-mindedly proffered one to Janice.

"No, thank you," she said politely.

He blinked. "Oh, right."

I felt laughter starting to well up and hurriedly left the room.

People often did forget she was only ten.

ON SATURDAY MORNING, we loaded into my Suburban for our trip to 100 Mile House and the 4-H competition there. It wasn't an event where the kids brought their animals but one where they judged other animals and competed against each other in public speaking. Janice had prepared a speech. Glen would think about what to say just before he was called upon. He didn't usually do as well as Janice, but he was competent and his way suited him. I refrained from nagging.

Parents would collect the animals to be judged from their herds and transport them to the stockyards ready for the competition. Judges who would rate the competitors had been chosen from the parent group with an outside judge as the overseer. This judge was from Kamloops, about two hours southeast.

The 4-H club members pledged: "My head to clearer thinking, my heart to greater loyalty, my hands to larger service, and my health to better living, for my club, my community, and my country." The parents committed to hours of work to support them.

I deposited my desserts in the kitchen and was told by the head organizer working there to report to the judges as they needed someone to record the results. I handed David over to Carl with strict instructions. "Hold onto his hand. Do not let him run loose. There are cars, trucks, horses, and kids everywhere."

"Yes, ma'am," Carl said, but I expected he'd get into conversation with someone or lend a hand fixing a fence or a car motor and forget David. I was going to be walking around the site with the judges, so I'd try to keep an eye on him. That worried me. David could easily escape supervision. I spotted the older sister of one of the members. "Adele," I called to her.

"Hi, Mrs. Crook."

Adele had graduated from high school and was working in the Royal Bank.

"Can I hire you to mind my three-year-old? Ten dollars plus enough extra for you to buy yourself and David some lunch?"

"You're on. It'll give me something to do."

I brought her over to Carl and David, introduced them, and transferred David to Adele's care. That relieved me, and Carl could enjoy his day.

"I'll get you lunch," Carl said to me. "I'll find you and deliver it."

"Thanks."

I spent the day following the judges and tallying their written figures that declared which 4-H member of all five clubs represented here won each class and the overall trophy.

I watched both Janice and Glen in their classes. Janice was impressive with her logical and adult approach to judging. Volunteers led four yearling calves around a pen. Five 4-H members of various ages stood in the pen, watching the calves intently. They each had a judging sheet attached to a clipboard in one hand, usually clutched to their body, and a pencil in the other. They watched the calves move and stand. Then they approached each calf and ran their hands over it. Parents hung over the edge of the corral, observing, but all were quiet. When Janice's group was finished, another five kids took their place.

Glen was entertaining and easily distracted, but he participated and was much like many of the other boys there, constantly moving. He was quick in his assessments of the animals and quick to write down what he'd seen. I tried hard not to compare Janice and Glen as they each had their own skills and different personalities. When Janice won a class, I took the tally sheet to another parent to have them check the figures and sign off on it. I didn't want her disqualified because I was recording the numbers, and I wanted it to be clear the competition was fair. Fairness matters to kids—and to their parents.

At the end of the day, we all met in the hall for dinner and the awarding of prizes.

Our Soda Creek club sat together. The kids talked about their experiences and were amazingly kind to one another. Janice and her friend Ray had both done well in their classes, so the kids speculated on who would win.

"It might be someone from another club," Janice said. "We don't know."

"Maybe," Ray said.

It didn't seem to occur to them that I did know.

When the award was announced, the highest score for the day, Janice received it. The whole club, including Ray, burst into cheers. She'd won it for the club and they were proud of her. I was so grateful to them. Some kids would have made her feel precocious and an outcast, but they embraced her as part of their club group. Everyone had something to contribute. Others were smart as well. Others contributed consideration and kindness. Others had skills with their animals. They all appreciated one another.

On the way home, with David fast asleep in his seat, I congratulated Janice. "Well done, honey."

"Thanks," she said. "I wasn't sure about that pen of yearlings. But I got it right in the end."

"Yes, well done, Jan," her dad said.

"I won four marbles," Glen announced.

"Did you?" I said with interest. "Who did you play with?"

"Mike and George. I won two off each of them."

Carl glanced at me. Was that gambling? Or was that a legitimate accomplishment?

"Well done, Glen," I said. To each his own skill.

CHAPTER EIGHT

FLYING TO PAN PHILIP'S RANCH

I DON'T KNOW what kind of law work Pan Phillips needed, but Carl almost bounced into the kitchen one Sunday afternoon in late May, asking, "Do you want to fly out into the Chilcotin with me next Saturday?"

My first thought was *Yes!* My second was: *Will Colleen babysit?* She was a neighbour, the oldest of six at sixteen, and unflappable. I thought about the Chilcotin, that broad, vast plateau to the west of us. It would be green now, with sunflowers in the meadows. "I'd love to. What's the reason?"

"I can deliver some papers to Pan, get his signature, and speed up the transaction."

"Faster than Canada Post?"

He grinned. "Of course."

There was no practical reason; he just wanted to get the plane out and fly. Colleen agreed to sit with the kids. I was eager to meet Pan Phillips as I'd read *Grass Beyond the Mountains,* written by Pan's friend and ranching partner Rich Hobson. I admired the tenacity and vision of the men. They'd come to this area in 1934 searching for good grazing land for cattle. Pan had established his Home Ranch and had many a gruelling cattle drive to market.

The weather cooperated, and we arrived at the airport before nine in the morning on a fine, sunny Saturday. We had owned a plane since just after we married. This one was a Navion, a Ryan product, built in the 1940s and held together with thousands of rivets. "Solid and reliable," Carl had assured me. It was a low-wing, four-seater aircraft with a sliding canopy instead of a door, a Lycoming 260 engine, a variable pitch prop, and retractable gear. It could get speeds of 120 miles per hour comfortably. This day, Carl agreed to let me take off. He cleared us with Air Flight Services and we were safe to leave. The Williams Lake Airport runway was seven thousand feet long, so a beginner pilot like me had a lot of time to get the aircraft up to take-off speed. I didn't need much runway; we were up and flying quickly. I levelled out, lifted the landing gear, trimmed back the flaps, and headed west.

Carl took over the column and handed the navigational book to me. He had plotted out the route. I checked the instruments to make sure he was on the heading he'd chosen, then relaxed. I'd spent the first few years of our flying adventures terrified of crashing. I read all the accident reports and worried. But once I'd learned to fly myself, I stopped having palpitations every time we took off. I suppose it was all about feeling in control.

The Chilcotin country was dramatically different from the air than it was from the ground. Here, if I just turned my head, I could see the miles and miles of conifers to the east and the miles and miles of grasslands to the west. When I was on the ground, I saw what was in front of me and had to imagine the rest. Flying high above the earth expanded my vision. I existed in a different dimension.

Carl turned his head and grinned at me. "I feel like I'm playing hooky."

I laughed. I also had that feeling of escaping all responsibilities. No kids. No ranching chores. No phone calls. No work. I liked all that, but it was fun to leave it behind.

Pan Phillips's ranch was at the west of the Chilcotin Plateau near the mountains, so over an hour's flying time. As we approached, I could see the conifers, probably spruce and pine, crowding the grasslands. The airstrip was a length of level land, some of it lined by conifers.

"Look out for fences," Carl said.

We never talked much on an approach to landing as the pilot needed to concentrate.

I peered below me. There were fences in the meadows but not on the approach to the landing strip. I wasn't even tempted to try to land on this field. Carl could do it. I wanted smooth asphalt before I landed. Carl, with eight years more flying experience, had no trouble.

By the time he had switched off the ignition and the prop had stopped turning, I saw a vehicle approaching from some distance away. When Carl slid back the canopy and we stepped onto the wing, I realized it was a tractor. Pan was coming to fetch us in his tractor! I could see as he came closer that he was shorter than Carl, probably about five foot ten. He looked every inch a cowboy even on a tractor, with his black stetson pulled low over his forehead, wearing a plaid work shirt and jeans. Carl reached into the back seat of the plane and lifted out his briefcase. I slid off the wing and waited for our ride.

Pan shook Carl's hand and nodded to me. He was polite, but he was intent on his business with Carl. I think it involved property, but I hadn't asked Carl for particulars. I felt as if I was in the presence of a celebrity. Carl stood beside Pan, and I hung onto the back of the tractor seat with my feet wedged on top of the hitch. Pan drove slowly over the smooth meadow grass. It was a huge meadow, over fifty acres, I guessed, ringed with alder and what looked like spruce and pine. The blue Itcha Mountains rose in the west.

I knew Pan was married, but when we got to the house, his wife, Betty, wasn't there. His daughter, Diana, gave me coffee and left me to wait in the large living room. I got the impression that planes frequently landed at their air strip and she couldn't entertain everyone who came. I appreciated the coffee. The men sat at a table and talked.

The log cabin was large, the biggest I'd ever been in. It was dark like most log cabins, even on such a bright day as today. From the air, the ranch had appeared isolated; their cabin was the only one I'd seen. I had thought our ranch, which was a quarter mile from the nearest neighbour, was isolated, but it was positively urban compared to this.

Carl's business didn't take long, and soon we were back on the bone-shattering tractor—Carl standing beside Pan again and me with my toes wedged into the back of the tractor seat and hanging on like a limpet to a rock.

We took off into the wind. Carl did that as well; I was not going to chance hitting a pothole on this grass strip and having the controls wrested out of my hands. Once airborne, Carl made a wide turn and headed west. I watched the trees and meadows fall away. I saw the lake in front of the Phillips ranch, and then as we got higher, I spotted a lake not far to the west. They would have all the water they and their cattle needed. It was beautiful but isolated. I thought about the pioneer settlers in the Cariboo and Chilcotin.

Some settlers—most, I presumed—wanted land. Some wanted large tracts of land where they could fence off their holding from others and control it. Some wanted only a bit of land to live a subsistent life. Few settlers lived the seasonal life of the Indigenous Peoples who congregated in villages for some of the year then dispersed to their territories following game, berries, or fish—a kind of land ownership, or at least an agreed-upon territory, that their families had used for generations. Those two types of land use didn't harmonize well. As long as there weren't many settlers it was workable, but we were beyond that easy accommodation now. When the first settlers arrived, they were tolerated by the Indigenous Peoples, but few of those settlers respected the Indigenous view of territorial control. Settlers wanted deeds of ownership, and they didn't recognize prior claims. Perhaps it was still possible to coexist, but the two groups had different philosophies about land. From the air, it had seemed as though there were hundreds of acres of uninhabited land still free. Although huge, free land was an illusion.

We landed, left the Navion in the hangar, and were home by three in the afternoon. I listened to the kids talk about their day and got supper ready.

THE LAST WEEKEND OF MAY was planting day. The trees were in leaf and the sunflowers were starting to show on the sides of hills. I was optimistic that the warm weather was coming; I'd seen snow in every month of the year, so planting was a gamble.

Carl had turned up a section of the hillside for a garden, and I had worked it over with a shovel and a rake until it was fairly smooth. The previous week, he'd dumped a load of cow manure on the plot and levelled it with the blade of the tractor. Chicken manure was too "hot" according to my uncle who was a farmer, but we had our choice of pig, cow, sheep or horse manure. I'd have liked to experiment with a different one each year, but Carl was committed to transporting the variety that was easiest to access, and that was the cow manure from the corral. I spent some time on Wednesday digging the manure in and raking it smooth.

Today, David and I were going to plant potatoes, lettuce, carrots, and radishes. I'd wait until mid-June to plant the corn, squash, and beans. I brought the bag of seed potatoes, a knife, a couple of trowels, and a shovel to the garden. I gave David a trowel. I dug into the loose soil and created hillocks in a long row. Then we opened the bag of potatoes, and I cut them so there was an eye—the white root-like runner—on each segment the way my dad had taught me years ago. David took the segment and placed it in the hillock, burying three or four in each one.

We worked there until we had buried them all, then planted a row of lettuce and one of radishes.

The songbirds were back, and I tried to identify them so David could learn to tell them apart. The red-winged blackbird had a distinctive call, so it was easy to identify. We were lucky and heard a Swainson's thrush; they sounded like bells chiming in the woods.

"Listen to that, Davie," I said. It was the spring song of the chickadee, with its musical *phoebee, phoebee*.

"Nice."

It was nice. Magical even. Warm sun. Warm earth. Loving child. Peace.

CHAPTER NINE

WORKING AT THE PRESCHOOL SCREENING FAIR

I T WAS A LAZY SUNDAY afternoon in the middle of June—about as lazy as it gets on a ranch—and I had climbed into the big recliner chair in the living room with last week's local paper. If I looked up, I could see down the valley, green now, the sky a hazy blue. My public health instructor had told me years ago it was vitally important to read the local paper in order to understand your community. I read it for that reason and also because I was insatiably curious. The paper reported who had achieved something, who had been charged with a crime, what events were coming up locally, and the usual births and death notices.

The Stampede Committee was still looking for volunteers. The Stampede, our rodeo, was an international competitive event with cowboys from the US, Alberta, and the local settlements like Alexis Creek, Alkali Lake, Riske Creek, and Anahim Lake. Carl and I didn't usually work at the Stampede; our 4-H activities took most of our spare hours, but I'd keep that volunteer opportunity in mind. I read there was a vehicle crash at McLeese Lake. One death. Was this someone I knew? Not this time. I read through the paper, sipping coffee and enjoying the quiet. Carl had all the kids outside working on cleaning up the croquet field, which was our picnic area below the house where we had level ground, trees for shelter, and a fire pit. It was Glen's birthday at the end of the month and we were planning a party.

I remembered reading like this years ago when Carl was in law school. We were at the university in Vancouver then, and I found an old *Williams Lake Tribune* and perused it with the same kind of pleasure until a name grabbed my attention: Lorne Decker. I remembered him. He'd been in grade six when I was the nurse for the school at Lac la Hache Station at the end of the lake. Lorne was the eldest of six kids who were orphaned when their parents died in an accident; he lived with his siblings and grandmother. They were Indigenous but must have been non-status because they attended public school. I'd loved going to Lac la Hache Station. This was a tiny community, consisting of a school and a couple of houses. I assumed there was a railway station there at one point to service the Lac la Hache community, about two miles to the east, but there was none there now. The teacher at the one-room public school, Elsie Henderson, was experienced, intelligent, and inventive. She taught calmly and seemingly effortlessly, and I'm sure behind that organized tranquility, she worked hard. She brought all the children to Williams Lake to the music festival every year, where they competed in the spoken verse category. The kids were happy in that school. I remembered them clearly.

As I read on, I realised that Lorne had been arrested, charged, convicted, and sent to Oakalla Prison for rustling. He'd shot a steer. He was sixteen. They sent him to jail at sixteen! He must have been trying to feed his grandmother and the other five kids. He was a young kid who hadn't developed good judgement, and he went to prison.

After I read the article, I wrote to him at the prison and told him I would get him a lawyer and would visit him, but he never replied. He may never have gotten the letter; Oakalla had a poor reputation. I should have gone to the prison and checked on him and not just waited for a response. But I didn't. I didn't do anything more. Over the years, I wondered what happened to him. He'd been such a lively, curious, kind boy. The school was closed now; Elsie was gone, and all the children had been dispersed to different areas. I sighed. I still felt as if I had let Lorne down.

I continued to read this week's *Tribune*. On a middle page, I saw that the Preschool Screening Fair was advertised for this Wednesday. Edith was willing to take David for the day and I had agreed to volunteer my time to help. I read on. There was a sale on mosquito repellent at Spencer Dickie's Pharmacy. *I should stock up.* The mosquitoes were vicious here on the ranch and the season had started. They weren't so numerous in town, but were part of the landscape at home. I checked the obituaries and the birth notices. Janice came in for more mosquito repellent and I put down the paper to prepare lunch.

"I'm going to take Flip out for a ride," Glen announced. Flip was the perfect pony: gentle and easy to catch.

"Fine," I agreed, "after lunch."

Glen knew how to saddle and bridle Flip, and he could stick like a burr to her no matter what fence or ditch she jumped. I didn't worry about him. He looked after Flip as well and didn't bring her back lathered and heaving.

After lunch, everyone dispersed. I caught up on the laundry; Glen was out on Flip; Carl went to repair the fence in the bull pasture, taking David with him. Janice was reading. It was a peaceful afternoon.

After the kids were in bed, Carl put on some big band music on our stereo. He'd made that stereo from a kit and the sound was clear. He reached out and pulled me from the sofa.

"Isn't this my dance?"

I smiled. We'd danced at the Break-Up Celebration in April, after the competition for the date of the ice breaking up on Williams Lake, and again at the 4-H dance last week. We tried to attend the fundraising dances in Williams Lake about once a month. I'd had dancing lessons as a child and felt the music in my bones. Carl said he'd figured out in high school that a good dancer got to meet girls. He was easy to follow. Big band music wasn't popular on the radio now, but it was still played at dances and we had many records. The house was quiet except for the music. Carl turned the lights down low so we danced in the soft semi-darkness. It was dreamy.

ON WEDNESDAY, I deposited David at Edith's house and then drove the two blocks to the health unit. All the public health nurses and office staff were on hand to work at the Preschool Screening Fair. The home care nurses didn't participate in this.

Marlene, the public health nurse with the best organizational talent, ran the screening fair. Ellie managed the registration of the children as they arrived; Ann would hand out the passports we'd designed, which the parents would take to the individual stations. The results of the screening would be written in the passport, so we needed a volunteer at each station to record the information on the health unit chart. Marlene assigned one person to a room and made sure they knew their duties. Laura, the speech pathologist, was setting up in one office; three nurses were arranging to give the Denver Developmental Screening Test; a dental assistant from one of the clinics in town had brought in a dental chair, which her husband carried into Paul's office; a volunteer from the mental health clinic was setting out her mental health questionnaire.

"She has to leave just before three to pick up her kids from school. We'll need a volunteer to cover after that. Can you get one?" Marlene asked me.

"Sure." I was acting as Marlene's assistant and general dogsbody.

Children began to stream in. It was busy. The many little bodies moved from one station to the next in fairly good order. We had stamps and stickers for the little ones and had only the occasional crying child. We kept our staff room free of visitors, so we were able to retreat there for coffee and something to eat. Paul had gone to Famous Bakery and supplied us with doughnuts and Danish pastries which were delicious and gave instant energy.

By two-thirty, all was well, except I didn't have a volunteer to hand out the mental health survey.

"I'll collect Janice and Glen from school," I told Marlene, "and be right back."

I sped up to Cataline School and intercepted them before they got on the bus. They were willing to help.

I deposited Glen in the waiting room area, where he immediately began to play with the children and help keep them amused. He could use puppets in a way that mesmerized the children and some parents as well. I left him to it.

I deposited Janice in the mental health office and instructed her to hand the questionnaire to the parents, ask them politely to fill it out, then place it in the box on the desk.

She agreed to do that.

Marlene poked her head in the door. "Thanks, Janice. You're a real help."

Janice smiled. "No problem."

"I'll bring you a doughnut."

"Thanks."

I'd have to be sure Glen got one as well, but he'd have to eat it in the staff room and not in front of a room full of four-year-olds.

We closed the fair at five. I called Carl and asked him to pick up David from Edith's then Janice and Glen as I was staying on for an evaluation of the day. He arrived in half an hour with David.

"It's busy here." Carl looked around at the scurrying staff. Janice and Glen were ready for him.

"Look, David," Janice said. "I saved you a doughnut."

"Mine?" David said with wonder.

"All yours," Janice said.

Carl raised his eyebrows. Doughnuts before supper were not a good idea. But sisterly kindness was quite wonderful. I kept my mouth shut on any criticism. Parenting is a series of moral dilemmas.

"See you later," I said and waved them off.

The volunteers left for their homes. The dental assistant's husband came back and wrestled the chair to his truck. The nurses and office staff cleaned and tidied until we had the health unit back in order.

Paul had gone to Wong's and returned with about twenty containers of Mr. Wong's excellent Chinese food. I could smell sweet and sour pork. Ellie set chairs around the table in the waiting room and Paul set out the food. He had paper plates and plastic forks as well as chopsticks. We fell on it.

When we all had had enough and had shovelled the detritus into plastic bags for disposal, Ellie brought the paperwork to the table.

"Before we start, Marlene," I said, "Janice picked out one mother she thought someone should see."

"Why did she think that?"

I handed Marlene the questionnaire that included the woman's name. "She said she didn't act like a normal mother. She didn't seem connected to her child." I shrugged. "That's what Janice said."

Marlene read the name aloud.

"Oh, she's mine," Sophie said, meaning the woman was in her district. "She's on antidepressant drugs. I'll check up on her." She took the paper from Marlene.

There was a short silence. Then Marlene said, "How old is Janice?"

"Ten," I said.

It was hard to explain Janice's ability to communicate with people and animals, or her sensitivity to their emotions, so I didn't try. I changed the subject.

"Do we know where people heard about the fair?" I asked. That would tell us where to concentrate our advertising effort next year.

Ellie read from her tally sheet. "About a third of them said Mrs. Harbinger told them to attend."

I knew she'd supported it. She'd said, "Saves us diagnosing problem kids. If you could screen every child before he or she arrived in school, we'd save ourselves exasperation and the kids years of frustration."

She had certainly promoted it. It had been advertised in *The Tribune* as I'd seen, and Paul had talked about it to the doctors' group.

We tried to get a sense of how many referrals to professionals for future care the whole team had made.

"Even if their child wasn't referred for anything," Angela said, "the fair made them aware of what services there are for children in Williams Lake, and they will be more likely to ask for a referral if and when they need one." That was one of the intangible, non-measurable outcomes.

"The Denver Developmental Screening Test takes too long," Marlene said. "It's inappropriate for a quick screening fair. We need a shorter version that screens faster. I'll look into it."

Ellie would check all the stats. Marlene offered to write the report and send it around for additions and editing before she passed it on to the head office in Victoria.

"There were very few Native people," I said. "We'll have to improve there. It's possible there's a deep-seated attitude that provincial health services are not for First Nations people." Some nurses might not accept Indigenous patients, not necessarily because they discriminated against them but because they saw Indigenous people as belonging in a separate health system. There wasn't anything in our rules that said we *couldn't* accept them. I'd checked.

"You look into that," Angela directed.

"All right." I'd ask around.

I WAS TIRED when I got home but stopped at the barn to shovel oats into the trough. I spotted one new lamb, a late one, outside without a mother nearby. I checked and saw Number Forty-Nine at the trough with the remnants of afterbirth on her backside. I herded her into a separate pen and gave her extra oats. Her lamb was cold but alive. I picked it up and brought it into the house.

Everyone was in David's room listening to Carl read a bedtime story. When it was finished, they came out into the kitchen.

"Your meal's in the fridge," said Carl, then turned toward the oven and reached for the knob.

"Don't turn it on!" I almost screamed. He stopped.

"I've got a lamb in there."

He laughed. "Roast lamb."

"Not if I can help it. She's cold."

"A lamb?" Glen said, peering in. "There's a lamb in there."

"Let me see," David crowded in.

"What's it doing in the oven?" Glen asked

"It's cold. It's warming up."

"Why doesn't the mother warm it up?" Janice wanted to know.

"Because the mother is Number Forty-Nine," I said.

"Oh, the stupid one."

"Right."

"You'd better take it back soon so she doesn't forget she has a lamb."

"Good point."

Scatty Number Forty-Nine had taken fright one day when a neighbour's dog had chased her. I got the dog out of the pasture, but Number Forty-Nine shook and bleated and wouldn't move. I had to drag her back to the barn where I thought she'd feel safer. Over the next week she dropped all her wool. She looked peculiar with wool around her face and nowhere else. It grew back, but she was an emotionally sensitive ewe or, as Janice diagnosed, a stupid one.

Carl gave me a quick kiss.

"Hungry? Or is that Mr. Wong's special I taste?"

"Not hungry. You're right. But thanks for saving something for me. I could use coffee, though."

He poured it from the pot he'd kept warm and handed it to me. He and David returned to David's room to start another story.

Glen and Janice were quarrelling about something. I left them to it. They would settle it one way or another. Like most siblings, they knew how to trigger each other.

After coffee, I trekked back out to the barn with the lamb bundled in a towel. I put more oats in a trough and Number Forty-Nine went for it with single-minded intensity. You'd think I was feeding her a drug instead of grain. I unwrapped the lamb and positioned her under the mother. The lamb rooted. Number Forty-Nine paid no attention to her, just concentrated on the oats. I guided the lamb's mouth to the teat. The lamb grabbed on and tugged. That worked. I hoped Number Forty-Nine would accept her. She seemed to.

It was about ten o'clock but still light. The birds had stopped singing and all was quiet. The yard was quiet. None of the animals called out. No mosquitoes buzzed around me. No cougars or wolves cried from the woods. The quiet enveloped me like a comforter. I stopped for a few moments to appreciate the solitude. Dusk was prolonged at this time of year, and the trees at the edge of the woods blurred into the dark beyond. Night would slowly pull the daylight away until the only light would be from the ranch house. It was magical.

CHAPTER TEN

PICNICKING IN THE USA

T HE WHOLE FAMILY was invited to lunch with a group
of pilots and their families who owned Navions, planes
like ours. It was to take place in Oroville, Washington, just
across the border from Osoyoos, BC, in the Okanagan Valley. Janice
and Glen were to attend another 4-H rally on that Saturday, so it
would just be David with us. I arranged with Verna Dennis, their
leader, to look after them for the day. I wanted to go to the 4-H rally
because I enjoyed them and felt that Glen and Janice should have at
least one parent there to show an interest and support them. I had
to talk to myself to make this decision because I felt guilty leaving
them. But this was a rally where they didn't need us to transport
animals, and Carl was keen to spend the day flying. So this Saturday morning, we dropped off the two older kids at the Dennis
ranch and drove ahead to the airport.

David was used to flying and had his ear protectors clamped on.
In a bag on the seat beside him were his toys, an apple, a carton
of juice, and a snack bar. The weather was clear and the forecast
called for sun for the next two weeks. We lifted off the runway.
What a feeling! Parting from the earth was exhilarating, as if I were
untethered and free. We headed south and a little east, over the
miles of forest-covered hills and over the Thompson River. The
plane bobbled a little over the wide, dry Kamloops Valley; the usual
turbulence in the air around Kamloops might be caused by the cool

river air meeting the heat rising from the hot desert alongside it. Carl checked in with air traffic control at the Kamloops airport and again with the Kelowna air traffic control farther south. We passed Penticton. Fruit trees covered this valley with lush green on either side of Okanagan and Skaha lakes. Occasionally, I saw a vineyard with rows of grapes. It wasn't turbulent here. We passed over the desert country of Oliver and Osoyoos and landed after an hour and forty minutes at the Dorothy Scott Airport at the end of Osoyoos Lake. The international boundary crossed the middle of the lake.

It was a short, four-thousand-foot runway but paved. Carl brought the plane close to the small terminal building, slid open the canopy, and waited.

David had snapped open his seatbelt and was ready to climb out.

"Just wait, David," Carl said. "We have to go through customs."

"What's customs?

Carl explained while I watched a tall, rugged-looking officer approach us. He wore a stetson, a brown uniform, and a gun on a belt around his waist. The RCMP carried their guns in a Sam Brown, an under-the-arm holster with leather covering the gun. Our border guards did not carry weapons. This officer's gun was hanging, ready for use. He looked intimidating.

He gestured for us to climb out.

Carl went first. I followed him and turned to help David. He reached out for me to lift him to the ground, but he couldn't take his eyes off the officer's gun.

"Morning," the man said affably. "Here for the lunch?"

"That's right," Carl said. "With my wife and son."

"I just need to see all your identification. Are you carrying?"

I stared at him. *Carrying what?*

Carl understood. "Nope. No guns."

"Good. I need your ID and your plane registration."

Carl produced it. I fished out my driver's licence and passed it to Carl. The officer glanced at them.

"Do you have anything for the boy?"

I searched my purse again and came up with David's birth certificate. Since the adoption had come through, I was so thrilled to have the birth certificate that I'd carried it with me ever since.

"Just wait here a moment. I have to phone our central data info centre and check that you aren't on any wanted list."

We stood and waited, but it wasn't long before he returned with our plane registration and IDs. He gestured to a field on the other side of the small terminal building.

"Lunch is in that tent over there. You can park your plane in that field."

I could see several planes already lined up in a huge field. It looked like the site of a private party: a marquee tent stood in the middle; people were sitting at the picnic tables nearby; a fire truck was parked near the tent.

"What's the fire truck for?" I asked. There weren't any races scheduled for today. This was just a picnic.

"It's a good idea, a precaution, in case there are any problems. But between you and me, the guy driving just wants to look at planes."

I smiled. Often, people came out to look at our plane when we landed at a small airport.

"Washrooms are in the terminal?" I inquired.

He smiled. "Sure thing"

"Thanks." I nodded to Carl. "We'll meet you at the tent." I took David with me to the terminal building. The flight hadn't been long but it felt good to stretch our legs. We were quick, then left the terminal building and headed over to the tent, stopping occasionally to talk to friends and acquaintances. We didn't join this group often, but enough to have made some friends.

"Hiya, Davie." We joined Ollie Sanderson from Oregon; he played the accordion and so was a favourite of David's.

"Hello, Mr. Sanderson." David smiled. "Did you bring your squeeze thing?"

"I did. We can have some music later. They have hot dogs for lunch. Do you like those?"

David was enthusiastic about hot dogs. "Yes, I do."

"Better ask your mom if you can have two."

He looked at me, his brown eyes wide and hopeful.

"We'll see," I said.

Carl had parked our plane at the end of the row and had started to walk toward the tent, but I could see he'd been waylaid by two men who were examining an engine. Lorna, a friend from Victoria, was seated at a picnic table with a cup of coffee.

"Sit down, Marion. I have a big Thermos here. Want a coffee?"

"I do. Thanks."

I checked on David. He and Lorna's eight-year-old son, Mark, were exchanging toy trucks. Mark had discovered a pile of dirt and the two of them squatted there, constructing roadways.

"Good flight?" Lorna asked.

"Uneventful, which is good," I said.

"Us too. Lovely trip over the strait."

"You had to come over the mountains too," I said. The Coast Mountains in that area were high, but a plane would clear them at less than ten thousand feet.

"We went above the Hope–Princeton highway into the Okanagan Valley and then south."

I thought about it. "That's a narrow valley."

"A little uncomfortable, but it's a clear day. I wouldn't want to do it in the rain. Definitely not in the fog."

We were silent a moment, both of us likely thinking of the harrowing situations we'd been in while flying.

"Who's hosting this event?" I asked her. "I know the Navion Society sent out a letter, but I am afraid I didn't get around to reading it."

"The Seattle chapter. Nice of them to have it here. It's so much easier in the Okanagan than having to fly through all that busy traffic near Seattle."

"Mrs. Crook?" Mark came up to me. "Can David and I go look at the planes?"

I glanced at Lorna. She nodded her permission.

"Just between here and the fire truck, Mark. And don't go anywhere near the runway," I said.

"We'll be able to see them from here," Lorna reassured me.

I watched as they walked through the field, stopping to talk with the men who were polishing their planes or looking at engines.

There were about fifteen Navions, all combinations of colours and with some obvious differences, such as wing fuel tanks. They were parked on the field and, as we watched, three more landed one after the other on the runway and taxied over. I shifted my eyes to check on Carl's whereabouts. He was still at the plane with the open cowling. He was a happy man peering at an engine with buddies to discuss the intricacies of the mechanics.

"What's the problem down there?" I asked Lorna.

"They're diagnosing it," Lorna said. "Judy, John's wife, told me that the problem is the O ring, but she knew John wouldn't accept her assessment so she's waiting for the guys to tell him."

I remembered that Judy had her pilot's licence and knew a lot about planes.

"Engines are not my field," I said.

"Not mine, either," Lorna agreed.

Suddenly, the ear-splitting fire siren blasted the air. I leapt to my feet, looking for David.

I saw Mark near the fire truck and the fireman walking out of the food tent. Where was David? I ran to the truck. There he was, sitting in the front seat, hands on the steering wheel, staring at the dash. The siren wailed in my ears. I pulled open the door.

"David! Get out of there this minute!"

He slid along the seat reluctantly. I held his arm and almost dragged him to the ground. I turned. The fireman was in front of me, young, tall, broad like a wall of muscle.

"I'm very sorry," I yelled.

He smiled. "I'm the one who's sorry." He reached into the truck and did something that cut off the siren. He turned back to me.

"Crazy of me to leave the keys in the truck. We're lucky he didn't drive it away."

I shivered. "Oh."

The driver looked at David, then back at me. "Could he have started it? Does he know how?"

"I'm not sure. We live on a ranch. He knows a lot of things."

We both studied David, who remained silent.

"His legs are too short," I finally said. "He'd have to engage the clutch, wouldn't he?"

"On this vehicle, yes."

"Thank God." I squashed the image of David careening down the runway in a fire truck.

The fireman squatted down and looked at David, who by now understood he was in trouble.

"Listen, son. Don't do that again."

"Okay," David whispered, slowly looking up at the fireman. His eyes travelled over his uniform. I wondered if he was looking for a gun.

"Sorry, Mrs. Crook." Mark came up beside me. "I didn't see him go into the truck."

Mark was only eight. He couldn't be held responsible. I should have kept my eyes on David. "It's okay, Mark. No harm done."

"Pretty loud, though, wasn't it?"

"Yeah!" David said, his natural buoyancy restored. "Really neat."

"You two play in the dirt," I shoved David toward his trucks and the engineering project he'd started.

I sat back down with Lorna. She started to laugh. She laughed so hard I finally joined her.

"Kids," she said. "You never know what they're going to do next."

"True enough." David was fine. The fire truck had not moved. No one was harmed by the siren. I relaxed.

"More coffee?" Lorna asked.

"Please."

I spent a pleasant hour with Lorna and several other people who wandered over to chat. I wondered how Janice and Glen were getting on. I was sure they'd have a good time at the rally, but I wished I could be in two places at once.

Carl finally left the engines and joined me. "Are you ready for lunch?"

"Sure. Did you hear the fire siren?" Of course he'd heard it, but I wanted to know if he'd heard David had caused it.

He hadn't. I told him.

"No kidding? I wonder which button he pushed."

"Don't ask him. He already thinks he is quite the big boy for doing it."

"Oh. Okay. I guess I should tell him not to go into other people's vehicles."

"Good plan."

I called David and took him into the terminal for a bathroom break and to wash the dirt from his hands. By the time we got to the tent, there was quite a lineup for lunch.

"It's hot dogs and hamburgers, salad, soft drinks, and coffee," Carl said. He'd been saving our place in line.

"Sounds good."

"I want a hot dog," David demanded.

"Okay."

"I want *two* hot dogs."

"I'll see." I smiled at him and then at the man in front of me who had turned when David spoke.

The man did not smile back. That was unusual. Most Navion people were friendly.

The line moved slowly, and David was impatient to get his hot dog. He moved closer to the man and his wife in front of us. Then he bumped him.

"David." I pulled him back. "Sorry," I apologized.

The man turned, looked at David, and said, "Keep that Indian kid away from me. He shouldn't even be here."

I pushed David behind me, staring at the man, shocked.

Carl moved up and leaned toward the man. "He's three years old. Want to pick on someone your own size? Because I'm available."

Carl didn't raise his voice. He didn't even sound unfriendly, but he was issuing a serious challenge. There was silence all around us.

The line moved, and the man turned back and moved ahead with it. The silence continued. The line moved a little more. I kept David behind me. Then a man who had been just in front of the aggressor came back to me, looked at both at me and Carl, and said, "I apologize for my friend."

Carl nodded. I just stared.

He returned to his place in line, but there was not a word spoken by anyone in front of us. David got his hot dog. The bigot and his party moved to a picnic table far from us. I darted a few glances that way and saw that the man who had apologized had picked up his meal and moved with his wife to another table. He might have learned something about his friend that day.

We left the picnic at three o'clock, took off, and headed up the Okanagan Valley. David fell asleep just over Kamloops.

"Carl, that guy who picked on David. He doesn't like kids?"

"He doesn't like *Indian* kids," Carl said.

I knew that. I just hadn't wanted to face it.

Carl reached over and held my hand. "Don't let it get to you. He's an asshole."

"Still . . ."

"The rest of the people there like David. He has lots of friends in the group."

"True."

Carl put his hands back on the column. As far as he was concerned the incident was finished.

Maybe I was foolish to dwell on the one idiot in the bunch, but his attack was so illogical, so unprovoked, so shocking. There were more people like that in the world. How would David cope?

WE PICKED UP THE KIDS at Verna and Bill's. They were full of stories of their day with the 4-H club. They had participated in a practice rally at the Dennis ranch and told us all about it. It wasn't until we were almost home that Janice asked, "How was your day, David?"

"I drived a fire truck."

"No!" She was impressed.

"How did you get to do that?"

"I just did."

"Did the fire guy help you get in?" Glen asked. He knew the seat of a fire truck was high off the ground.

"No. I climbed in all by myself and I hit the button."

"The button?"

"The thing that makes the noise."

Janice and Glen looked at me for an explanation.

"The siren," I offered. "The truck didn't move." I wasn't going to get into the excitement of the whole escapade.

"Wow!" Glen was envious. "We had doughnuts," he said, trying to compete.

"I had a hot dog. *Two* hot dogs!"

"Good for you," Janice said.

We drove into the yard and were getting out of the Suburban when David said, "A guy called me an Indian kid."

"So?" Glen said.

"It didn't sound nice."

"Oh." Glen looked at David. "Maybe the guy wasn't nice. That sounds dumb."

"Yeah. Dumb," Janice said.

Glen helped David out of the Suburban. "Did you really make the siren go?"

"I did."

"Was it loud?"

"*Really* loud!"

Carl unloaded his map briefcase from the back of the vehicle. We followed the kids. They were chattering.

"I'm glad he hit the siren," Carl said. "It's obviously more important than some dumb guy."

CHAPTER ELEVEN

EXPLORING THE WEST SIDE OF THE FRASER RIVER

O N A WARM JULY DAY, I drove north toward McLeese Lake. This was Cathy's district, but she was on holiday—half the nurses took their holidays in July—and I was covering for her. There was a new baby already a month old on the other side of the Fraser River. We didn't want the mother and baby to wait until Cathy returned, which would be yet another month.

Carl took two weeks off from his law practice in July to get the hay in, so, as usual, Colleen would mind the children while I worked. She was off school for the summer, as were my kids, and happy to have a paying job. Colleen was competent and reliable, and the kids were sensible most of the time, so I didn't worry about them. Besides, Colleen's mother was at home with her fourteen- and fifteen-year-olds to help with her kids—all of whom were available as a back-up.

I had loaded the metal scale in the back of my car. It was an old friend by now, riding over rough roads with me, clanging and rattling as if singing accompaniment to the bangs and rattles that had developed in my Suburban. I had my black bag and the patient file on the seat beside me. I'd read the file: a young mother, Roxanne Taylor, with her first baby. No problems with the birth or the baby, but they were a long way from a doctor; she would need some support. The family lived on a ranch on the west side of the Fraser

River. There was no direct road to it from Williams Lake, so I had to drive up the east side of the river on Highway 97, go down to the river at Marguerite, take the cable ferry across, then drive north up the road to the ranch. The mother told the hospital staff she didn't have a phone, but I could leave a message at the main ranch house and the rancher would convey the message to her. I'd phoned yesterday and given my approximate time of arrival. The rancher said she'd let Roxanne know. I had to assume Roxanne had gotten the message and would be waiting for me. Once I left the health unit, no one could contact me. I hoped I wouldn't make this long trip to find no one at home.

I had never been in this area and was looking forward to travelling to new territory. I had friends in the 4-H club who ranched near here, so it would be interesting to see the country they'd described. I hoped I wouldn't get lost, but there was only one road and surely I wouldn't be leaving it. I'd packed coffee and a lunch; if I did get lost, I wouldn't starve.

The turnoff to the ferry was about forty miles north of Williams Lake with only a small directional sign to indicate there *was* a ferry. I took the short road slowly as there were some potholes that jarred the car. The scale protested. I slowed even more. I didn't want the scale to bounce off the seat and fly around like a missile. The open side windows caught some breeze. It was hot, which Carl would have liked as he couldn't cut and bale hay in the rain, but which I found uncomfortable. As well, the Cariboo in July held dust in the air no matter where you were—and mosquitoes. It was all bearable when I was driving.

The road ended at the edge of the river. I stopped, set the emergency brake, and got out. The river wasn't wide at this point, just swift with brown water surging past me. The nearby Soda Creek Band members spear-fished for salmon here in August. I imagined men and boys hanging onto rocks, leaning over the river with their spears poised. Dangerous, but exciting. I stayed back from the edge and away from that fast-moving water. I could see the ferry travelling toward me, a flat, open boat, almost a barge, with room for two cars or three small ones. It looked fragile, like a small raft floating on the water. Two passengers alighted, an older Indigenous woman and a young girl.

"Good morning," I called as I headed back to my car.

"Morning," the older woman called back. "You the nurse?"

"Yes, I am." I wasn't in uniform, and there were no decals on my vehicle, but I wasn't surprised she knew who I was.

"Going to see Roxanne?"

I nodded. She must have known Roxanne was expecting me and assumed the only person coming over at this time would be the nurse. There weren't many secrets in the back country.

"She's a good little mother. Lonesome, though."

I climbed into my car but left the door open. I waited a moment. If Roxanne was lonesome, this woman might know more. The silence stretched. I glanced at the ferry. I was going to have to board it. I rolled down the window, shut the door, and put the car in gear.

"She should come for coffee," the woman said.

"I'll tell her," I replied, and moved off.

I didn't learn the woman's name but I had no doubt Roxanne would know who she was.

The ferry operator waved me on.

I manoeuvred up the short ramp onto the ferry, all the time imagining the river pulling the ferry away from me and dumping me into the river. That didn't happen, and I rolled on safely. I turned off the ignition and set the emergency brake. The ferry operator put chocks in front of the wheels, which would help keep it from moving, and I got out. This felt precarious, although I knew people crossed all the time without any disasters. Once we were away from the shore and in the current, the river rose up and bulged on either side of us. The water was so close.

I turned to the operator, determined to distract myself from imagining a catastrophe. "I'm Marion Crook, the community health nurse."

"I'm Willie Lee."

"Captain Lee?"

"Yeah. That's what they call me." He smiled.

"This is an interesting ferry." It was. As far as I could see, there was no motor. The ferry was caught by the current and pulled into the river and was prevented from rushing downstream by cables that ran through it. The ferry ran on the cables, but the river current supplied the power to move it across. Captain Lee managed levels connected to chains which pulled us along on cables so we didn't corkscrew.

"Yep. Been in operation since 1921."

"How long have you been running it?"

"Four years now."

I took a deep breath, enjoying the sunshine and the absence of mosquitoes. The breeze over the river was too strong for them. I smelled the hot oil from my vehicle, a tang of pine from the trees on the shore, and sunshine—at least I was sure I could smell sunshine.

"Nice in this weather."

"Sure is."

I looked at Willie Lee. Obviously of Chinese descent. I remembered a conversation I'd had with Sally about him.

"His dad, Sing Lee, owned a ranch on the west bank," Sally had told me. "The whole family got moved off during the war. Chinese was the same as Japanese to the government."

I knew about the incarceration of Canadians of Japanese descent and expropriation of their property. I hadn't known Chinese Canadians faced the same injustice.

"But they came back?"

"Yeah. Bill Webster's ranch is adjacent. He took over the Lee ranch, bought it from the government, and gave it back to Mr. Lee after the war. He said Lee was a good neighbour and he didn't know what kind of riff-raff the government would give it to if he didn't keep it for him."

Bill Webster must have been a man of firm principles. I doubt that happened very often. My grandfather took over the land of

Japanese Canadians when he returned from the war. He didn't have the same sense of social justice that motivated Bill Webster.

"Do people use this ferry at lot?"

"Yep. The river divides the Alexandria Indian Band land, so they go back and forth quite a bit. And the government people like you don't want to drive all the way to Quesnel and then back down on the west side, so they use the ferry. Pretty much everyone on the west side comes over at some time."

"Handy," I said.

"It is, that."

When we bumped into the riverbank at the other side, I climbed into the car and Willie removed the chocks.

"Bye," I called to Willie as I left. He grinned and waved.

The gravel road was dry, and dust swirled behind me as I drove. It would have been tolerable if it stayed behind me, but the dust kicked up into the cab. The car fan only brought the dust inside, so I didn't use it. I had to close the windows. I had ten miles of this ahead of me. The scale clanged and rattled.

"I know. Sorry."

I did talk to my scale. I sometimes imagined having reciprocal conversations. The scale would complain, *Can't you find a smoother road? You're shocking my parts.*

I'd answer, *No, I can't. The patient lives on a gravel road. Your parts have lasted this long; they'll survive.*

I wasn't so far into fantasy that I actually heard any response. I didn't think the scale was magical, just indestructible.

There were open fields on either side of the road, and I could see active haying in one field. A tractor with a mower was cutting swaths of tall hay, laying down feed for cattle.

Ranchers would be happy with this weather. I drove through a conifer forest, pines mostly, then into ranch land again.

Twice a week, I checked with mothers in the hospital, but I missed those who came and went between my visits. The hospital nurse had thought to get directions from the mother and had tele- phoned the health unit to give the information. "Drive north about ten miles on a gravel road. There will be cleared ranch lands, then a cluster of ranch houses on the right. If you go too far, there will be ranch buildings on the left."

It was almost ten miles on my odometer, so I should see the ranch buildings soon. Everyone along the road would see me coming as a dust plume rose behind me.

I saw a collection of three small houses on the right side of the road and turned into the long driveway to the yard in front of three small cabins. Which one? Diapers flapped behind the cabin closest to me. I drove slowly, trying to create as little dust as possible. Roxanne wouldn't thank me for sending dust over those clean diapers. I pulled up in front of the cabin and waited a moment for the dust to settle.

The door opened before I could knock.

"Roxanne Taylor?" I asked. She was about eighteen, thin with long blond hair.

"You're the nurse?"

"Marion Crook," I said, "from the Williams Lake Health Unit." It was called the Cariboo Health Unit, but there were several offices. People who lived on this road were arbitrarily assigned to the Williams Lake office, but they might prefer to get their medical care from Quesnel, which was also in the Cariboo Health Unit area. The trip to the Quesnel clinic would be quicker as there was a direct road with a substantial bridge and no ferry at the end. Roxanne had chosen to have her baby at the Williams Lake hospital, so she was referred to me. If Roxanne would rather have her records in Quesnel, I could send them there.

"Come in. Michael is sleeping."

I assumed that was the baby.

"Coffee?" she asked. On the kitchen table were china cups with saucers accompanied by a delicate creamer and sugar bowl that matched the cups. A wedding present? There were cookies on a plate. My visit was a social occasion. If that's what she needed, that's what I'd provide.

"Lovely," I said, setting the scale on her low coffee table, well away from the fragile china. The cabin was bigger than it appeared from the outside. The kitchen and living room were one room with a sofa but no television. She might not be able to get TV reception here. We could get CBC at our place, and the kids watched one program a week, but it wasn't available everywhere. I glanced around for books but didn't see any. The woman at the ferry might be right—Roxanne could be lonely. Her husband worked for the ranch and would be spending long hours in the fields getting as much hay in as possible before the weather turned. There looked to be two bedrooms with a bathroom in between. I asked to use the bathroom and found it also bigger than I expected, and spotless. A washing machine sat against a wall.

"Coffee would be wonderful," I repeated when I returned.

She smiled and bustled around. She gave me the impression of a little girl playing house, but I reprimanded myself for the thought. She obviously worked hard at being a housewife and a mother.

We'd just finished our coffee when the baby woke. Roxanne went to pick him up.

"Leave him naked," I said, "and we'll weigh him."

I set up the scale on the coffee table, making sure it was balanced at zero with a small blanket on it. That cold metal was a shock even on a hot day.

I weighed him—he was gaining weight—discussed feeding, gave Roxanne his immunization schedule, and answered her questions. She had written them down and we went through them all. Roxanne would benefit from having an experienced mum around her who could answer her questions. Nothing she wanted to know required nursing expertise. But unless the woman I'd met at the ferry dock or another neighbour turned out to be that helpful mentor, Roxanne would need another visit.

"Are you able to come to Williams Lake? You can use the scale at the health unit if you want to weigh Michael." It would be best if she could come to us; I doubted Cathy would make a visit out here when mother and baby were doing well.

"I can after haying is finished. Then we'll go in once a week." By the look of the fields I'd seen, haying should be over in about two weeks. She was young, but she was doing a good job with Michael. She might be lonely here, though. She had some neighbours, but not many.

I relayed the invitation from the woman at the ferry.

"That's Sarah Charleyboy." She was quiet.

"She seemed friendly."

"She is. She lives on the ranch just up the road."

"Easy for you to get there, then."

"Should I go?"

I looked at her. "Why not?"

"I've never gone to an Indian home before."

"Do you think it's much different from yours?"

"It might be."

True, it might be. It might even be better. Roxanne was reluctant to socialize with an Indigenous woman, probably because she never had done so before.

"What do you and Sarah have in common besides two hands, two feet, and working parts?"

Roxanne grinned. "Well, we're both interested in quilting. She's an expert quilter and I'm just learning."

"Anything else?"

"I can make trifle. She had it once and wants me to teach her."

"That's enough to start a friendship. You just have to sling Michael on your back and hoof it over there."

I wasn't a psychologist, but the nearest one was Dr. Peggy MacFarlane in Williams Lake. She would be almost impossible for Roxanne to access when factoring in the distance and the waiting list.

"You're doing a good job with Michael."

She beamed.

I DROVE BACK to the ferry with the windows up because of the dust. It was hot in the car, and I was happy to stop at the ferry dock and lower the windows. The breeze on the river was a relief. It was a long way to go visit one mother and babe, but a first-time mother could make mistakes if she didn't have good advice. If she had a visit and talked with a public health nurse, she'd be more likely to bring her child to town if she was worried, or at least more likely to phone and ask questions.

I unloaded my car at the health unit, did some charting, did the rounds at the hospital, then headed home.

Colleen stayed long enough to reassure me that all was well—Janice was reading in her room, David was playing with trucks in his room, and Glen was out riding Flip—before she headed off through the woods to her house. I got supper going and Carl came in for a drink before going to the tractor shed to hook up the baler. He'd cut the hay in the bull pasture two days ago then gone on to cut the far meadow. Now the hay in the bull pasture was ready to bale. The Cariboo air was so dry it pulled moisture from the grass quickly, and from our skin. I was always slathering on moisturizer.

After he'd finished in the tractor shed, Carl stood on the porch swiping at his jeans and shirt trying to get the dust and pieces of grass off. When he came into the kitchen, he looked tired. His curly hair was even tighter, with bits of twigs and grass stuck on the top. I reached up and picked them out. He hugged me.

"You are one smelly man."

"So true," he said and kissed me.

"Sit down. I'll get you a beer."

"And water."

I nodded at the sink and he got his own water. Then he sat at the corner table, accepted the beer, and sighed. "That's good."

I bustled around getting the spaghetti and meatball meal on the table. I added a salad and some buns from the freezer, defrosting them quickly in the microwave. I don't know how I survived before the microwave.

Glen arrived home.

"Did you brush down Flip before you let her loose?" I asked him.

"I did." He went to wash before supper.

Everyone ate quickly. Janice and Glen told us about the hike they'd taken with Colleen. David tried to partake in the conversation. He knew many words and was rapidly adding more. I sometimes stopped everyone else from talking and let him have our attention. Janice had started talking at one year of age and was speaking full sentences at eighteen months. Glen had been like David. He hadn't said much at all, just learned and stored up the words until he was three, then started talking when he decided to. He still had problems finding the words he needed.

After I loaded the dishes in the dishwasher, I grabbed the truck keys.

"Apples are dessert for now," I said. "I'll bring cookies with us."

"Where are we going?" Glen asked.

"To the bull pasture."

Janice said, "To pick up bales, I bet."

Glen was happy with that because he would stand on the back of the truck and shove bales into place while I threw them up. Janice would help him, and David would stay out of the way.

Carl had gone on ahead, and he was on the tractor at the end of the bull pasture, pulling the baler with short bales in a crooked line strung out on the ground behind him. I stopped the truck and we all got out and waited for Carl to make his way back to us.

I thought about Roxanne as we waited. Perhaps this is what she wanted—ranch life with her husband and child—and was willing to deal with isolation to achieve that.

"Up, Daddy," David said, holding up his arms when Carl stopped the tractor in front of us. I lifted him, and Carl settled David in front of him. I worried Carl would concentrate on the bales and not keep an eye on David, but David was sensible and was unlikely to move much on that shaking tractor.

"Why did Dad leave that piece of grass in the centre uncut?" Janice asked.

We stared at the patch of long grass surrounded by a shorn expanse. We watched as the tractor and baler approached the opposite side of the field. A bird flew from the long grass and landed on the ground. It dragged its wing and hopped away.

"It's a killdeer," I said. "I bet it has a nest there."

"It's doing that with its . . ." Glen flapped his arm.

"Its wing," I said.

"Yeah. Its wing. It wants us to think it's hurt," he said.

"I think so."

"Listen to it cry," Janice said. "It's trying to lead the tractor away from the nest."

We all listened, and above the growl of the tractor and the metal clanking from the baler we heard the keening of the killdeer.

"It's acting!" Janice said.

"Yes. We're disturbing it. But your dad spotted it and left its nest. We'll be done here by tomorrow and we'll leave it in peace."

"It's smart," Glen pronounced.

It was smart. We tried not to get too close to the nest as we picked up bales.

The hay was dry, so the bales were relatively light, but by the time I'd thrown twenty of them up to the kids in the back of the pickup, my shoulders were aching. The first two layers weren't difficult, but the next two took a lot of strength.

Janice and Glen climbed onto the roof of the truck cab with their feet wedged into the pile of bales. David, after being handed over to me from Carl, sat inside the cab, and I drove very slowly over the dirt trail home.

At one point, Janice and Glen yelled and pounded on the roof.

I stopped and stuck my head out the window. "What happened?" I was suddenly apprehensive.

"We lost a bale," Janice said.

"We'll pick it up on the way back." My heart rate went back to normal. Neither of the kids had fallen off. A bale? Fine. My son or daughter? No.

I backed the truck into the barn, which was built into the side of a hill that sloped down and away from the driveway. The first half of the upper floor of the barn was level with the driveway and was a storage space for equipment. The last half was elevated about three feet and was for hay storage. The animal pens were underneath it, so it made feeding hay a matter of shoving the bale to the hay chute and letting it fall into the manger below. Carl had imagined and built it; I thought it was an ingenious design.

Unloading the bales was much easier than loading, and we were back in the field within a half-hour, picking up the lost bale on our way. I called Carl over, and everyone had tea and cookies before we collected a second load of bales. By the time we had the truck full, it was past eight o'clock and time for the kids to go to bed. I backed the truck into the barn and unloaded it quickly. We all went into the house except Carl. We'd left him doing the final round of the field.

Once the kids were in bed, I ran the bath. I was going to need a long soak. I heard Carl come in while I was luxuriating in rose-scented hot water. The shower came on in the lower bathroom. I hoped the kids had left dry towels for him. The water stopped running. I heard a curse. They hadn't.

CHAPTER TWELVE

VISITING A BABY IN HORSEFLY AND SHEARING SHEEP

T HE KIDS SLEPT in the next morning. Carl was up and out to the far meadow with the baler. He would likely finish the baling and pick up all the hay before I got home from work. I waited for Colleen, who would cook breakfast for the kids and mind them until three-thirty, when I should be home. This week, only Marlene, Sophie, and I were working as well as the home care nurses who had staggered their holidays so they could manage the patient load. We had enough patients on the home care list to justify another nurse, at least in my eyes—but not in the eyes of the supervisors in Victoria. The nurses' union was in negotiation with the provincial government over many issues including wages, so I didn't expect any more help this year. At the moment, all was running well.

It was hard to describe the worth of the program. In fiscal terms, the home visits provided supervision for the frail elderly and prevented hospitalizations, which reduced costs to the government-funded health system. It reduced the number of doctor visits, which were also paid by the government, so it was cost efficient. In medical terms, it was sometimes hard to record exactly what the nurses did. We could chart blood pressure results and any doctor's orders that we followed, but often the nurses did much more. I charted "Health Supervision," but I didn't chart "the nurse went through the fridge and threw out all rotting food and thus prevented poisoning," or "dropped off a kitten to a lonely senior, which sparked a renewed interest in life and caused a reduction in her high blood pressure." The home care nurses knew they were improving the lives of the patients, but there were no guidelines to help them record *all* the ways they were helping.

My phone rang at ten o'clock. Ellie said, "I have a woman on the line who wants to speak to any nurse."

"Put her through," I said. People phoned the health unit for information on wide-ranging subjects.

"My name is Susan Anderson," a soft voice spoke.

"I am Marion Crook. How can I help you?"

"I don't know if you can, but I have a delicate problem, or at least a confusing one."

"Yes? Why don't you tell me about it?" This sounded like an anxious woman.

"I will." She hesitated, then began. "I am a member of the Anglican Church Women. I have been for thirty years. My friends are there. I'm part of the church community." She stopped talking.

"Has something happened?"

"Yes. We had an application to join by someone called Brenda."

I had an idea where this was going. We didn't have a crisis centre in town, and people tended to call the public health nurses for help because they saw us as knowledgeable and willing to listen.

"And?"

"Brenda was a man. His name was Brandon. He was my plumber. I knew him. He was a man." She stopped. I waited. Brandon had indeed been a man. As far as I knew, he was the first person in the area to change his gender. He'd done it surgically as well as socially. We'd talked about it among the nursing staff.

She continued, "My problem is this is a women's group. He isn't really a woman. I can't pretend he is, and I don't want to just stop going to the group, not after all these years."

I could hear her crying. I didn't think she'd respond to any efforts on my part to show how brave Brenda was and how hard she was trying to adapt to her new life. A psychologist could probably help, but that wasn't likely an option. We did have a mental health office on Second Avenue, but they had only one psychologist available, Peggy, and she was busy with programs, planning, and school kids' assessments and had little to no time for phone conversations. The nurses tended to get calls from the anxious and the depressed. I wasn't qualified to deal with much in terms of mental health, but I'd had a four-month immersion course of theory and practice at a psychiatric hospital as a student nurse, so I had some background. Most of the time, I simply listened.

"You're uncomfortable around her."

"Very," she said.

"And you've never faced this situation before, and you don't know how to act."

"I guess that's some of it," she said. "The other part is I don't know what a good Christian would do. I want to just pretend he's not there, but is that kind?"

No, it wouldn't be kind. "That's a good question. Do you think you could talk to your minister?" Did Anglicans call them ministers or priests?

"Maybe I should?" She sounded as though she was trying to choose an ethical stand.

"Your reactions are honest, and you're trying to find a solution. What outcome would you like?"

"I'd like him not to come." She was quiet for a moment. "But then I'd feel guilty for driving him away." She sighed. "I'll have to think about it some more. Thanks."

"You're welcome." I hadn't helped her with her decision. She had to convince herself of the right thing to do, and she wasn't ready to do that.

"Can I call you again?"

"Yes. You sure can. Good luck. It's a difficult dilemma."

She disconnected. That was a problem I hadn't anticipated, and one I couldn't solve.

ANOTHER PROBLEM no one had anticipated was the loss of our supervisor. Angela had become increasingly distressed in the last few months following the death of her friend, Aileen, a speech therapist from Quebec who had moved to Williams Lake at Angela's instigation, as Angela knew her family. Aileen had been travelling to Vancouver with her husband and brother-in-law in their pickup truck. Their vehicle's right front tire caught in the ridges on the shoulder of the highway; her husband overcorrected, trying to get it back onto the highway, and they spun into an oncoming truck. Her husband was wearing a seatbelt. His brother, beside her, was also wearing a seatbelt, but Aileen was in the middle of the bench seat without one. On impact, she went through the windshield and died. It was a shock to everyone, including the staff. She was only twenty-three, committed to her patients and friendly to the staff. We were all so sorry for Aileen's husband, his brother, her family, and Angela, who had been like an aunt to her. There was enough guilt around the tragedy to depress several people. Angela left at the end of June, and we were without a supervisor.

The head office in Victoria sent a supervisor to assess the situation. Vanessa Craddock was an intelligent woman and spent two days with us observing and talking to as many as she could find. She spent quite bit of time with Paul, who probably missed Angela badly as she had done most of the organizing of program delivery. Vanessa had been a supervisor for at least ten years and was wise in the ways of administration and field work.

"You seem to like your work," Vanessa said to me when she rode along on a well-baby visit.

"I do."

"How would you like to take on something more challenging?"

I glanced at her. Was she was offering me Angela's job? I didn't want it—all that paperwork and little contact with patients.

"This job is challenging enough."

"You're not ambitious?"

I considered that. I wanted my master's degree, but perhaps not in nursing. "I want to go back to university."

"That's hard to do here."

"Impossible."

"So what about an administration job?"

I pulled into the yard at a small house on Western Avenue. "Sorry." I said.

She shrugged and smiled. She'd probably ask Marlene next, if she hadn't asked her already.

When Vanessa left, no one had taken the supervisor's job, and she told us to rotate the supervisor's duties. I took the job for the rest of July. We designated Cathy for August, and Marlene for September, although we'd revisit the problem at that time.

"If we're still without a supervisor in October," Sophie said, "you three can do it again. It's not my thing."

"We'll worry about it in October," I said.

There was only a week left in July and very little planning to do as most agencies we worked with were in caretaking mode over the summer, not starting new programs. Planning would recommence in late August when Marlene would be in charge.

I didn't anticipate much added work. Ellie would collate all the statistics that had to be delivered to Victoria at the end of the month. I'd read them over then sign them. With Ellie's stewardship, we would keep on top of the paperwork.

I headed out to Horsefly at lunchtime. There was one baby visit there, and I wanted to do it before my holiday. It was forty miles to Horsefly. The first section of the Horsefly Road was paved, but when it divided, the left-hand road branching to Likely and the right road to Horsefly, I was on dusty gravel with teeth-jarring potholes. The scale rattled and jangled as if it were muttering curses.

Mrs. Chubb, the mother of four, lived in a large cabin just before Horsefly. After I parked in her yard, I took a moment to gaze at the Cariboo Mountains rising over the miles of fir trees. Horsefly Lake was a few miles east past the town, but I couldn't see it from here. Mrs. Chubb had a phone, so Ellie had called and arranged the time. I grabbed my black bag and hauled out the scale. Mrs. Chubb was waiting for me, holding the baby in her arms as she opened the door. A little girl of three peeked around her mother's knees. Julie. I'd read the chart quickly before I'd left. The two older boys were not visible.

"Where are the boys?"

"Their dad has a day off and they've gone fishing. It's lovely and quiet here now."

I followed her into the large cabin. I remembered my mother, the mother of six, saying that one less child in the house was peaceful.

I put the scale on the table, which held the remnants of lunch: the crusts from a cheese sandwich, a small glass with a film of milk on the bottom. Mrs. Chubb waited while I readied the scale. I saw her nod at Julie, who carefully gathered the dirty dishes and carried them to the sink. She was about David's age. It was too bad they lived so far from us as she'd be a good playmate for him. I knew he needed other kids to play with, but he was going to leave Edith's care this fall and go to nursery school. He'd find playmates there.

I weighed baby Jordan, did a physical exam, and pronounced him healthy.

"I thought so," Mrs. Chubb said with satisfaction.

She dressed the baby, soothed him back to sleep, and put him in the cradle by the table.

"How have you been?" I asked her as I charted Jordan's name, length, head circumference, weight, and general observations.

"Pretty good. I made it into the hospital on time. I got Dr. Wilson this time." I glanced at her chart; Dr. Craisson was listed as her doctor.

"Dr. Craisson wasn't available?"

"He hasn't made it to any of the births. He lives a ways out of town, but I don't think he likes births. Too messy."

I stared at her. "But you went to him for prenatal care?"

"I did. I was four months along. He felt my tummy and told me I had a tumour."

"No vaginal exam? No test?" I was shocked. It is quite easy to diagnose pregnancy at four months.

"Nope." She nodded at Jordan's cradle. "Meet my tumour."

I stared at her. Her eyes twinkled and she laughed. I was speechless. I wasn't allowed to criticize a doctor, but this was negligence. Luckily, Mrs. Chubb hadn't believed him. What happened to those patients who did? Why didn't his colleagues supervise him or report him or curtail him in some way? He'd been a problem since I came to work here.

Mrs. Chubb was not bothered.

"Have some coffee," she said, standing to grab the pot off the stove, where she had it warming. We sat with our mugs of coffee for fifteen minutes and chatted about her children, the school, and the work opportunities in the area. She was a competent mother, one of those who could teach me how to raise children if I paid attention.

I PULLED INTO OUR RANCH AT FOUR, relieved Colleen of child supervision, and got supper ready. Tomorrow was Wednesday, my day off. I planned to shear all twenty-six sheep. I hoped Carl had finished the baling so he could help me.

I wasn't lucky. In the morning, he told me he had two more hours of work left.

"I just have to pick up the last of the bales. Janice and Glen can help me."

They groaned. Haying had lost its appeal.

"David will stay with me, then."

David was willing. He'd be a help fetching things while I sheared the sheep. Carl could use the electric clippers to strip the fleece from the sheep, but those clippers were too heavy for me. The hand shears were easier to use, although they were slower. Carl could shear two sheep while I was shearing one, but I was still fairly fast. Twelve minutes was my record time.

David and I headed for the barn with Ben accompanying us. He would get in the way of the haying crew, so he stayed behind. I anticipated he would sit above us in the top part of the barn and watch us work.

"Mommy! Mommy! Here comes Charlie!"

I looked to my left and saw Charlie, our mischievous wild crow, hovering about ten feet above the ground and lining up above the driveway. Ben's ears perked up and he stood, one foot raised as if pointing to the bird, then raced to the driveway. Charlie came in low over Ben's head, pacing him. Ben yapped and jumped, a whirling blur of golden yellow, trying to catch the crow. Charlie stayed just out of reach, enticing Ben the length of the driveway, then swooped up over the house, leaving Ben frustrated and barking. Ben never learned. Charlie simply waited for an opportunity and swooped down again. When I stopped laughing, I called Ben.

"You'd better stay in the barn with us, Ben. I don't think Charlie will come in there."

David and I enticed all the sheep into the barn by the simple ruse of pouring oats into the trough. Sheep will do almost anything for oats.

David perched on the manger and watched. He could be trampled by so many sheep milling around. I separated one ewe and nudged her into the pen I'd prepared for shearing. I had two pairs of shears, a blade-sharpening stone, a long wool sack, some twine, and a darning needle. I'd swept the floor so I wouldn't drop the clean fleece onto a dirty floor and have to pick out bits of hay and twigs.

Once I had the selected sheep in the pen and David had shut and latched the door, I grabbed the ewe by one leg, braced her against my knee, and tipped her onto her rump. She leaned against me and was quiet.

"Bring me the shears now, David."

He scrambled over to the bench I'd placed in the pen and lifted the shears.

"Careful," I said. "They're sharp."

He stopped and stared at the shears, then brought them over to me.

"Stay well away, David. She might decide to kick and struggle."

He moved toward the manger and settled there, watching me.

I started at the neck and worked carefully, clipping away the wool near her face. Number Twenty-Three was an older ewe and a sensible one. She had twins who were gaining weight.

"You're doing great, old girl." I talked to her as I worked. Once I finished her neck area, I clipped in a line, the wool falling away and revealing the next row just the way grass in a field falls before a scythe. Once one row was cut, the second was easy to shear. I did one side, belly to the centre of her back, then rolled her to brace against my other knee and sheared the remaining side.

I clipped off the dirty wool on her backside and threw it in a garbage can. I checked her teeth and her feet. All looked heathy, so I let her out into the barnyard. She bawled for her twins. I looked through the sheep waiting to be sheared and spied them. They had ear tags Number 231 and Number 232. I picked them up one at a time and deposited them outside. Archie the ram was butting the door, but I didn't let him out. I'd do that later.

David had pulled the wool sack from the manger to the fleece.

"Good job," I said. I knelt down on the floor and proceeded to fold the fleece. First, I stretched it out; then I brought one side to the middle, trying keep it from separating, then the other side. Then I rolled it as tight as I could and stuffed it in the bottom of the sack. I would take it down to the feed store tomorrow. They'd send it away for me, and eventually I'd get a small cheque.

I got the next ewe into the pen, Number Forty-Nine. She bleated and complained, but her wool wasn't as dense, so the shearing went faster. It was peaceful doing a repetitive task. The regularity of it, the *snip, snip*, the repeated path of the shears, relaxed me.

At ten-thirty, we went into the house for a quick break. I had coffee, David had juice, and we both had cookies. David collected a couple of books and some toy trucks and followed me back to the barn. I was concentrating on making a smooth cut on the wool, over and over, when I heard David cry, "Mommy!"

I looked up. David wasn't there. I dropped the shears, dumped the ewe, and leapt for the pen where his voice was coming from.

David was backed against the manger, and Archie—all 150 pounds of muscle with a battering ram for a head—was squared off in front of him, stamping his feet.

"Get up into the manger!" I yelled as I scrambled over the fence and shoved sheep out of my way trying to get to David. Archie had not been distracted by me and reared up to charge. I turned, threw David into the manger, and dived in after him. Archie crashed into the side of the manger. David wailed.

"We're fine," I said. I gathered him close. "We're fine, honey. That was scary."

"Scary," he repeated. He'd stopped crying. I rocked him in my arms for a moment.

I wanted to say, *Why didn't you stay in the safety of the pen?* But he was only three. Why didn't I watch him more closely? Why didn't I let Archie out earlier?

I boosted David up through the opening to the hay storage area above us and crawled up after him. I sat on a bale and hugged him some more.

"Why did you go into that pen, David?"

He sniffed. "I wanted to see the twins."

"What twins?"

"The last ones. The small ones."

"Number Fifty-Six's?"

"Yeah." That would seem a reasonable plan to him.

"It isn't safe when Archie's there. He's usually okay outside, but not when he's in the barn."

David nodded.

I took his hand. "Let's go."

We went back to the small pen. David settled on the manger. I doubted he would move from there. I manoeuvred Archie to the yard gate and let him out. No one had been hurt. We were all fine. When my hands stopped shaking, I resumed shearing.

By noon, when Carl and the kids drove into the yard with the last load of bales, I had sheared ten sheep. I was going to need Carl's help to get them all sheared that day. David had recovered enough to tell the story of terrifying Archie. Janice and Glen were impressed.

I put pizza into the oven for me and the kids. Carl hated pizza, so he made himself a fried egg sandwich.

Shearing went much faster in the afternoon. Carl was quick with the electric shears. Janice and Glen rolled the fleece and stuffed them into the wool sack. David sat on the manger and watched everyone, responding to requests for the needle and twine to sew a wool sack shut or to fetch a cup of water, but otherwise just enjoying the activity. I clipped steadily. By five, we had finished. I had a blister on the inside of my right thumb.

Everyone headed for a shower. Sheep have lanolin in their wool, and while it's a good cream for human skin, it smells. I found a band aid for my thumb, put the chicken drumsticks in the oven, and set the table. I had a potato salad and a green salad already made. There was ice cream for dessert. That's all I had the energy for.

We ate quietly without the usual chatter. Janice and David were yawning over their dessert. I sent them to bed. Even Glen, who seemed to have constant energy, was flagging. The house was quiet by eight-thirty. I was asleep by nine.

CHAPTER THIRTEEN

SALLY, DETERMINED TO GIVE MEDICATION

T HE HEAT ROLLED across the country through to the end of July. While I was glad to see the grass growing and the livestock getting fat—except for the sheep, who stubbornly refused to get plump—I found the temperature in the high eighties uncomfortable. Canada had implemented the Celsius system, but I found it hard to adapt; twenty-seven degrees Celsius didn't mean anything to me, though I supposed I'd get used to it eventually. The ranch house caught the breeze coming up the rise, so it cooled off at night and was bearable, but my car was stifling. I was glad to get to the health unit, where we had air conditioning.

I did one baby visit in the morning and caught up on my charting. I needed to leave everything completed when I left for my vacation.

Just before noon, Sally came into the office.

"How's everything?"

"Okay," she said. She gave me a report on her patients.

"How's Melody's abscess?" We were treating a thirty-year-old woman for a pilonidal cyst that had developed at the base of her spine. It's painful and, if not treated, could get worse.

"What a circus that was yesterday!"

"What happened?"

Sally leaned back in her chair and let out a long-suffering sigh.

"I couldn't find her. She's usually hanging around the Lakeview Café, and she knows I come looking for her at ten in the morning. She needs that antibiotic, and every other day I change the dressing."

"Where do you do it?" I was curious.

"I bring her here."

"Okay. So what happened yesterday?"

"I couldn't find her, but I found her sister Martha. Do you know Martha?"

"Short, plump. Laughs a lot. Nice woman."

"That's Martha. Melody doesn't have Martha's nice nature. Anyway, Martha said Melody was at the Stampeder Motel—entertaining."

"Uh oh." We had suspected Melody had a small business going on, but she hadn't appeared on our list for sexually transmitted disease, and it was our policy to ignore how people made their income. The Stampeder Motel wasn't far from the health unit, on the hill just off the highway.

"Well, she can entertain if she wants, but she still had to have her shot. So I packed Martha into my car and drove to the Stampeder. I sent Martha in to tell Mel to come out for her shot."

"And?"

"And Martha came back and told me Mel said *I* had to come to her. Like she was some kind of queen. She annoyed me, but I went. What else was I going to do?"

I thought she could have left without giving the shot but didn't say so. Sally was used to making quick decisions and following through on them. As well, she had the determination of a beaver. She'd accomplish what she set out to do, no matter what obstacles were in her way. She knew how to work around problems, but she sometimes just plowed through them.

Sally stretched and settled back in her chair. "I went into a kind of a suite where there were easy chairs and a kitchenette. There were two guys there, but I ignored them. The bedroom was separate, and that was where Melody was.

"'Melody,' I shouted at her, 'Come out and get your shot.'

"'You come in,' she shouted back.

"I felt like grabbing her and dragging her out, but she's a lot heavier than me, so I yelled at her, 'Get that guy off you and roll to the edge of the bed and stick your butt out.'

"I put my bag on the counter and got the syringe and med out and prepared it. Then I went into the bedroom. Sure enough, she'd done what I said. I gave the shot and got out of there."

"You are intrepid. How many more doses does she need?"

"Another five. I told her she had to come to the health unit tomorrow for her shot or I'd report the whole lot of them."

"For what?"

"I'll think of something." She looked fed up.

"So sorry. You didn't have to do that, you know. It was beyond the call of duty." As soon as the words were out of my mouth I regretted them. It sounded as if I was criticizing her.

"Yes, I did."

Knowing Sally, of course she did, but most nurses would not have ventured into that motel room.

"That's not all," she said as she stood to leave.

"What else?"

"When I was leaving, Silas Moore—you know Silas?"

"Just to see him, and by reputation."

"He blocked my path to the door and said, 'Gimme a kiss and I'll let you out.'"

I stared at her, imagining Silas looming over her, his broad shoulders and shovel-sized hands hanging down at his sides. "What did you say?"

"I said, 'Get real, Silas. It'd be like kissing your mother.' He stared at me for a moment. I know he was taking in my grey hair and wrinkles, then said, 'You're right.'"

"Sally," I said, "you deserve a medal."

"So I do," she agreed.

I spent a moment or two after she left wondering if the nurses who had designed the home care program ever anticipated some of the situations the nurses who delivered the program ran into. The head office in Victoria seemed a world away both in distance and culture.

I drove to the south edge of town where Dr. Allan had asked me to visit a young woman patient of his, Harpreet, who recently immigrated from India to marry a young man here. She was living with his family. Dr. Allan suspected she was being abused.

"She has a couple of bruises on her arms. Nothing major, but it worries me. Just see if you notice anything."

"You speak Punjabi, don't you?"

"A little. I asked her if she was being harmed, but she said she fell. I don't have enough evidence to report it to a social worker, and I don't want the family to know I suspect anything for fear they'll keep her from coming to the office. If you find abuse, then I'll risk the social worker going in."

I agreed to go on the pretense of checking her immunization status.

A South Asian woman of about thirty opened the door and let me inside. She was all smiles until I asked for Harpreet.

"Why?" she asked me.

I had my excuse ready. "Just routine government immunization inquiries."

She looked mistrustful. "She doesn't speak English."

"That's unusual," I said. Most young people from India spoke some English. "Where is she?" I did know enough about the culture to leave my shoes at the door. I padded into the room. It's a good thing I wasn't trying to exert authority. That's hard to do when you're barefoot.

There were four women sitting in the living room, three on a blue couch and one on a matching easy chair. They were dressed in saris and seemed a blur of bright blue, yellow, and gold. The woman who had answered the door pulled a young woman from the corner of the couch.

"All your men are at work?" I asked and nodded a hello at the women. They said nothing, but the older woman smiled at me.

"We could go to the kitchen," I said to Harpreet and headed there. I could not think of a way to have a private interview with her. Perhaps they'd leave us alone in the kitchen? That didn't happen. The woman who had answered the door followed us. I'd had the foresight to create a file for Harpreet. I pulled out her records and checked her name and address.

"Is this your correct name?"

"Yes, that's right." I knew then she both spoke and understood English.

I stared at the file.

"Oh dear," I said. "My pen stopped working. Could you get me a pen?" I asked the woman who I took to be Harpreet's sister-in-law.

She frowned and yelled something in Punjabi. There was no answer from the other room. She went to the kitchen door.

"Tell your doctor what is going on," I whispered to Harpreet. "He can get you out of here."

Harpreet stared at me. I don't know if she understood me, but it was the best I could do.

Her sister-in-law returned quickly and I went through the immunization status slowly, hoping our guard would get bored, but she stuck with us.

I called Dr. Allan when I returned to my office.

"I think it is the sister-in-law who might be abusing her, grabbing her and pulling her around. She's much bigger than Harpreet. She was so hostile and determined not to leave Harpreet alone with me. You could send the social worker in. They will think it is because *I* suspected something—which is true."

"We don't have any evidence. Maybe it won't escalate and Harpreet won't be physically harmed. And maybe she will be hurt. Nothing terrible has happened yet. I suppose we have to wait until it does. I'd like to prevent that, but I don't know if the social worker can help."

"I don't know neither. Harpreet is in a difficult situation. She is in Canada because she was sponsored by her husband. His family is the one she has to get along with for the rest of her life. There isn't a temple here, so there's no organized religious leader available to the family; do you know anyone who would represent spiritual authority to them?"

"I do know a well-respected man in that community. I might be able to talk to him—not that he will be able to do much. If she comes in with broken bones or contusions, I will get the Ministry of Human Resources involved."

We were both silent for a few moments. It wasn't a satisfactory plan, but we didn't have any other.

Paul popped his head into my office just before I left for home.

"Is there anything you need before I leave on my holiday?"

He sometimes signed standing orders for the home care nurses and the public health nurses when we needed them. I mentally reviewed my caseload. "No, all is well, thanks."

He smiled, waved, and left.

Paul was the only medical health officer I'd ever worked with. When I started here, in my first nursing job, Rita was the supervisor and took care of all the medical health officer duties she could. After she left, Angela had been doing that job. I didn't know exactly what it was Paul did aside from attending the monthly meeting of doctors at the hospital. Perhaps Paul had discussions with the head office about policy. Perhaps he was taking on some of the nursing supervisor's duties. We'd all have to look at those duties if we didn't have a new supervisor soon.

I STOPPED AT THE BARN to feed the sheep before I went into the house. I didn't need to drop hay into the mangers as the sheep were grazing in the pastures. I could see them on the rise of land beyond the barn. They looked like white dots in the field, with the yellow-green aspen leaves beyond them shimmering in a slight breeze at the edge of the woods. I put some oats in the trough in the vain hope I could get their weight up. The barn smelled sweetly of the new hay, now stacked to the rafters. I checked that the water trough was full, although they could drink from the pond. All was well in the barn.

I admired the sunflowers on the sunny rise past my vegetable garden. They were a flower I'd never seen at the coast where I grew up, but they were abundant here. Every late spring and summer when they bloomed, I remembered Glen at about three years old running up to me with his gift of a handful of sunflowers—sunny day, sunflowers, a sunny smile from my son. Lovely. The memory still warmed my heart.

No one was home; I presumed they were all together on some project or adventure. It was a rare moment of quiet in the house. Missy the cat occupied a square of sunlight in the living room, but no one else was there, not even Ben. I put some food in Missy's dish. She padded over to investigate it. I changed into shorts and a T-shirt and checked the time. Carl hadn't left a note, so it was likely he and the kids would be coming home for dinner soon. I knew I'd better start something. I made a salad. If they had already eaten, it would keep until tomorrow. I had the fixings for macaroni and cheese if supper was needed.

They trooped in about six, the children full of their day, Ben bustling around his food dish.

"We went to Tyee Lake," Glen said. "We went swimming."

Everyone but David could swim. I was teaching him but he hadn't yet managed the head-under-the-water trick.

"The water was warm," Janice said, "and you could see right to the bottom. We saw a mother loon teaching her baby to fish—all underwater. I mean, *they* were underwater; we were on the shore."

I smiled at Carl. "A good day?"

"Nice," he said, and gave me a quick kiss.

"Dinner in forty minutes," I said.

"What's forty minutes?" David asked.

I reached for the timer by the stove, set it for forty minutes, and handed it to him. "When that rings, come to supper with your hands washed."

"Okay." He went to his room happy now that he understood the plan. He always had to know what was going to happen. I was pleased that they had managed to get to the lake. I did feel at times that, with my work and Carl's, they didn't get the holidays others kids did in the summer. I'd try to give them more experiences in August when I was on vacation. I had only to finish out the week before my vacation started.

THE NEXT MORNING, I loaded my car for a well-baby clinic at Miocene. It was an hour's drive up the Horsefly Road and scheduled for ten o'clock. I usually did that clinic in the school, but school was closed for the summer, so one of the ranchers had offered her house. Once I got on the gravel road, the dust rose up around the car. I opened the front window. I didn't know if that helped or just let fresh dust pass through. I pulled into Maryanne Herbert's yard and parked beside the three pickup trucks near her kitchen door. I reached for my black bag, the scale, and the silver aluminum suitcase that held the syringes, first aid kit, flashlight, gauze, and tape. No suitcase. The back seat was empty. In my mind, I could see the loaded suitcase resting beside my desk back in Williams Lake. Blast!

I trudged into the house. Maryanne opened the back door for me.

"Come on in, Nurse. We've got four babies here today. Janine came with Anne."

I nodded at the women and set the scale on the table.

"I am really sorry," I said. There was no way out of this that would save my dignity. "I forgot the syringes." And the vaccine.

There was absolute silence.

"The kids can't get their shots today?" Janine asked.

"I can go back to town, collect the syringes, which are sitting beside my desk, and return. It will take me two hours."

I waited.

They looked at each other. "Put another pot of coffee on, Maryanne," Janine said. "I got more gossip."

"You go," Maryanne said to me on behalf of the group.

"I'll balance the scale and you can weigh the babies while I'm gone."

"Good idea."

I did that and left.

I was immensely grateful that not one of them had condemned me for stupidity or even carelessness. I was inconveniencing them, but perhaps they were glad of it. They would have few opportunities in their busy lives to have two hours of unscheduled time. *You are not doing them a favour, Marion. They are just amazingly tolerant.*

It wasn't the first time I was absentminded. I'd been dealing with periodic incidences of this all my life. I can remember my mother saying, "You'd forget your head if it wasn't screwed on." Sometimes, like today, my forgetfulness was highly inconvenient.

I slid in and out of the office, trying to be invisible, but Ellie saw me. I held up the suitcase on the way out and she raised her eyebrows. Obviously, I'd forgotten it. I was back at Maryanne's in exactly two hours. I spent an hour and a half giving immunizations and talking to the mothers. They had rehearsed all their questions, and the group had given advice while I was fetching the syringes and vaccine so the conversation with the mothers was a group affair.

"Sherry's little girl sucks her thumb and she's three years old," one of the mothers, Brita, said.

"Put mustard on her thumb," Maryanne said. "That cured my Bobby."

They looked at me. Maryanne was my host. She was providing me with clinic space. I couldn't contradict her—but mustard?

"What seems to work is to substitute the thumb with something else, like a teddy bear or a favourite blanket, and give her a hug. She may be feeling afraid or just anxious."

"Yeah, that works with the old man," Sherry said. "He wants sex and I turn on the hockey game. Distraction."

"Doesn't work for long," Brita said.

"You'll have a little lunch before you leave," Maryanne said, plunking a ham sandwich in front of me. "What do you take in your coffee?"

"Milk." I wasn't going to turn down lunch. Homemade bread, home-cured ham, and home-preserved pickles were impossible to resist. I didn't deserve them, but I ate them.

Maryanne carried my scale to the car, accompanying me as if I were a guest leaving her party. "We all had a really good time. You are coming back in August?"

"No one needs immunization in August. I'll come in September."

"The school will be open then." She sounded disappointed not to be hosting the clinic.

"Thanks for having us here."

"Oh, it was no problem. You watch out for the logging trucks, you hear? Jacobsons have some on the road this week."

"Thanks, I will."

I rattled along the gravel road on my way back to the office, noticing the dust on the aspen trees on either side. The colour of the leaves went from dull green near the road to bright green in the distant trees. Ponds beside the road mirrored the colours. In the fall, the aspens wore a brilliant yellow, shimmering in the autumn breeze, but today they were still, laden with the heat and dust of summer.

I wondered at the generous spirit of Maryanne and her friends. Not one complaint nor any criticism of me when they would have been justified in voicing it. They just adjusted to the problem I presented and made the most of the delay.

CHAPTER FOURTEEN

4-H COMPETITION, NEW PATIENTS, AND FISH HEADS

FINALLY, in the first week of August, I was on holiday at home, and Carl was back at work. Aside from the usual ranch work and cooking for the family, I took the kids to Tyee Lake for picnics. The gravel boat-launch site was a good swimming area, and we had the place to ourselves most of the time, with only one or two boats launching during the afternoon. Those were of great interest to Glen, who squatted on his haunches out of the way and studied everything about the mechanics that allowed the boat to be winched down into the water.

Janice was more interested in the fish and birds that were all around us.

"What's that song?" she asked.

"A yellow-headed blackbird." That raspy, loud call was one of the few I could identify. "They live in the reeds."

She crouched at the edge of the water and stared at the reeds.

I watched all the kids, but especially David. Janice and Glen could swim enough to keep afloat, but all kids could get into trouble in a lake very quickly. I went into the water with David and dropped a small stone. "See if you can pick it up."

He cheerfully put his head underwater to reach for the stone. He dropped it into the pail I held. That kept him busy for several minutes and taught him how to hold his breath under water. But it was too soon for him to be safe on his own.

"Okay, everyone, out of the water," I said. "Here's a sandwich. Stay on shore while I have a swim."

This was our usual routine. The kids would swim and play in the water for an hour or so, then sit on the shore while I swam.

The air was hot and the water inviting. I slid into it without the shock I got from the ocean. This lake wasn't deep, so it warmed up quickly during the day to swimming pool temperature. I struck out with a fast crawl, making the most of my reprieve. I trusted the kids to stay on shore for about ten minutes.

They were still contentedly raiding the picnic basket when I waded through the reeds and up the shore. I dried myself and sat down to have my lunch. They'd left me a sandwich and an apple. Good enough.

The water of the lake was turquoise, with dark blue streaks where it was deeper, and ringed with pine and alder, their leaves trembling in the gentle movement of air from the lake. There were cabins in a bay around a point, but we couldn't see them from here. Friends of ours had a ranch at the far end, also out of sight. *Carl and I should consider buying a lot on this lake and putting a cabin on it.* It was only forty minutes from home and might be a great place when the kids were teens.

In the interest of surveying lot possibilities, I persuaded the kids to take a walk with me through the trees along the lakeshore before we returned home. There was little underbrush in this part of the country, just grass under the pines. We had gone only a short distance when Glen said, "There's smoke."

We came up to the remnants of a campfire. A thin wisp of smoke rose from a charred log. Around us was dry grass and dry pines. *A forest fire could start at any moment. Should I get my kids out of here, race home, and call the Forestry department? Or try to douse this fire?* Leaving this was not an option.

"Janice, run to the car and get the bucket in the back. If there's anything in it, empty it."

She dashed away.

"Glen, use your hat to get water. I'll do the same. David, sit on that rock and don't move."

Everyone obeyed me.

Glen and I brought up small hatfuls of water and poured it on the log. When Janice returned with the bucket, we used that and soaked the log.

"Me too," David said.

"Just wait." I appreciated he wanted to help, but I had to know where he was at all times and I didn't want him wandering away and complicating the situation. When I thought we'd soaked it thoroughly, I helped David use his hat to scoop up some water and pour it on the now wet ground.

"There," he said as if he'd personally completed the job.

"Will it stay out?" Janice asked.

There was no more smoke rising from the site, but that didn't mean the fire was out. There could be a smouldering root. We may have poured enough water on the ground to reach a root, but I couldn't be sure.

"It should be good," I said, "but I'll report it."

I'd call our friends at the ranch at the end of the lake when I got home and tell them about it. They could check on it. They'd probably come with shovels and make sure no root was smouldering below ground.

We put on our soggy hats and walked back to the car. We were hot, so the cool damp felt good.

"We stopped a . . . a . . ." Glen said.

"A forest fire," Janice supplied the words.

We probably had.

WE WERE BUSY IN AUGUST with 4-H competitions and ranch work. Janice sold her piglets when they reached a weight that satisfied her, but kept one weaner pig for 4-H competition. Glen was still struggling to feed his calf. He didn't spend much time grooming it or training it, so it was difficult to catch.

I was in the barn one evening when I heard him talking to his calf. He didn't know I was there.

"Why are you so much trouble? Why don't you come into the barn when I call? The sheep do, and they're a lot stupider than you are." His voice took on a pleading tone. "Come on, Pedro. Can't you act better?"

I snuck out of the barn quietly. Pedro didn't obey Glen because Glen hadn't spent enough time training him. Animals were not the passion for Glen that they were for Janice. If Pedro had been a motor with wheels, Glen would have spent hours with him.

The big week, the 4-H Show, ended with the 4-H Sale on Saturday. The 4-H kids had their animals in peak condition for sale—at least they were supposed to have them ready—and were gathering with their parents, families, trucks, and all the paraphernalia animals needed to look outstanding.

Janice and her friend Ray had trained their weaner pigs, named Rosie and Pansy, to respond to the tapping of a cane on their cheeks, so the ten-year-old handlers were able to herd the pigs around the ring while the auctioneer pointed out the pigs' good points. At least they herded them, more or less. The pigs were not instantly responsive. They were intelligent and tended to make their own decisions, contrary to the direction of their handlers, about where and when to go exploring. So the best-trained pig could suddenly scamper toward an opening.

"Rosie here topped the scales and won the champion rosette for her weight and her overall good condition. Pansy was a close runner-up with the Reserve Championship." The auctioneer spoke with enthusiasm. Since they were the only two pigs in the competition, it wasn't particularly impressive, although everyone understood that if they had been underweight or miserable specimens, they would not have gotten an award.

"They're our first pigs for sale here, folks, not our usual Hereford calves. Let's support this sale so more kids can get into 4-H."

The bidding was fast and moved to unheard-of high prices in minutes. It was hard to resist those two kids. Both wore their 4-H uniform of jeans and a denim vest with the Soda Creek 4-H emblem and their badges of accomplishments sewn on every available surface. Janice, with her short pigtails and intense concentration, worked hard to keep Rosie contained in the ring. Ray wore a small stetson and a matching intent expression. Carl and Jake, Ray's dad, were in the ring with them holding rectangular shields of plywood ready to separate the pigs if they started fighting.

There were no fights. Janice's pig fetched an amazing price from Freddy Westwick, a rancher from Pea Vine Ridge; Ray's also did well.

I knew Janice was going to be upset at losing her pig. Freddy might keep Rosie for breeding, or he might butcher her when she was fully grown, but either way Rosie was leaving our ranch. I walked into the barn area where Rosie was back in her steel pen. Janice was standing by her, talking to Freddy.

"She likes apples," Janice was telling him.

"I'll see that she gets some," Freddy promised.

I didn't intrude; I waited until Freddy left then joined Janice. She was sitting on the straw beside Rosie talking to her. "I can't keep you, Rosie. I already have Cleo. Mr. Westwick will be good to you."

"At least she'll probably be raised for breeding," I said as I sat beside her.

"Yes. I'm glad Mr. Westwick is taking her. But" she turned to me, tears in her eyes, "she's my friend."

"And you'll miss her."

She sniffed. "I will."

We sat in silence. She would miss her. There wasn't much I could do about it. The 4-H kids raised animals for sale.

I managed to make it to Glen's class just as it started. He looked up and smiled when he saw me in the bleachers. His smile always lifted my heart.

I watched while he and Pedro joined the other 4-H kids and their calves in a circular parade. He hadn't spent enough time with Pedro, and the calf bucked and struggled to free himself from the halter. Glen wrestled him back in line and managed to line up with the others. I could see Pedro was not up to weight. I should have snuck in extra feedings so the calf wouldn't have suffered such a weight loss. I suspected Glen hadn't been feeding regularly.

"I'm sorry," I said to Bill Dennis, from whom we'd bought Pedro. "I should have paid more attention."

"Probably," Bill said. "I'll buy him back and feed him up. I was hoping Glen would show off how well Charolais cattle do in this world of Herefords, but Pedro isn't going to convince anyone."

I'd really let Bill down. I just hadn't noticed how underweight Pedro was.

The judge lined up the calves in order of his preference. Pedro was second from the bottom, but he certainly didn't want to stay in the order the judge had placed him. He fought Glen. Glen struggled with him and brought him back. Every time he did that, the judge moved him up a placement, so Pedro and Glen ended up in the middle.

I went to help Glen put Pedro back in his pen. Bill Dennis had bought him, and Glen was happy he was going there.

Glen had done a good job grooming Pedro; his hooves were polished and his coat well-brushed. Parents were not allowed to help before the sale, only 4-H members could assist.

"Janice helped me," he said.

"Well, Pedro looked very nice."

"A little skinny, though."

"Right."

I didn't say any more.

There was a banquet and dance that evening, which we all attended, tired but excited, anticipating the awards. To my amazement, Glen won the showmanship trophy. The judge said he'd done very well with a difficult calf. The Soda Creek parents knew the calf was difficult because Glen hadn't trained him, but no one said a word. They were a kind bunch.

We all let Glen enjoy his trophy. He had controlled Pedro, after all.

LATE AUGUST was a time of abundance, harvesting, and preserving. I froze wild blackberries and saskatoon berries and our own raspberries. I even coaxed the kids to come wild strawberry picking with me. It was impossible to collect enough of those tiny, sweet berries to freeze as we ate them as we picked them. I'd canned tomatoes and peaches from the Okanagan earlier in July; Sophie and her family had picked up boxes of fruit when they were holidaying in Penticton and brought some back for me. I also froze as many vegetables as I could buy since I didn't raise enough in my garden to provide for the winter.

My friend Cynthia called to say she had fish for me. Because she was Indigenous, she could fish for salmon in the Fraser, but she wasn't allowed to sell it. She did, though, and I bought it.

That evening, I told Carl that Cynthia was bringing me some salmon.

"Don't tell me about it. Lawyers aren't supposed to do anything illegal. Tell her to come when I'm at work."

That seemed a bit like hair-splitting to me but easy to arrange.

Cynthia drove her truck into my yard with a tub full of fish on ice in the back.

"How many do you want?"

"Twelve will do me. Have you got that many?"

"Sure."

She carried the tub into the house. I had the coffee on, poured her a cup, and gave her a cheque.

"Stay and visit while I wrap these in freezer paper."

"I can do that."

David wandered in from his room and inspected the fish.

"Did you catch them?" he asked Cynthia.

"Me and my family," she said.

"Cool," he said, and headed for the back door.

"Where are you going?"

"To the pigpen."

"Is Janice there?"

"Yes."

"Okay, then."

"What Nation is he?" Cynthia asked me when he had left us.

"The Welfare told us he is Tsimshian, from Port Simpson. They told us Glen is British, Polish, and French. I'm not sure any of that is true, but it's the only information we have. It's hard to figure out where he fits in with so little information."

"Can you find out?"

"No. I tried with Glen. I went to the town office and got the clerk to search the file. She was willing but came back saying the file was labelled 'secret.' I can't try that again. Adoptions are secret. It's crazy."

"It would be nice to know where David's relatives are."

"It's important, I think." I always felt as if I had a place in my huge McKinnon clan. David should know about his clan.

"I remember you have a lot of cousins. Your own tribe." I had sixty first cousins on my dad's side of the family, so yes, I did have a tribe.

She sat at the counter while I reached into the tub and brought out the first salmon. It was silver and about two feet long. I sliced off the head and opened the garbage lid. I thought about letting Missy have it, but she'd play with it and I'd have blood splatters all over my house.

"Hey!" Cynthia said. "Aren't you going to eat the head?"

"No. Does anybody eat the head?"

"We do. It's delicious."

"Eyes and all?"

"Eyes and all."

I stared at the head then back at Cynthia. "How about you take all the heads home?"

"The kids will love that," she said.

So we drank coffee and talked while Cynthia helped me decapitate the salmon and wrap them in freezer paper. We dumped all the heads back into her tub. I gave her more ice to keep them cool, and we finished quickly. I waved and watched her truck trundle out my driveway. The trees on either side of the driveway were turning a faint yellow. I hoped the frost would hold off for some weeks yet. I saw the brake lights flash on Cynthia's truck as she slowed to drive over the cattle guard. She might have been kidding about eating fish eyes.

WITH THE FLURRY of 4-H competitions and dances, preserving, and freezing, August flashed past, and David turned four on the last day of the month. I wished I knew where his birth mother was so I could call her or write her and tell her that he was thriving. He was happy with his gifts: a toy car from Glen, a book from Janice, a small bicycle with training wheels from Carl and me, and a lavishly decorated chocolate cake. Glen had had his ninth birthday at the end of June. We'd had five boys here with water pistols. It was noisy but fun. David's birthday was quieter, but he seemed happy.

School started and I was back to work. David started nursery school. I was grateful to Edith for her care of him over the last two years, but he needed to socialize with kids his own age and the nursery school was a good choice. I dropped him off on the way to work.

All the public health staff met at nine for a planning meeting. We still did not have a nursing supervisor.

"We're going to have to figure out some way to handle all the administration," Marlene said.

"I can't do it," Paul said. "I can't do the medical health officer's work and the nursing supervisor's."

"Besides," Sophie said with a warm smile, "you don't know what we do."

"Not day by day, that's true," Paul agreed. "I mean, generally I know, but not specifically."

"So nurses will have to supervise nurses," Sophie said.

"Yes. Yes."

Having neatly dealt with Paul, Sophie turned to the rest of us.

"I don't feel I've got the administrative skills, so I don't want to make a fool of myself trying to manage this place, but I can pick up staff nursing from someone who does and so give that person more time for supervising."

"Okay, Sophie," Marlene said. "That might be crucial."

We talked for some time and decided Marlene would act as supervisor for September. I would act as supervisor for October and Cathy for November. By then, head office in Victoria may have hired a supervisor.

The first week of work was busy. Ellie collected our school class lists and parcelled them out to us. A few weeks before we planned to immunize a class, we called for the records and read through them to make sure we immunized only those who needed it.

I had a meeting with the home care nurses. Cathy had acted as their supervisor when I was on my holiday, but she told me they hadn't asked her for anything. I'm sure Sally oversaw all the care. I was relieved that Pam had been able to take her shifts. She lived out of town about six miles up the Horsefly Road on a small farm. Both she and her husband worked, but they also ran about twenty head of cattle and had chickens and a pig. Their two boys were teenagers and helped out as well. It was a big commitment for Pam to show up for work, but she had done it.

"We got two new patients while you were gone," Sally told me. "They're different because they originally came from Social Welfare."

"A referral from Human Resources?" The name of that government department had changed, and we all had a hard time remembering it.

"Yeah. I got both their doctors' referrals as well, but it was the social worker who pushed for us to visit."

"What's the diagnosis?"

Violet answered, "Both need health supervision. Mrs. Barnston has high blood pressure and a bit of COPD."

"She was a smoker," Kate said, "but she doesn't smoke now, thank the good Lord. We'll have to watch for signs of heart disease or cancer." I imagined Kate's mind like a filing cabinet where, once she had the diagnosis, she accessed the accompanying symptoms.

Chronic Obstructive Pulmonary Disease. "That can restrict activity," I said. "What's her mobility like?"

"She'd like to stay in bed all day," Pam contributed.

"Coughs like an engine," Sally said.

"Most COPD patients do," Kate agreed.

"And the other patient, Mrs. Michelson, has allergies," Sally continued.

"That's all? I mean, that's her diagnosis?"

"No," Violet said. "She also has mild dementia."

They would not take a lot of nursing time. "Where are they?"

"The Welfare got them an apartment across the street," Sally said. That was a building with about twenty units directly across from us. "They're sharing it. It's really just a big room with a bathroom and a kitchenette. They're sharing," she repeated.

"And how's that working out?"

Pam had an opinion. "Badly. Mrs. Barnston is a bully."

"Physically?"

"Not so far. At least, I haven't seen bruises. But she's nasty."

I thought about it. "Let me know when you think we should intervene."

The nurses nodded. They would watch out for Mrs. Michelson.

"What about Mrs. Westin? She lives in that same apartment house, doesn't she?" She was a patient of Dr. Patterson and she had been on our list for a month.

"Yes. She's okay, but she has a lot of side effects from her meds," Sally said.

"Let me see her chart." I studied it. The nurses waited. "She's on seventeen different medications for heart disease! She's grossly overweight, which doesn't help, but seventeen?"

"She's got Dr. Patterson," Jane said, as if that explained it, which it did to some extent.

"He's almost as old as she is." I hoped he'd retire soon.

"He's pretty good most of the time, but he gives a lot of meds." He was Sally's doctor.

"Maybe I should talk to him?"

"He's set in his ways," Sally warned.

I didn't make an appointment to talk to him. He wasn't going to pay any attention to my opinion and, to be fair, I didn't know if all those medications were necessary or unnecessary. I wouldn't blame him for ignoring me or for being insulted if I challenged him. I went to the pharmacist instead.

We sat at her small office in the back of the pharmacy. She looked at my chart.

"Well, this one is given for high blood pressure. And this one is given to combat the side effects of the first drug." She studied it for some time. "I would probably recommend deleting this one and this one." She pointed to the ones she thought unnecessary.

"Thanks."

"But I *wouldn't* recommend you talk to Dr. Patterson about it. I've already tried."

"Oh." I was disappointed, really disappointed. Some of those drugs were making the patient dozy. There was no reason for her to have to live in a drowsy state when it wasn't necessary. It was frustrating. If Dr. Patterson didn't listen to the pharmacist, he wasn't going to listen to me.

A week later, Sally told me Dr. Patterson had gone on vacation.

"Who's taking his patients?"

"Dr. MacDonald." He was my family doctor. I got an appointment with him and presented Mrs. Westin's chart.

His eyebrows rose.

"I think we can eliminate some of these drugs."

Mrs. Westin's drug regimen was reduced to five medications. I was delighted. I hoped it would make Mrs. Westin more alert and more able to enjoy her life.

"Is she better for it?" I asked Sally two weeks later.

"She is better, and she likes being what she calls 'happier,' but she worries she isn't taking enough. She trusts Dr. Patterson. He's been her doctor for years."

"Maybe her improved health will convince her."

At the end of the month, Dr. Patterson returned.

"You won't believe it," Sally said, plopping Mrs. Westin's chart on my desk. "She's back on seventeen meds."

We stared at each other, then Sally shrugged. "Lost cause."

I agreed, but I was frustrated.

DAVID HAD BEEN almost a month at nursery school and seemed to enjoy it. The teachers were kind and kept the kids busy with activities, games, and art projects. They taught them songs, which I thought was wonderful until I chanced to hear David singing his new song to Janice. I was coming down the stairs with laundry, and I heard David in Janice's bedroom singing, "Old Joe Jacob had a little Indian."

I stopped in shock. The nursery school was teaching him that?

I didn't say anything to David. Four-year-olds don't understand slavery or prejudice, but on Monday morning, when I brought David to nursery school, I asked to speak to the teacher.

We sat on tiny chairs while I explained the problem.

"I don't want David to sing 'Old Joe Jacob *had* a little Indian.'"

Her eyes grew wide and she stared at me. "I didn't think. '*Had* a little Indian'? Of course he can't sing that song. No one should. I won't teach it anymore, and I won't have them sing it. How could I have been so insensitive? I just forgot he was Indian. I don't really look at skin colour."

I was quiet for a moment. I understood her point of view; I used to have it myself. I tried to explain. "We think if we are colour-blind, we are accepting, but we aren't really. We are just ignoring the difference."

"As if everyone is white?"

"Yes, and '*had* a little Indian' is condoning slavery."

"Oh, my God. I am so sorry."

"Racism is insidious," I said. I might as well name the problem. Most people never used that word.

Her face flushed red. "It is. I'm so sorry," she repeated. "I never meant to be racist."

She was defensive, and I was angry but trying hard to be civil.

"Thanks for getting rid of the song."

"Glad to," she said.

I drove to work relieved the teacher had been receptive, but facing the fact that there were going to be more incidences of racism. I had thought David would be protected by our family and friends, that people would know him and not see him as a stereotype of their prejudice. That was a kind of hubris on my part, I expect. He was going to meet prejudice. Obviously, he was.

CHAPTER FIFTEEN

TAKING ON HOME CARE

SEPTEMBER WAS A WARM and beautiful month. The poplar leaves had turned bright yellow and were a stark complement to the sapphire-blue sky. The temperature dipped close to freezing at night, nudging us toward the next season. At the coast, winter came after a gentle and prolonged period of rain and gradually cooling weather. Here, it descended with a snap. One day, warm breezes lulled us into thinking the environment was benevolent; the next day, the thermometer plunged, vegetation died, hoses plugged with ice, and everyone dug out sweaters and long johns because the cold could last until April.

I fed oats to the sheep, trying to give them enough protein to keep them healthy, continually frustrated by their inability to gain weight. Verna Dennis, the Soda Creek 4-H leader, had persuaded me to supervise two club members who wanted to raise lambs as their projects. As long as Verna supervised *me*, I was willing. I studied to keep ahead of the children as they had to understand how to feed the lambs, trim their feet, and keep the ticks off their coats. I had the theory; I was just shaky on the practice. I felt more competent as a nurse than I did as a rancher.

At the health unit, Marlene had arranged for an instructor to come from Vancouver to teach us how to do a physical exam on adults. We were all adept at examining babies but didn't have much knowledge or practice with adults. I asked permission from Paul to pay the home care nurses for their time to attend the workshop with the public health nurses. The only day the instructor could come was Saturday, so we all dutifully turned up on Saturday. The public health nurses wouldn't get paid for the extra day, but most of us planned to snatch an hour or two from future workdays to compensate.

Nora, the instructor, was young, in her late twenties, dark-haired, about my height, with clear skin and large brown eyes. She was beautiful and seemed to carry that knowledge unself-consciously as if it were just one aspect of her life. I didn't know many truly beautiful women, but some I did know gave the impression they were important because of their beauty. Not Nora.

We listened to her and took notes. It wasn't long before she told us we would divide into groups and examine one another. Marlene had set up the offices so two could examine and two observe and coach. Then the positions would be reversed. Before we dispersed to do this, Nora demonstrated what she wanted us to do. She stripped off her shirt and bra, as the preliminary move for the examination, revealing scars covering her torso—pink, shiny, and numerous.

"I pulled a pot of boiling water over me when I was two," she said. She asked Marlene to do the exam and coached her through it. Once we had the theory and the practical demonstration, we went into our groups of four to exam one another.

It occurred to me that we were used to babies and their perfect, unblemished bodies. Adults were different. I had a deep, twelve-inch-long scar over my left hip, the remnant of a wild race bareback on my untrained horse on the Cloverdale racetrack when I was fifteen. My horse bucked me off. I landed on my feet. My hip snapped, and the surgery in those days wasn't as efficient as it currently is, so I ended up with a slightly crooked leg and a huge scar.

"I had a hysterectomy," one nurse said, "so you're only going to find a vault."

We were all carrying the experiences of living.

We worked through the day to learn what was normal and what was not so we could make more confident referrals.

The next week, I approached Dr. MacDonald and asked if I could practice my new physical assessment skills by examining a few of his patients. I would check them over and see what I could discover about their physical health, then he could do the same thing and either concur with what I found or show me where I had gone wrong. He agreed, and I set up the appointment for a day later. I did the same with Dr. Herren, the internist, who allowed me to practice in his clinic. By the end of the month, I was fairly confident of my ability to see any obvious abnormalities. If I never used the skill, I appreciated the education.

I WAS AT MY DESK at the health unit on a Tuesday when I got a call from Janice's school.

"She's hurt her finger. Can you come and get her?"

"Badly hurt?"

"Not sure. She says it hurts, but there isn't any blood."

"I'll be right there." Janice didn't fuss over minor injuries. This one must be painful. One of the positive aspects of my job was that I could usually readjust my day to respond to my kids. I told Ellie where I was going and headed for the school. Janice looked a little white-faced but stoic.

I stood by the open car door with her on the seat facing me.

"Show me your finger."

She held it out.

I gently pulled the finger toward me. "Does that hurt?

She shook her head.

Slowly I pushed the finger back and moved it.

"Ouch! That hurts."

"I think you've broken it. We'll go to the emergency room."

I drove her to the hospital.

"Hi, Marion," June, the ER nurse, said. "Who do we have here?"

"My daughter, Janice. Janice, this is June Lake. She's a friend of mine."

"Hello," Janice said.

"What's wrong?" she asked Janice.

"I think I broke my finger."

"Who's on today?" I asked June. If it was Dr. Craisson, Janice and I would come back when his on-call shift was over. All the doctors did regular on-call emergency room shifts, as well as hospital visits, office visits, and the occasional visit to a home.

"Gary MacDonald."

"Good." I respected his knowledge and his approach to medicine. Janice had not met him before now.

"Hello," he said to me when he arrived. "Got a problem?"

"My daughter hurt her finger. We're looking for a diagnosis."

"I see." He sat in front of Janice and reached for her finger. He moved it then turned back to me. "I don't think it's broken. She didn't react."

"Look at her," I said.

Tears were streaming down Janice's face.

Gary looked horrified. He leaned toward Janice and said, "Why didn't you tell me it hurt?"

"You didn't ask me to tell you," she said with some anger.

Gary sent me a look of apology. "We'll get you an X-ray."

I took Janice to the X-ray department, where we sat to wait our turn.

"I don't think much of that doctor. He didn't even introduce himself!" Janice was no longer crying, but she was angry.

She had a point. He'd only spoken to me.

"You can have another doctor if you want. I'll see to it."

"This one is *your* doctor?"

"Yes." She meant: Is this the doctor you go to for your own health?

"That means he's the best one here?"

"Yes."

She was silent for a few moments. "I'll keep him, then."

Once they took the X-ray, we returned to the emergency room. Gary sat in front of Janice but spoke to me. "It *is* broken."

He reached for Janice's hand.

She pulled her injured hand back and put her other hand in front of it like a guard. She stared directly at him. "Exactly what are you going to do?"

Gary stopped and sat back. This time he spoke to her.

"I'm going to gently wrap it and the finger beside it in a bandage. The unbroken finger will act as a splint. There isn't much else to do. Put ice on it to prevent swelling. Keep it above your heart level when you can."

He was talking directly to her now. She nodded.

"It's called a jammed break. Did a ball hit the end of your finger?"

She nodded again.

"Sometimes that breaks the finger. It should heal in a few weeks. Protect it from getting another bang. Don't play soccer for a while."

Her team would be sorry; she was a good player.

"All right." She headed for the exit. I lingered for a moment.

"She's quite disgusted with you. She complained to me that you didn't even introduce yourself."

He stared at me. "I didn't, did I?" He rolled his eyes.

I grinned at him, softening my criticism. "She's a person, you know."

"I got that. I won't forget."

THE NEXT SURPRISE concerned a child also, but this was more serious. I was home in bed, and it was an hour before I planned to wake from a comfortable sleep when the phone rang on my side of the bed.

"Marion, it's Pam." She was the home care nurse scheduled to work that day.

"What's up?" She wouldn't be calling me unless it was an emergency. I blinked and was alert in seconds.

"I'm sorry. I can't come in today or tomorrow. You need to get someone to cover my shifts."

I swung my legs over to the side of the bed and sat up. "What's happened?"

Carl stirred and stretched.

Pam said, "My son was killed last night."

I was stunned silent. Then, I gathered my wits. "Oh no. I'm so sorry." She had two sons, one about sixteen and one about fourteen.

"It's Dan. He was walking on the road. That's all he was doing. On the side of the road. A man didn't see him and hit him." She spoke in measured tones as if she was forcing herself to get the words out. She must be almost numb with grief.

"Oh, Pam. I am so sorry." What could I say? Nothing was going to help. Dan was her sixteen-year-old. "Don't worry about work. I'll cover for you today and make arrangements for tomorrow. You take all the time you need. Let me know when you want to return."

"All right." She disconnected. I sat with the phone in my hand and stared at the wall. It had probably happened quickly. So unexpected. So tragic.

"What is it?" Carl said.

I told him.

"That's pretty awful. Anything we can do?"

"I don't think so."

It was horrible. I couldn't help myself. I stumbled to my feet and opened David's door, then went downstairs and opened Glen's and then Janice's. They were safe. Of course, they were safe.

I LOOKED AT THE HOME CARE ROSTER when I arrived at work to decide how I would handle Pam's work. I created the list of patients for the day, then pulled their charts. I adjusted my public health appointments to the next day. At nine-o'clock coffee, I told the public health staff what had happened.

"We need to collect for flowers," Marlene said.

"Good idea." I hadn't thought of it.

The staff gave me the money and I ordered the flowers. I called Sally to tell her about Pam's son and to ask if she could work the shift the next day.

She agreed. "Did you get flowers?"

"Yes, I did."

"I'll take them to her."

Pam's farm was at least a forty-minute drive. I wouldn't have time to go there today. In any case, I thought Pam would prefer to see Sally.

"Thanks. That would be a big help."

Sally came by just after lunch. I'd collected the flowers and had them ready for her.

"Hell of a thing," she said. "Can't help thinking how I'd feel."

Sally had two sons and a daughter.

"Me too." Devastated. Unbelieving. As if my world had crumbled around me. No child should die before their parents.

Sally stood. "No way to help her feel better. She's going to hurt like someone's beat her with a bat."

She would be stunned, disbelieving, then overwhelmed by incredible pain. We were silent for a moment, then Sally said, "I'll let her know we're thinking of her."

I handed Sally the flowers and the card. "Tell her not to worry about her job. It will be here when she wants to come back."

In spite of what she thought about her ability to help, Sally would be a comfort to Pam. She'd be a solid and reliable presence in a world that had suddenly become precarious. I'd heard my grandmother say once that having children made you a hostage to fortune. She had thirteen children, and six of them served in the Second World War. She must have had many fears for them. She probably spent the war years on her knees, slipping rosary beads through her fingers. Miraculously, they all came home unscathed.

I started on Pam's work by going first to the two elderly ladies, Mrs. Barnston and Mrs. Michelson, who lived across the street from the health unit and who did not get along with each other. The Welfare had been asked by the families to find a placement for them, and this shared living arrangement was their idea of a solution.

I'd read their charts and sorted in my mind that Mrs. Barnston was the one with COPD and Mrs. Michelson was the one with mild dementia.

Mrs. Michelson answered the door.

"Hello, dear," she said. "Who are you?"

"I'm Marion Crook. I'm the home care nurse today."

"Where's Pam?" Mrs. Barnston shouted from across the room.

I walked in, shut the door, and put my bag on the table.

"She's got an unexpected problem at home," I said. I wasn't going to tell them anything about Pam's son's death. She might confide in them and she might not; that was up to her.

"Oh, poor thing." Mrs. Michelson said. "I hope she'll manage all right."

"Probably looking for a day off." That was Mrs. Barnston. She was not going to win my affection.

I'd deal with her first.

"Would you like a cup of coffee?" Mrs. Michelson asked, acting as hostess.

"She's not here to socialize, Ethel. She's here to work." Her voice was hoarse as if she'd smoked too many cigarettes. It was not the seductive, husky voice cigarettes sometimes produced but the rasping voice of a longshoreman or a master cook used to shouting orders.

"Oh, have I said something wrong?" Mrs. Michelson looked across the room at Mrs. Barnston, who was established comfortably in an easy chair.

I answered before Mrs. Barnston could. "No, Mrs. Michelson, you didn't say anything wrong. I appreciate the offer, but I just had coffee at the health unit."

"Sitting around getting paid with government money, drinking coffee."

"That's right," I said. "It's a snap job."

Mrs. Barnston blinked at me.

Humility with this despot would just get me abuse. "I need to take your blood pressure. How have you been?"

Now she had my attention, she was cooperative. Her blood pressure was fine and her lungs seemed clear. Her respirations were faster than normal and her heart rate a little high, but she wasn't in distress. She would have times when her condition was worse and times like today when it was tolerable.

I listened to Mrs. Barnston's litany of complaints—most of them about Mrs. Michelson: "She's stupid." "She smells." "She can't even make a decent cup of coffee."

Then I sat with Mrs. Michelson, held her hand, and tried to assess her level of dementia. It was surely aggravated by Mrs. Barnston's attacks. Mrs. Michelson seemed fearful and confused. We'd have to get her away from Mrs. Barnston. Sally had told me that both their families had found it impossible to take care of them in their own homes, and neither patient was able to manage alone. This apartment was the best the Ministry of Human Resources could do, at least for now.

I thought about the problem as I drove to a road parallel to and above the highway to my next patient. There was a bed available in the assisted living home—but only one. Which patient should we recommend taking it? Mrs. Barnston would benefit from more nursing care and oversight, but that would leave Mrs. Michelson alone, and she would be even more confused and lonely. If Mrs. Michelson went to the assisted living home, she would be happier, but that would leave Mrs. Barnston alone, and there must be a reason Human Resources didn't want that. I'd talk to Sally.

THE NEXT PATIENT lived in a small house on a lot near about seven other houses under some lodgepole pines above the highway. They had a view over the town but could hear the noise of the traffic. The ground floor looked as though it was used for storage, with no obvious door at the front and boarded windows. I climbed the stairs to the second floor, which was where the couple lived. Mr. Watson answered the door.

"The wife's in the bedroom." He indicated a door to his left. Both Mr. and Mrs. Watson appeared to be in their late sixties. He was short and almost round. She was short and thin.

"Come in, Nurse," Mrs. Watson said. "Where's Pam?"

I repeated my story about a family emergency. The bedroom was a sunny yellow room with white accents. It was cheerful and neat, a contrast to the outside of the house, which seemed drab and neglected. I wondered if Mrs. Watson was responsible for the inside of the house and Mr. Watson for the outside. Or perhaps their pensions only covered some of their needs. She had a table near the bed ready for my equipment.

"Can you change my dressing?" Mrs. Watson was used to the regular home care nurses and wasn't sure about me.

"Oh yes," I reassured her. "Certainly."

She had had a mastectomy the previous week and the surgical site was still oozing. Pam had requested a dressing set from the home care aide who sterilized and packaged up our equipment. Everything I needed was in the package except gloves, which I'd remembered to bring.

I set the package on the side table and opened it. Mrs. Watson lay back on her pillow and watched me. When I removed the soiled bandages and exposed the surgical site, she turned her head away.

"It's healing well, Mrs. Watson. You won't need us much longer."

She kept her head resolutely turned. I applied the clean bandages and taped them onto her chest. She didn't say a word during the procedure. I bundled up the used bandages and gloves and put them in a plastic bag. I'd leave them in the house so Mr. Watson could depose of them. I wrapped the haemostats and scissors in the wrapping I'd come in with and put them back in my bag.

Then I sat on the edge of her bed and took her hand in mine. "You won't look at yourself."

"I can't. I just can't. I used to have such lovely breasts—the girls, I called them. I was so proud of them. I was so feminine. They were lovely still. Now I'm mutilated."

There was no point in telling her to be grateful she was alive. She probably was grateful but she was mourning the loss of her breasts. Some women would be glad to see them gone as they represented a threat to their life, but she saw their loss as a diminishing of her identity.

"It's hard," I said. For her it was.

She squeezed my hand.

"It *is* hard. George says I should be grateful they caught the cancer in time, and he'd rather have me without breasts than any other woman, so I *should* be grateful."

George was doing his best with her.

"But you're not grateful."

"No. I'm not. I'm mad. Really mad. Why me?"

She wiped her eyes with her free hand and half laughed.

"Why not me, I guess. I just miss them so."

"And you are entitled to miss them and grieve for them," I said.

"You don't think I'm stupid? I mean, I know I'm a bit silly about this."

I waited a moment trying to find the right words.

"I don't think I can tell you what feelings are right," I said. "You say you miss your breasts and you are mourning them. I believe you. I can't really understand it because I haven't experienced it."

"And I hope you never shall." She smiled at me and squeezed my hand. "Thank you," she said.

She disengaged her hand and sat back in the bed. I stood and gathered my purse and black bag.

"Sally will be here tomorrow."

"Oh, she's a character." She smiled.

I thought about Mrs. Watson as I drove back to the health unit. I was used to dealing with babies and schoolchildren at the beginning of their lives—that was a big part of my work—but most of the home care patients were older, sometimes very old. Mrs. Watson's situation reminded me that life was quite different from that end. I don't know how I'll adjust to the losses that come with aging.

CHAPTER SIXTEEN

FLYING
TO VANCOUVER

CARL ARRIVED HOME one September evening excited by an idea. He dropped his briefcase on the counter, grabbed me by the waist, and swung me around. I held onto his shoulders. "What?"

He kissed me and set me down.

"Let's fly to Vancouver for the hockey game. The Canucks are playing the Maple Leafs, and I'd love to see that game."

I wasn't the hockey fan Carl was, but I loved the idea of going to Vancouver for a weekend. The air would be much warmer. There would be flowers in the park and friends to visit.

"When's the game?" I asked.

He named the weekend, two weeks away on a Friday night. I'd need to get that Friday off. I spent the next day on the phone arranging my work schedule and phoning Vancouver numbers. I got tickets to the game on Friday night and the opera on Saturday as well as a room at the Four Seasons Hotel. I phoned my friends Janet and Paul, who were in Vancouver for a year while Paul worked on his master's degree. They would join us for the opera. We'd return Sunday. Colleen agreed to babysit for that weekend; her mom would come and stay overnight and be on hand from her house during the day. Colleen's dad would check the cattle and help Janice and Glen with feeding the stock. I felt like a high-powered executive arranging details of a corporate coup. There were a lot of moving parts to my life.

The Friday weather cooperated as it was crisp but sunny. The air in the Cariboo was light and dry, almost intoxicating. It wouldn't be the same at the coast, but I was ready for a change. I wore my ski pants, sweater, and parka for the ride down. The plane had a heater but it could get cold at nine thousand feet. Besides, I'd be dressed for the hockey game.

We packed everything in the plane including a Thermos of coffee and sandwiches. Carl got clearance from the Air Radio, which acted as our air traffic control, and accelerated down the runway off to Vancouver. I poured us each a half cup of coffee. There was always a chance we'd hit an air disturbance, so a full cup was tempting fate. The smell of the coffee was almost as satisfying as its taste. We had flown about twenty minutes when Carl said, "Look at the gauges."

I looked at the indicators that told us how much fuel we had in the tank.

"The needle on the main tank isn't moving," he said.

"What does that mean?" Why wasn't it moving? My brain processed the problem. If it wasn't moving, we weren't using the gas from that tank.

"It means that when the Art worked on the plane last, he must have put the control on the tank in backwards, so the lever can only access the auxiliary tank. There's no way to switch it to the main."

"And?" I said. We had two tanks: the main tank and a small emergency auxiliary tank.

"It means we're running on the auxiliary. I'm going back."

The auxiliary tank had only a small amount of gas in it. I looked down outside the plane to the terrain below. Miles and miles of forest. No place to land. If we ran out of gas and went down here, we'd crash into those sharp, pointed trees. I took some deep breaths. There was no sense in having hysterics. Carl needed to concentrate on flying. I sat perfectly still, concentrating on pouring the last of the coffee back into the Thermos, tidying the cabin so there was nothing that could fly around on impact—and praying, as if my own desire to live could keep the plane in the air. Between scanning the ground for a meadow we could land in— there weren't any—and imagining a forced landing where Carl had to try to aim the plane between two trees so the wings would take the impact, I could only hope that we wouldn't be thrown to the ground. I reviewed my will. Carl had told me that, if we died together, I would be deemed to have lived the longest after the accident because I was younger, so it would be my will that was enforced. I'd named their aunt and uncle as guardians for the kids and made sure I had a sharp executor. The plane jerked. My heart leapt to my throat.

"Just an air pocket," Carl said.

It was hardly a bump. I closed my eyes and took several calming breaths. Then I looked ahead at the miles of conifers, willing the runway to appear. We didn't talk. I didn't want to distract Carl as he may have to face an emergency at any moment. We landed back at the Williams Lake airport before we ran out of gas. As Carl pulled up in front of the hangar, the engine quit.

I looked at him. "Did you turn it off?"

"No. It ran out of gas."

Only then did I start to shake. Carl reached over and took my hand. "Are you okay?"

I squeezed his hand, took a couple of deep breaths, then nodded.

Carl slid the canopy back. We got out. He opened the hangar and we pushed the plane inside.

"What do you think happened?" I asked him.

"I think Art put the fuel selector valve in backwards, so that instead of it resting on the main tank and being capable of moving to the right to access the emergency tank, it was resting on the emergency tank and couldn't move left to access the main tank. He'll shit himself when I tell him."

I expected Art, the mechanic, would be shocked at his mistake. If Carl hadn't noticed that the main tank indicator wasn't moving, we might have run out of fuel above the Fraser Canyon, where there was no place to land. It was all trees, rocks, railway tracks, and river there.

"What do we do now? Go home?"

"Naw!" Carl grinned. "I saw Matthew fuelling up a Beaver. He's working for Wilderness Air. I'll ask him if he's going to Vancouver." Matthew was a young pilot, about nineteen. I knew Carl had taken him up in our Navion when Matthew was learning to fly.

Carl asked him, and Matthew was agreeable. We transferred our luggage to the Beaver, a much bigger plane than ours but not as comfortable. This one had seats for the pilot and co-pilot and one small seat behind for me. The rest of the plane was a hollow cavity used for freight. Matthew was flying empty to Vancouver.

We took off and headed southwest. It was noisy in the plane, and I couldn't hear the men's conversation. After about an hour, we were over Whistler and heading toward Squamish and Vancouver. Matthew tried to raise Air Traffic Control at the Vancouver airport. He spoke into his mic, fiddled with dials, and shook his head. He and Carl turned dials and listened to their earphones. Eventually Matthew turned to me.

"I have to go back. My radio's quit."

I looked ahead and caught a glimpse of the ocean. We were so close, but he couldn't go into the Vancouver air traffic without clearance.

Matthew banked the plane, levelled it, and headed north. We lumbered along, the plane noisy and shuddering a little in a brief patch of rough air. My bladder didn't like it.

I touched Matt on his shoulder. "Do you have a potty back here?"

He glanced at me. "Just a plastic bag under your seat."

The men probably had a bottle they used, but that wouldn't do for me. I grumbled to myself about the unfairness of biology that made this process so difficult for women.

I struggled with the zipper on my jeans and managed to get positioned above the plastic bag. It was a relief. I tied the top securely and was just congratulating myself on accomplishing a difficult manoeuvre when I saw a wet spot at the bottom of the bag. It was leaking. Urine was going to drain out onto the floor of the plane, warm and aromatic. Damn! I reached under the seat and found another bag. I put the leaky bag into the new one and hoped for the best. The men didn't say a word.

We arrived back at the Williams Lake airport at about noon. I handed my luggage to Carl but held onto the waste bag. I emptied it in the washroom at the airport and threw the bag in the garbage. What a morning—flying for hours and getting nowhere.

When I returned to the waiting room, I found Carl pacing impatiently.

"Come on. I've got Phil to fly us in his 182."

"Is he going to Vancouver?"

"He is now."

"We're chartering the plane?" I knew Phil had a charter business.

"We are."

We were off in fifteen minutes. It was a lovely plane, a Cessna 182, with leather seats, a working heater, and loaded with instruments. Carl was fascinated with the various updates Phil had made to his panel. I sat back and dozed. We landed at the Vancouver Airport at two in the afternoon. I stepped down from the plane to the tarmac at the South Terminal and breathed in the moist, coastal air. It felt thick, as if was laden with ocean spray. I could almost hear my hair and skin thanking me. I smelled salt and the oil from the cooling engine. We had time to taxi to the hotel and the luxurious room. There was even time to hold each other and celebrate being alive, then have supper and taxi to the arena.

I was energized by the crowd pouring through the turnstiles and up the ramps to the seats above the sparkling, white ice where we joined the many people who were crazy about hockey. I smelled hot dogs and onions, cotton candy and coffee, and a certain excitement. Could I smell adrenaline? Probably not, but I smelled something that I equated with excitement. The tickets I'd secured on the phone were at the centre line and gave us a good view. I couldn't help but cheer wildly with the crowd and yell at bad calls from the refs. It was a glorious, exuberant experience. Vancouver won.

Our flying challenges belonged in the past, and I wasn't going to let it spoil my holiday. The welfare of the kids, though, was always a worry. I called home about four in the afternoon on Saturday to get a report from Colleen.

"All's good here. We went over and had dinner with my mom last night. I took her a pie from your freezer. Was that okay?"

"For sure. I'm glad you thought of it."

I talked to Janice, who gave a report on all the animals. Glen told me about how far it was to walk to Colleen's house, and David just listened while I told him about Vancouver. Everyone was fine; I could enjoy the rest of my weekend.

We met with Janet and Paul for dinner for a completely different experience from the previous night's hockey game. I wore my long, formal black lace gown that had cost the earth, and my red velvet evening coat that I'd had since college days. I felt elegant and a different woman from the screaming hockey fan. The opera was *La Bohème*, a romantic, lyrical opera that had me crying—not because the heroine Mimi was dying but because she was dying so beautifully.

Sunday morning breakfast was a feast, with eggs Benedict and coffee. It felt luxurious to have someone else make and serve it. We flew back to Williams Lake on a regular commercial flight and arrived home Sunday at six in the evening. I felt I'd been through a lifetime of emotions in one weekend: from the anticipatory excitement to the near terror at the fear of dropping out of the sky, the tedium of the aborted flight, and the exhilaration of the hockey game—to say nothing of the romance and resonance of *La Bohème*. Work was going to be a relief.

CHAPTER SEVENTEEN

ACTING SUPERVISOR AND TAKING ON WHAT I SHOULDN'T

OCTOBER ARRIVED and the weather committed to winter. The temperature hovered around freezing in the daylight but below freezing at night. It wasn't cold enough to plug in my car's block heater or the heat tapes—those tapes with an electric wire embedded, that kept the pig and chicken water from freezing—but it was cold enough that we grabbed our parkas and toques in the morning.

"I'm not wearing boots," Janice said. "There's no snow."

That was fine with me. I wasn't wearing them either. I avoided putting on boots until I had to as we were condemned to them for the long winter months.

The first of October also meant I was the acting supervisor for the month.

Marlene and Ellie joined me for an early morning meeting, during which Marlene gave me the list of unfinished business that I needed to complete. I was lucky to follow her as she was meticulously organized. What she hadn't done Ellie had, so I simply took their recommendations and hoped I could carry on.

"There are several forms for you to sign." Ellie passed me a stack. I glanced at the top one. It was a report on the statistics for immunizations for the month of September. There also would be reports of home care statistics, mileage recompense requests, requisitions for home care supplies, and medication supply requests to sign.

"It's all yours," Marlene said as she rose to go.

"Are you glad to be shuck of it?" I asked her. We watched Ellie leave the office. Marlene turned back to me.

"I don't mind the paperwork. I'm not happy with staff problems."

I raised my eyebrows.

"You'll see."

I hoped not. I assumed my fellow staff nurses were considerate and cooperative. All the public health nurses had their own districts and were away from the health unit working much of the time. We got together for meetings and several times a week for coffee, but I knew the home care staff better because they kept me informed every day.

Pam had returned to work after being off for a week. She was quiet, but then she'd always been quiet. No one spoke of her son as she didn't. We were trying to do whatever was easiest for her and were careful around her, as if she were a frail candle whose flame might blink out at any moment. She spoke very little but arrived on time and did her work. I didn't think the patients noticed much difference in her. In any case, it wasn't Pam a patient called to complain about.

Violet came into my office about noon.

"You're going to get a call from Mr. Burns." She was slim, almost delicate, but must have been deceptively strong as she moved some heavy patients when she worked. She placed her bag carefully on the counter and stood before me a bit like a pupil at the teacher's desk. This wasn't like her. Something had upset her. I gestured to the chair.

She sat.

My desk faced the wall, so when people came in to talk to me, I swiveled to face them with no desk between us.

"What's the problem?"

She touched her face. "He doesn't like Chinese."

I stared at her, trying to absorb the problem. He doesn't like Chinese? Violet was born in Canada, so the patient wasn't concerned about immigration status or language, just race. Vi was an experienced, reliable, valuable nurse, and he didn't like Chinese? I felt a surge of anger. That bigoted asshole.

My phone rang.

"There's a Mr. Burns on the line," Ellie said.

"Oh, do let me at him."

"I beg your pardon?" Ellie said.

"I'll take the call." I raised my eyebrows at Violet. She bit her lip. I didn't like to see her disturbed, especially by a bigot. I made a huge effort and held onto my temper.

"Mr. Burns? This is Mrs. Crook, the home care supervisor. What can I do for you?"

"You can send me a normal nurse, not a Chink."

I took a deep breath. "You are going to have to be polite here, Mr. Burns, or I will not talk to you."

There was silence, then, "I don't want a Chinese nurse."

I looked at Violet. She looked resigned. That made me angrier. *She should not accept this. Not at all.*

"Do you have any specific complaints about her work?"

He was silent for a moment. "No," he said that reluctantly. "I just want a white person."

Diagnosis confirmed: He was a bigot.

"Here's the deal, Mr. Burns. Mrs. Lee is a well-respected and competent nurse, so she was assigned to you because your treatment requires a proficient caregiver. I do not assign nurses by race. That is against nursing ethics. If you don't want Mrs. Lee as your nurse, you will have to make other arrangements for your dressing change."

His dressing change was for a pilonidal sinus, which took daily attention and some skill.

"What would 'other arrangements' be?"

"You could go to your doctor's office every day and wait there until they have time to do the dressing change."

"That'd take hours. I'd have to get someone to drive me, and it's painful to sit!"

"Just so," I said.

"Why don't you just send me another nurse?"

"Because I already sent you a competent nurse. As a matter of fact, if Mrs. Lee won't take you on as a patient because you have been rude, you will *have* to go to your doctor."

"She can refuse to see me?" He sounded incredulous.

"Of course she can refuse. She's not required to take abuse from patients, and I'm not obliged to take abusive patients onto our caseload."

There was silence, a long silence. I didn't break it. Finally he said, "Will she take me back?" He didn't sound apologetic, just resigned.

"I will ask her and call you back. But if she *does* consent to continue with your dressing changes—which is not a sure thing—you are going to have to commit to being polite and cooperative." I sounded stiff and formal, even to myself. "And an apology might be a good start." Idiot.

There was another long silence, then he said. "I don't like what you're saying. It sounds like a threat."

"Does it?" I said pleasantly and waited.

Finally, he said, "I guess I'll have to."

"Yes, Mr. Burns, you will. I'll call you shortly." I hung up the phone.

Violet looked amazed. "That sounded like blackmail."

"Not at all. Just reasonable nursing ethics." Racism was ugly. I wanted to stamp on every tiny scrap of it. "What do you want to do about Mr. Burns?" I asked Vi.

"I can refuse to see him?" She looked straight at me, judging whether I would support her.

"Yes, of course you can refuse. Don't feel obliged to nurse him. He's the one with unacceptable behaviour."

She thought about it. "I'll take him."

"I can't guarantee he'll apologize, and he probably won't change his prejudice, but he has to be polite. If he gives you any trouble or makes you uncomfortable in any way, let me know."

"Will do. Thanks." She smiled at me and left quickly.

PAM GAVE A REPORT on another patient. At our weekly Thursday morning meeting, when all the nurses came in for an hour to plan patient care, she complained about Pete Gates.

"You're going to have to send a taller nurse."

"A taller nurse?"

"That rat bag felt up my leg while I was taking his blood pressure. I'm short, so he could get quite a way."

We all stared at her, shocked. Then, as we could see she was more annoyed than worried, we relaxed.

"And what did you do to him?" Sally asked.

We knew she would have done something.

"I told him I was used to castrating calves on the farm and was really, really good at it, so to stop annoying me."

"That ought to sort him!" Sally said.

"If you have any more trouble, let me know," I told her, "and *I'll* sort him."

She smiled. "I don't think I will."

It was good to see that smile.

Ellie told me once that she loved Thursday mornings because smoke and laughter billowed from my office where the home care nurses crowded in for a meeting. All but Kate used to smoke. We put her by the door and cracked it open a smidgen so she could get fresh air. Now just Sally smoked, and she no longer lit up in the meeting. The laughter, though, was still part of Thursday morning meetings.

After the meeting, I drove along Williams Lake and south to 150 Mile House. The leaves on the poplars on either side of the highway had disappeared and left the bare branches ready for winter. The dark-green conifers stretched across the hills beyond. I wondered if those hills had been logged in bygone years and if the forest I was seeing was a second growth. Directly in front of me was the lodge and local store, and beyond it a pond and open grass-lands. I turned off the highway and drove up the hill to the school.

Hal was the principal: tall, with dark hair and eyes that lit with enthusiasm.

"I've got a problem for you, Marion," he said as he ushered me into the staff room, deserted at this time of day. I could hear a buzz from a classroom nearby but otherwise the school was quiet.

"What's up?" I put my bag and purse on the table.

"It's the Thompsons," he said. "The kids are truant a lot."

"Why?"

"No idea. I think the parents just don't see any need for regular attendance."

"Have you talked with them?"

"Sort of. I met Mrs. Thompson once at the store. She had Sam with her. He's the oldest and in grade six. I told her Sam needed to come to school, otherwise he'd always be behind the other kids."

"And?"

"She wasn't impressed. 'My Sam is smart. He'll do fine.'" Hal mimicked Mrs. Thompson using a falsetto voice.

"Not your favourite parent?"

"She's nice enough. Just clueless. And Sam is a smart kid. It isn't fair to him."

"That's a shame, Hal, but where do I come in?"

"I thought you could go to the family and tell them they have to send their kids to school."

I stared at him. "That's the job of a social worker."

Hal looked uncomfortable. "I'm not that happy with the social worker for here."

I'd heard the new social worker was officious and brusque. I hadn't met her yet.

"Still . . . sorry, Hal. Not my problem."

"Look at it this way," he argued. "If the kids don't come to school, they will fall behind. If they fall behind, they'll feel like failures and they'll miss opportunities. Their future will be dim and they will feel badly about themselves, so they'll start drinking and end up with mental health problems. There you are. It's a health problem."

With that specious argument behind me, I drove the short distance, less than a mile, up the Horsefly Road to the Thompsons' cabin. I had phoned Ellie from the school and asked her to pull the file on the Thompson family and read me the immunization status of all four children. They were up to date. The Thompsons were conscientious about immunizations. This interview could go several ways, some of them disastrous. Mrs. Thompson could berate me for shoving my nose in where it wasn't wanted. She could complain to my supervisor. I was the supervisor this month. I wondered how that would play out. She could refuse to let me in. I was feeling guilty because I shouldn't be doing this visit.

The cabin was on a slight rise. They had a lovely view of the surrounding woods and pastures.

Mrs. Thompson, about thirty-five, tall, with long dark hair, wearing jeans and a blue shirt, was pleased to see me and invited me in. That was a good start. The cabin was large, with rooms off the main living area. It was sparsely furnished with old couches and a table that had a block of wood under one leg. The cabin was cluttered with clothes hanging over chairs, boots toppled over and lying in several places on the floor. Mrs. Thompson swept the crumbs off the table onto the floor before I put my bag down on it. I wondered if it had been washed lately. I considered putting a paper down first but decided that was too insulting. I'd wipe off the bottom with an alcohol swab when I got back to the car. Four-year-old Carrie played with a carton of macaroni and tin cups and plates. She smiled at me but didn't leave her play. Well-socialized, then.

"She'll be ready for school soon," I said.

"Not for another two years. I'm hard put to keep her occupied; she's such a bright one."

"The other children aren't attending school regularly." I might as well come straight to the point.

"They don't like to go when the weather gets cold like it did last week."

"Do they have warm clothes? Boots? Parkas?"

"They do, yes. They just don't want to go to school."

I suspected Mrs. Thompson saw the value of school for her children but not the value of regular attendance.

"I thought I'd warn you, Mrs. Thompson. The principal is considering writing to the government to complain that the children are not attending school enough. The government can withhold your family allowance if he does that." The family allowance was a set amount for each child and sent to the mother in her name. It would be an important subsidy to their income.

She looked shocked. "Can he do that?"

"Yes. He can." Principals rarely did, because the harm caused by depriving a family of income didn't justify it, but they could.

"Well!" She stared at the wall for a moment, then looked back at me. "Well, they'd better go to school then. I'm not doing without the family allowance!"

"Probably a good idea." I stood. I was going to leave before she changed her mind and before she started to wonder why I came and not the principal.

"Thank you for telling me, Nurse." She escorted me to the door. "Do the kids need any shots?"

"No, they are all up to date. You do a good job there."

She smiled. "It's a day out when Carrie here has an appointment. Charlie drives us to Williams Lake. She gets her shot, then an ice cream, and Charlie and I have coffee. Makes a nice outing. And I always make sure they're in school when you do the immunizations there."

I smiled at her. She was doing her best. Her own education was likely limited, and perhaps it was the same for her husband. The kids were happy, not troublemakers at school, and, as far as I could see, they were loved and looked after quite well. It was possible that Mrs. Thompson saw me as someone non-threatening and helpful, and so she listened to me. I was lucky. She could have seen me as a busybody. Still, I decided that Hal could manage his own problems of attendance after this; I wasn't going to do it again. True, I'd managed to get the kids to come to school, but he could have done that himself. He could work on being helpful and non-threatening and more engaged with the parents of his pupils. *He* could visit them. I'd keep that advice in mind for the next time he asked.

CHAPTER EIGHTEEN

ASSISTING RESPONSIBLE WOMEN

O CTOBER PASSED QUICKLY as I had a lot to do. On top of my regular home care supervision and staff nurse responsibilities, I had my new nursing supervisor duties, all the paperwork I had to sign, as well as meeting once a week with Paul to discuss any problems. He used the time to talk about his ideas, such as an integrated health records system for the province. It was an interesting concept. If records were centralized, any doctor could get the records of a patient no matter where they lived or who else they were seeing—but it was impractical. It would require acres of filing cabinets and a huge staff to keep track of it all.

"One day there will be that central system."

I agreed that one day it might be possible, although I didn't see how.

We couldn't go on for much longer without a supervisor. I didn't know how the nurses in the Quesnel office were managing without one, as the supervisor also oversaw the Quesnel office. I didn't know who was signing off the paperwork in Quesnel, but I resented having to spend time on all the paperwork in Williams Lake.

I DID GET TIME to conduct my regular weekly visit to Hannah Harbinger's school. I checked on the vision referral she had for me then stopped at her office to give her a brief report.

"Can he see?" she asked me.

"I think so." I had conducted a vision screening test on Harvey Dale, a grade five boy.

"Hmm. I wonder why he isn't paying attention." Hannah oversaw the learning of every child in her school. Whatever the boy's problem was, I was sure Hannah would discover it.

"How was your trip to the coast?" I asked her. "A meeting with the all the provincial principals, wasn't it?"

"Yes, it was. The meeting was fine. Hard to move those sticks-in-the-mud, but I got a bit of progress. No, the meeting was fine. The trip down was a bit of a hassle, though."

"What happened." I waited by her desk.

"I took the bus, you know, because the weather was bad and I didn't want to drive."

I nodded. The roads had been icy.

"Just before Cache Creek, an idiot across the aisle from me exposed himself."

I stared at her. It would have been almost night by then—the bus left Williams Lake about four in the afternoon—and dark in the bus. There wouldn't be many passengers. Probably no one around her. Hannah would have been threatened. Had that been traumatic for her?

"What did you do?"

She snorted. "Well, he didn't have anything special to show off, that's for sure. I told him to put it away. He didn't, so I took my umbrella—I was going to the coast. You know how it rains incessantly there?"

"It does."

"So I took my umbrella and whacked him right across his proud possession."

I dropped into the seat by her desk, astounded that she'd attacked a man. I imagined the scene: shock from the man, a howl of pain, Hannah indignant, umbrella raised, prepared to hit him again.

"Then what?"

"Then I yelled at the driver to stop and put the pervert out on the road."

"Did the bus driver do that?" Hannah saw only one choice in that situation.

"He did." I could see in my mind the bus driver pulling to the side, leaving the lights flashing, striding down the aisle, pulling the whimpering man from his seat, and shoving him out the door. It was winter. The temperature would have been well below freezing.

"So you left the man at the side of the road. Do you think he froze there?"

"No. I think he zipped up his fly, stuck out his thumb, and hitched a ride either to Vancouver or Cache Creek where he could wait for the next bus, which would come around six hours later. And I bet any money he will never try that again."

I expected the man would go the rest of his life eyeing well-dressed older ladies, complete with elegant hats, wondering if they carried umbrella assault weapons.

"You took care of the problem, didn't you, Hannah?" She was a woman who solved problems every day. That one had been well within her skill set.

She gave me a wicked smile. "I did."

I laughed then. She wasn't traumatized by her experience; she was energized. It was simple to her. The man hadn't behaved on the bus; therefore, he couldn't ride on it. She had insisted that there be immediate consequences for his actions. I wondered what the world would be like if she were in charge of it.

ON THE LAST MONDAY OF OCTOBER, I picked up David from nursery school, beat Janice and Glen home, and had the sheep and chickens fed before they arrived. Janice raided the fridge for an apple, but Glen went straight downstairs to his room. While I was staring in the cupboards wondering what I was going to make for supper, the phone rang. It was the principal from Cataline, the school Janice and Glen attended.

"Marion, it's Mike." Mike, the principal, was not my favourite person. He seemed to think that he was running a personal kingdom at the school and parents were only irritating, but I was polite. I was not the nurse for his school; Sophie was.

"What can I do for you, Mike?"

"Glen threw a rock and broke one of the windows at school."

"He did?" No wonder he went straight to his room. "Tell me about it."

"There were probably other boys involved, but Glen is the only one we caught," he admitted.

Glen was going to have to take responsibility for the broken window, but I would try to keep him from being blamed for all the problems in the school. Mike would be happy to scapegoat Glen.

"So he stayed. Did he admit it?"

"Yes. He admitted it."

"That's good, then. I'll talk to him. Let me know the replacement costs."

"I think the insurance will cover it. So that's not a problem, but this is deviant behaviour."

Glen was impulsive but so were many kids. He wasn't unkind and he wasn't mean. "I agree; a rock through a window is not ideal. However, we aren't concerned with bullying here or setting fires or . . ."

"Okay. Yes. All right. But you will talk to him."

"Definitely. And Mike, I am sorry about it."

"Oh. Yeah, well. Boys, you know."

I did know. That Mike agreed it was not a serious offence was more than I had expected.

I found Glen sitting on his bed. I'd always liked his room. His big window looked out over the valley and let in lots of light. There was evidence of his personality all around. He was a whiz at putting together models. Ships, cars, and trucks occupied the shelves and bookcases. He had a warm, yellow Hudson's Bay banket on his bed and, of course, a warm dog. I sat down on the bed and petted Ben.

"Tell me about the window."

He rolled his eyes. "It was a mistake."

"Obviously." I waited.

"You always say mistakes are there to learn from."

"I do say that," I agreed. "Tell me about the window."

"It was like this. See, me and Jessie and Marvin were throwing rocks trying to hit . . . that animal that runs up trees."

"A squirrel," I guessed.

"Yeah, a squirrel at the back of the school. You know where those trees come close to the wall?"

I nodded and abstained from going off on a tangent about harassing wildlife.

"Well, Marvin said he bet we could put a rock through the window, and I said I didn't think the rock would have enough speed to do that."

"And?

"And I was wrong. It had enough speed."

I controlled my face. Laughing was not what he needed right now. If he was trying to convince me he was conducting a scientific experiment, he failed.

"When you had the rock in your hand and were ready to throw it, did you say to yourself 'What if I'm wrong?'"

He shook his head. "I just threw it."

"And?"

"It broke in a million pieces." There was awe in his voice.

I kept my focus on preventing a reoccurrence. Glen rarely made a mistake twice.

"Could you fix it?" I asked.

He gave me an incredulous look. "No. It was in a million, maybe a trillion, pieces."

"So you broke it and you couldn't fix it."

"Yeah."

"Maybe next time you will think about what might happen *before* you throw a rock."

"Oh. Yeah. Maybe." He was quiet for a moment.

I spoke. "Marvin and Jessie? Do you think they'll own up to throwing rocks as well? I assume they also chucked a rock at the window."

"Yeah, they did. And no, they won't. Own up, I mean."

We sat in silence for a moment. Then Glen ventured, "What's going to happen?" He must have been imagining dire consequences from being expelled to going to jail.

"You are going to write an apology to the principal and promise never to do that again. Your dad and I will offer to pay for the window."

"It was a big window." He sounded worried. At last he was seeing the consequences of that rock.

"It would be."

He looked dejected for a moment, then brightened.

"I have five dollars."

"That will help." He went to his bookshelf, took down his wallet, and extracted the precious five dollars. I took it.

"Mom?" he said as I stood to leave.

"Yes?"

"Marvin and Jessie. They aren't real good friends, are they?"

"Because they left you to take the blame?"

"Yeah."

"I'd say they weren't real good friends."

I leaned down and hugged him. It had not been a good day for him. I tucked his five dollars in my jeans. It was part restitution, and I would return it if we didn't have to pay for the window. I hoped that was the right thing to do. Parenting is such an imprecise vocation.

THE NEXT MORNING I started my day at work by signing the stack of forms Ellie had placed on my desk: requests for travel reimbursements from the nurses, reports on immunization statistics, reports on tuberculosis contact tracing. About nine-thirty, she called me on the phone to ask if I'd take a woman who asked to see a nurse without saying why.

"Where is she?"

"In the waiting room."

I walked down the hall and invited the young woman to come into a clinic treatment room where it was private. She was short, about five foot two, with blond curly hair, clear fair skin, and blue eyes. She smiled.

"I'm Ramona. I'm pretty sure I have the clap," she said brightly. "It's a hazard, I know, but you can give me antibiotics, right?"

I could. "Do you have a doctor?" I asked.

"No, and I'm not getting one."

I wondered why. "I'll take a swab," I said. "Could you hop onto the gurney?"

She was quick to do that, and I took a sample, which I'd send to the communicable disease lab. I expected it to be positive as her symptoms were concurrent with gonorrhea infection.

"You'll give me the antibiotics, won't you? I won't have to wait a week for the results?"

"That's right." Our policy was to give the antibiotics before confirmation of the diagnosis because, in a week, a sexually active woman could infect others.

I pulled a contact form from the desk drawer. "Can you give me your name and telephone number?"

She did that quite readily.

"And your contacts?"

She started to recite names. After the twelfth one, I said, "Just those for the last, say, three weeks."

She added three more. With that much activity I assumed she was charging for her services but, since prostitution was illegal, I didn't want to know. The list would keep several nurses busy trying to find and treat these men or send them to their doctors.

"I can tell some of them." She took my pen and put check marks against four names.

"Thanks." I would trust her to do that.

"You seem to be an intelligent young woman," I said. "Why wouldn't you go to a doctor?"

"They moralize," she said.

I grinned at her. "You wouldn't take that well."

"No, I don't, then we have an argument, then I don't go back. Is there a doctor you recommend?"

"Nurses aren't allowed to recommend any particular doctor. Or criticize a doctor."

"Oh. Not helpful, then."

"You could ask me who my doctor is."

She smiled. "So, Nurse, who do you go to?"

"Gary MacDonald."

"Got it."

I went to the fridge for the antibiotic and returned to the clinic room to give it to Ramona.

She thanked me.

"Hazards of the trade," she repeated as she left. "I may see you again."

I studied the list she'd given me.

Men usually reported gonorrhea, then we looked for the women with whom they had shared the infection. They went to their doctors for treatment because gonorrhea caused them such immediate discomfort. Not so for women. They could be without pain for some time, so we were usually looking for female contacts as they could have the infection and not realize it. Ramona was aware of her susceptibility, so she was quick to diagnose herself. We were looking for men, some of them highly respected in town. I could probably get most of them on the phone.

The lab results came back in three days with a positive test result for gonorrhea. It took me three hours to make the phone calls. I was brisk, business-like, and direct on the phone.

"Please see your doctor and report that you have been in contact with gonorrhea."

I whittled the list down to only three and gave the last to my colleague Sylvia to chase down. I'd check in with her at the meeting at the end of the week.

ON FRIDAY MORNING, Ellie called me about another walk-in patient. This was a fifteen-year-old girl. Ellie kept her near the office and didn't send her to the waiting room, which was full of mothers with babies who were waiting for their immunizations.

I recognized her when I went to get her.

"Tania, how are you?"

"Good. I want to talk to you."

"Sure. We'll go to my office."

Ellie handed me the chart. I knew the family. Her father had suffered an injury and was not able to work. Her mother had no profession and had not worked out of the house for twenty years. I knew her mother was feeling overwhelmed looking after her husband.

Tania was blunt. "I want birth control pills."

"I see."

We did not have a regular clinic for teens. Minors were supposed to have the consent of their parents for any kind of medical procedure or prescription. But there was a designation of 'informed minor consent' where we could treat minors if we thought it was to their advantage and they understood the treatment. Obviously, birth control came under this. I couldn't prescribe birth control pills, but Paul could.

"I will need to ask Dr. Parker to examine you and prescribe for you."

"Who's he?"

"He's the public health doctor."

"Will he tell my mother?"

"I don't think so, but you can ask him."

"I don't want her to know. She's got enough to think about."

I felt sorry for Tania. She was at an age when she needed both parents, but they were preoccupied with serious issues.

I found Paul in his office. He was happy to help.

"We should have a teen clinic. These poor girls need to get some help. I wonder if she can afford the meds. I think there is a fund that will pay for the monthly costs."

"You've got a gurney in your office," I said. "I'll bring her to you and fetch a pelvic pack from the medical supplies."

"Okay, great."

I set up the room for the exam, then fetched Tania and explained the pelvic exam to her.

"You need to stay," Paul said.

"Yes, of course."

Physicians were wise to have a nurse witness the exam.

After the exam, I left them alone as Tania seemed to like Paul and he seemed eager to help her.

Tania popped her head into my office before she left. "Thanks. He said I could come once a month and collect the pills and check in with him. That's nice, right?"

I agreed. "You are taking responsibility here, so good for you."

"He asked me lots of questions about why I wanted sex. I just thought it would please Dar . . . my boyfriend. He really wants it."

I waited.

"Dr. Paul said that wasn't a good enough reason. I had to want it. Is that right?"

"Vital," I said.

"I might wait."

"Just because you have the pills doesn't mean you must have sex."

She grinned. "He said that too."

I thought about her for a few moments after she left. She was really young to start a sexual relationship, but she was surprisingly sensible. I suppose the trauma in her house demanded she grow up quickly. I liked Tania. I should keep in touch with her.

I joined the staff nurses for a quick coffee at two-thirty and asked Sylvia how she'd gotten on with her contact tracing.

"Got them all," she said with satisfaction.

"All?" Betsy said. "Not just one encounter, then?"

"No," I said briskly. "Lots."

"Can you report the woman for soliciting?" Betsy asked. "A woman like that is probably charging for her services. That's illegal.

Probably Native." Betsy wasn't one of our regular staff nurses. She was a student from the university with us for two weeks of public health experience. She was young and opinionated. She made my blood boil.

"She wasn't Native," I said curtly.

Betsy snorted as if she didn't believe me.

Ellie and Maria stopped talking and looked at Betsy.

Sylvia shot me a look that said, *You're the supervisor. You deal with it.*

I stood. "Betsy, come to my office, please." I'd have to forego my coffee break.

She held up her coffee cup.

"Bring it with you," I said, and left.

She followed me.

"What's this about?"

I gestured to the chair, shut the door, and faced her.

"Betsy, to start with, if we reported women who were charging for sex, they would not come for treatment. If they didn't come for treatment, we would be failing them and the community because the diseases would spread."

"Well, she shouldn't be doing it."

"The second thing your RN licence tells you—if and when you ever get one—is you can't put your own prejudices before good nursing practice. That means, whatever your private opinion, you treat the patient with respect. Your remarks in the staff room were not respectful."

I felt peculiar taking Betsy to task. I was only acting supervisor and only until the end of the week. This was definitely a supervisor's task but I was not going to let such prejudice go unchecked. Betsy resented me. I expect she saw me as a staff nurse, not someone with authority.

"The Bible says, 'The wages of sin are death.' She deserves to be criticized."

"It also says 'He among you who is without sin, cast the first stone.'" Trading Bible quotes was like fighting with playdough. You could create any shape you wanted and it was generally emotional, not rational. "Just stop it, Betsy," I said firmly. "No one is comfortable with that kind of blatant prejudice against those with sexually transmitted disease or against Native people. So stop it."

"Will you write me up?" She finally realized she was in trouble. She wanted to know if I'd register an official complaint with her professors.

"If I hear it again, I will."

She left without saying a word. Dealing with that kind of staff problem was not my strength; Marlene was better at it. I came across sounding pompous, and Betsy resented the criticism. I was right to turn down the offer of the supervisor's job. *Victoria head office had better find a supervisor for us*, I thought. What would we do if they just procrastinated and did nothing?

Before I left for the day, Cathy stopped into my office. She worked the north and western districts but had some town schools on her caseload.

"Did you hear that Annie Cavell tried suicide?"

I stared at her. Annie was my favourite social worker: older, sensible, caring. Suicide? I hadn't heard that. I gestured to the chair, and Cathy sat down.

"Tell me about it."

"She's been misdirecting funds from some programs to support the community living group home. She got caught, and her supervisor reported her. The Ministry in Victoria is going to prosecute."

"Oh, my God. Poor Annie. She is really devoted to that group home."

"Did you know she has a daughter in a group home in Kamloops?"

"No, I didn't."

"So I hear, anyway. No one thinks she used the money personally, so it seems harsh the department is going to prosecute."

It did seem harsh. "What happened with her suicide attempt?"

"Her husband found her, and they revived her at the hospital. She's home now on leave."

"Thanks, Cathy."

"I thought you'd like to know."

THE NEXT WEDNESDAY, with David in the passenger seat, I drove along the Horsefly Road to Annie's house to visit her. She and her retired husband lived on acreage in a tidy three-bedroom house. I had many dealings with Annie over the years, but we'd never been close friends. I didn't know about her life at home. I hadn't known about the daughter in a group home in Kamloops until Cathy told me. I wanted to help her, but I didn't know how.

Annie invited me in and offered me coffee and David some juice. She had a few toy trucks, which she brought down from a shelf for David to play with.

"I'm so sorry, Annie," I said. "I didn't know you were having such trouble."

I couldn't think of anything I could say that would help. I could have said, "Stealing funds from one account to put in another isn't such a huge offence," but her department thought so. Or I could have said, "You are such a wonderful person, the world can't do without you." Obviously, she didn't think that. She was a reserved woman who didn't communicate her feelings easily. That made it hard for me to say anything useful.

"Thanks. It was of my own making, but now the department is going to prosecute. They want me to pay back the money." She spoke matter-of-factly, as if we were discussing a patient's problem.

"And you can't?"

"Marion, it's thousands. I'd have to sell the house, and where would Michael go?" She sounded as if she were in pain. That was the first sign of feelings I'd ever heard from her.

"It's Michael you're worried about."

"Of course, it's Michael." She was impatient with me. "He needs the house and my pension to survive."

She wanted to protect her husband. That was clear. "The law could force you to sell this house to pay back the money." I could see the enormity of the problem. If she was convicted of theft, the court would want recompense.

"And send me to jail." She had reined in her feelings and again spoke quietly with great composure.

"So if you were dead, they couldn't prosecute?" I said slowly, trying to process what she had told me.

"That's right."

"Can't Michael buy you out so the property is in his name?"

She shook her head.

I suppose the courts would see that as an attempt to avoid payment. It was difficult speaking about this because Annie was so calm and reserved. She might not want to talk about it, but I knew enough about suicide prevention to know that talking helped prevent it. I persevered. "Why suicide? Isn't there any other option?" I asked.

"If I'm dead, they can't convict me, then they can't touch any of my assets, including my pension. Everything I own would go to Michael." She sounded as if she had come to the only reasonable decision. I watched her for a moment, noticing her neat brown hair framing her round face, her dark, tired eyes. She must have spent a long time going over her options. I searched my mind for some reason to deter her.

"Michael wouldn't want to keep the property without you." I didn't know him, but surely he'd rather have Annie than money.

"I wouldn't be here after a trial, in any case." She must have thought what would happen if she got caught manipulating the accounts. Jail for some years. She was thirty years older than me. Jail might be the rest of her life. She'd considered her choices. She didn't want my naïve opinions.

We talked of other things, and she kept her quiet composure. I had only glimpsed the feelings that she must have been dealing with; she didn't want to talk about them. Michael was in town getting groceries, so I couldn't talk to him.

It was so unfair. I knew she stole the money, but it went to the benefit of those who her department was supposed to look after. She wasn't eating caviar or taking trips on that money. I didn't see why the department couldn't offer her a more dignified way of making amends. She'd spent her whole working life helping others, and now she was trying to make a decision that would help her husband. She wasn't trying to help herself.

She gave me a jar of her homemade raspberry jam as I left and told David to keep the trucks.

I drove home worried about her. I couldn't think of any way out of the problem. It wouldn't help for me to talk to local supervisor, because by now the case had gone to the department in Victoria, and they were prosecuting.

A week later, I wasn't surprised to hear she had died by suicide. Sally phoned me at home and told me. I blamed her department, although I never knew all the facts. Surely they could have found a more humane way to deal with Annie than force her into such a desperate choice. Michael was safe on his property; the department couldn't touch him because Annie had never been convicted of anything. The mentally challenged people kept their group home. My friend Annie gave up her life for that. I found myself at the pigpen, leaning over and telling Cleo about it. I was crying. David was worried.

"Mom. You're crying."

"I'm feeling sad for my friend who died." She had a loving husband; she did good work for society, and she died because she didn't have money to pay for her theft. It was so unfair and cruel.

"Oh." He wrapped his arms around my leg and leaned in to comfort me. We stood there for a time until the cold drove us into the house.

CHAPTER NINETEEN

RESCUING
THE SITTER

I WAS HAPPY TO HAND OVER the acting supervisor's job to Cathy on the first Monday of November. She could sign all those forms and oversee the flow of paperwork. Head office in Victoria assured us they were actively looking for a supervisor but had not yet found one. It was as if they hoped we would muddle on without one and, since they were not paying any of us extra wages to take on the job, they were saving money.

"We may have to refuse at the end of November," Marlene said when we gathered for our monthly staff meeting. "If none of us will take on the job, and Paul won't do it, they will have to do something."

Marlene was our union representative.

"Best send them an official letter stating that," I said.

We were all there: Sylvia, Sophie, Marlene, Cathy, and me. We all gave a nod of agreement. We didn't know if a letter would help, but at least the head office would know we were unhappy and unwilling to keep on with this temporary strategy.

"I don't plan on doing it again." Marlene had a husband and three young children at home. She didn't need more responsibility, especially when it was unpaid. She'd make a good supervisor as she was supportive, intelligent, and understood the paperwork. But she didn't want the job yet.

"I don't want it again," I said.

"I'm sure once is going to be enough for me," Cathy said.

"Okay, we're agreed. I'll send the letter."

With that push, we might finally get a new supervisor. If they still refused to fill the position, we might have to come up with a stronger or more drastic plan.

THE HOME CARE NURSES were busy as the doctors moved more patients from their offices to our home care program. They also now appreciated that we were a dependable resource for overseeing the health of the frail elderly.

Pam was quietly efficient. There wasn't any way she'd ever be reconciled to losing her son, but she was living with the sorrow. Sally was as energetic as ever, as long as I didn't insist she come to work before ten. Since she did the work of two, stayed after four-thirty, and did impromptu nursing on her off-duty days—some patients stopped her while she was grocery shopping to ask advice—I didn't insist she start at nine. Jane was reliable and ready to take shifts and accommodate others if they wanted to change shifts. She lived in town with her husband and two school-aged kids. She was the one who encouraged me to take flying lessons a few years earlier, as she had done that and flew with her husband in their small plane. I studied with her for my ground school exam. Kate was an efficient nurse who managed to drop laughter into our meetings with her wicked Irish sense of humour.

Violet said she hadn't had any more trouble from Mr. Burns, which didn't mean he wasn't still racist; he was just silent on the subject. Violet said she could deal with that. "Prejudice is the other person's problem, you know."

I'd have to remember that and tell David when he was older.

November had come in with another cold snap, with temperatures dropping to below freezing overnight then rising to around freezing during the day. That meant snow overnight and often rain and sleet during the day. We got up in the dark and stumbled out to the barn, the chicken house, and the pigpen before daylight, contending with frozen water troughs and demanding livestock. The sun rose about seven-thirty, when we all left the house. I had to make sure Glen had his boots and parka. He didn't seem to feel the cold and never complained about it. Janice felt the cold and didn't forget to dress for it. David wore what I put on him.

I was back in boots. I carried a pair of shoes to wear if I was going to be in the health unit for long, but boots were going to be part of my ensemble until April. The cattle stayed outside all year long but had to be fed hay daily after the snow came. Horses could dig for grass, but cattle could not. The rest of the animals had shelter if they wanted to go inside. Most of them did, except sheep Number Forty-Nine, who didn't have much sense; we had to watch out for her.

The 4-H activity had settled to a once-a-month meeting after all the competitions of the summer. Janice was calculating when she needed to bring a boar to Cleo in order to have piglets in early April.

"Three months, three weeks, and three days," I heard her muttering to herself. Then she called out, "Mom, I need to get Cleo to the boar around the first of December."

"I'll attend to it. Do you have a boar in mind?"

"I hear Mrs. Blenkinsop at Sugar Cane has a good Berkshire boar."

"I'll go and talk to her."

"I'll watch for Cleo's next heat period. She's only in heat for two days, so we have to take her to the boar when I say. Cleo comes into heat every three weeks, so if we miss the first time, we'll have to take her back. Will you ask Mrs. Blenkinsop if that would be all right?"

"I'll check."

I drove to Sugar Cane Reserve the next Wednesday. Janice and Glen were in school, but David was always up for an adventure, and he hadn't been to the reserve before. We drove to the end of Williams Lake where the reserve land spread out into the valley from the collection of houses. The Blenkinsop's house was a little apart and closer to the highway than the main group of houses.

David expected to see farm animals but had to be content with a cat. The farm animals were on another area of the reserve, distant from the house.

A woman of about fifty, slightly plump and with short dark hair, opened the door to my knock.

"I'm Marion Crook, and I'm here on behalf of my daughter, who is looking for the services of your boar."

"Come in. Who's this?" she asked, looking at David. "Is he one of the Gilberts'?"

I was startled. I wasn't used to David being identified except as a member of our family.

"No, he's my son, David."

"Oh," she said. "I thought you might have picked up one of the Gilbert kids."

I shook my head. The Gilberts lived on the reserve. I expect they had children David's age. Mrs. Blenkinsop had gestured that we were to come in, but we stayed on the rug by the door. There was moment of silence, then Mrs. Blenkinsop said, "When does your daughter want Boris?"

"The first week of December. She said Cleo should come into heat then. My husband Carl will deliver her."

"Does she want to leave her here for three weeks if Boris isn't interested?"

"Carl will pick her up and bring her back. Is that all right?"

"Yes, that would be fine."

"Janice would like to know what she is expected to pay for Boris's services."

"What breed is the sow?"

"She's a Yorkshire."

"All right. That should give a meaty piglet. I'll take a weaner pig at eight weeks, castrated." This was the usual age at which Janice sold the piglets. They could leave Cleo's milk and do well on food pellets and grain. It was the usual payment.

"That's fair. Thanks."

I thought about her reaction to David as I drove away. She was surprised and seemed resentful, I thought. When the social worker told us she had a baby for us, she'd said, "Oh, and he's Native. Is that all right?"

Carl and I had looked at each other. It didn't matter to us. We didn't think that it might matter to others. Or that it might matter to his clan, his band, his tribal community, and one day, that it might matter to David. We had been incredibly naïve.

The usual process for adoption was to take the baby right after birth with a temporary custody agreement. At three months, the adoptive parents applied for permanent custody through the *Adoption Act*. When David was three months old and we applied for permanent adoption, we were told all adoptions of Indigenous children had been put on hold as the Indigenous people objected to them going outside their communities. I understood their concern, or at least I tried to, but this baby was in my heart and I could not give him up. I found someone who was willing to talk to me, and I drove to the Musqueam Reserve in Vancouver to talk to a chief at the Union of BC Indian Chiefs Association. He told me they were not interested in taking back children already placed but in preventing more adoptions outside the communities. That reassured me, but it was only after David turned three that his legal adoption came through. He was now legally part of our family. Indigenous people did not want their children going to white families; I understood that. David's life was going to be more complicated than I had expected. Mrs. Blenkinsop had resented David being part of my family. What business did a white family have in adopting an Indigenous boy? She hadn't said this—her manners were too good for that—but I understood her. I couldn't resolve this objection to our adoption of David. He was permanently part of our family. We'd have to weather disapproval from wherever it came.

David and I stopped at the restaurant just off the highway before Williams Lake. I had promised David an ice cream. He seriously deliberated between chocolate and strawberry, but I knew the outcome would be chocolate. I waved at the four men crowded into the booth nearby. Carl used to drop in for coffee with them but couldn't get away from the office now that he was lawyering. They nodded and smiled at David.

"Growing up, isn't he?" John said. He was the travel agent in town, and a friend.

I grinned at my pint-sized cowboy in jeans and a denim jacket. David stood taller.

"I am big now?" he asked me on our way to the car.

"Bigger than you were."

We sat in the car and ate our ice creams. Driving and ice cream always ended in a mess, so I didn't start the car until we had munched the last of the cones. The air was warm, perhaps four or five degrees above freezing, but it would drop overnight. Of course, any temperature is perfect ice cream weather.

I expected Carl missed his twice-a-week coffee with his friends. He had a staff of six now, so he had coffee with them, and we did have a social life. I'd booked Colleen for the upcoming Saturday night as Carl and I had been invited to Gary and Amy MacDonald's house for dinner. Our medical health officer, Paul, and his wife Tansey had been invited as well. It was the first time I'd socialized with Paul. I hoped it wouldn't cause any problems at work with other nurses thinking I might get preferential treatment, although Paul didn't have a lot to do with the nurses, so it shouldn't cause trouble. Besides, the town was so small that if you started drawing lines, you'd have few friends.

ON SATURDAY NIGHT, I dressed with care. We did go out every second week or so, but this was still an occasion. I had a soft grey Jaeger skirt and a red mohair sweater. I wore the silver dangly earrings Carl had given me the previous Christmas and brought along my silver pumps in a bag. I'd take my boots off at the MacDonalds'.

I knew everyone, but I'd only met Tansey once when she and Paul had first arrived. Amy MacDonald was tall, solid, almost stocky, with kind brown eyes and an easy manner. She smiled and thanked me for the flowers I'd managed to remember to pick up at the florist and invited me into her kitchen. She found a vase and arranged the flowers. I'm never sure if it's kind to bring flowers, as the hostess has to deal with them when she's occupied with dinner preparations.

"Lovely," Amy said. "I miss flowers at this time of year."

"Me too," I said. "Dinner smells fabulous."

"Lasagna," Amy said. "Easy to serve because it can wait in a warm oven for hours and still be eatable."

She picked up a bowl of salad and led me back out to the living room via the dining room.

"Gary, are you looking after the drinks?"

"Oh, yeah." Obediently, Gary attended to his host duties.

Tansey Parker was seated in a big easy chair. She looked lost in it as she was a tiny woman of about twenty-five. She had wavy auburn hair and the fair complexion that often goes with it. She was arguing with Carl about art. He'd be tolerant, polite, and bored.

I sat in a seat near Tansey and drew her attention. "Tell me about your paintings," I said to her.

Paul had mentioned his wife was a painter, or rather she had taken up painting, which wasn't quite the same thing. I found Tansey interesting. She'd come from a city and was trying to adapt to a small town. She didn't have children or property to keep her busy. She and Paul had moved from their trailer to a small rental house, so she must have been desperate to fill her days. As far as I knew, she didn't work outside of the house.

Amy served her lasagna, and the conversation improved as the wine flowed. We had finished dinner, including the flaming baked Alaska (which I had not yet attempted to make myself) and were settled around the fireplace with our Drambuie liqueurs when the phone rang.

"You're not on call, are you, Gary?" Amy shot a firm look to her husband.

"No, but I'd better get it."

He returned. "It's for you," he said to me. "Your babysitter."

Carl rose and accompanied me to the kitchen where the phone was.

"Colleen? What's wrong?" I held the phone away from my ear so Carl could hear.

"Jordan King is up here."

"Who's he?"

"An idiot in my class. He's outside, and he's been pounding on the door. I told him to go but he won't. David's asleep, and I left him, but I put the other kids in their rooms and told them to stay there."

"Tell her we'll be right up," said Carl.

I did that. When I was back in the living room, the men were standing.

"Hey," Paul said. "Let's rumble."

"What does this Jordan want?" Amy asked.

The men looked at each other. "Probably to get time alone with the babysitter without parents around," Gary said.

That did make me wonder about his behaviour in his teen years.

They looked excited, all three of them, like teenaged boys ready for some wild behaviour. That energy was infectious. I found I wanted to go with them.

"Who's sober enough to drive?" Amy asked.

They looked at each other.

"Carl, you drank the least," Gary said.

Carl agreed to drive, and they left.

"Do you think they'll be all right?" Tansey asked.

Amy thought about it. "Three grown men against one teenager. It was just one, wasn't it, Marion? They aren't going to meet a gang on your ranch, are they?"

"I'll phone Colleen back and ask her."

"What if there is a gang?" Tansey said.

"Then we'll have to go as well."

I felt a tingle of excitement. I've never participated in anything like this.

"Hah! Women to the rescue!" Tansey said.

In spite of my worry, I grinned at her enthusiasm.

Colleen answered the phone. "No, he's alone," she said in answer to my question. "Only Jordan. He's the only one stupid enough to pound on the door and yell at me."

"Three men are on their way. Carl and two doctors."

"Good," she said, more in exasperation than fear. "If they beat him up, they can patch him up."

I would rather hear anger than fear in her voice because she could act under anger; fear was often paralyzing.

"They should be there soon."

"I hear a car in the yard. I'm going to go look out the window." She was back in a moment.

"They're here. Sorry about this, Mrs. Crook."

"It's not your fault. Do you want us to come home?"

"No. But I'll hang up because I want to go to the window and watch."

"Okay."

"The posse has arrived," I told Amy and Tansey. "I expect they will sort it out."

We looked at each other, disappointed we weren't necessary, and laughed.

The men returned in about a half hour full of the excitement of confronting Jordan.

"He turned out to be a skinny kid who almost fainted when we surrounded him and read him the riot act."

"Who yelled at him?"

"That would be me," Carl said. "My property, my house, my kids."

"And who pushed him around?" Amy asked

"I did that, too," Carl said. "Just to help him get into his truck."

"Were the kids okay?" That was my chief concern.

"David slept through it; Janice and Glen were only a little scared. Colleen helped by being disgusted with Jordan and not afraid of him, although I think she *was* afraid he'd get in the house. She was right to be afraid."

"But the kids? Should we go home?"

"They're fine. If we go home, we make it too important."

I understood his point. Colleen had asked me not to return early, and I didn't want to spoil Amy's dinner party, but I was uncomfortable away from my children.

"He was just a kid," Carl murmured to me a little later. "Scared witless at what he had done. I told him I knew his father and I'd call him if I ever saw him on the ranch again."

"*Do* you know his father?"

"As it turns out, I do."

That made me feel better, and I could give attention to my fellow guests.

THE KIDS SEEMED FINE at breakfast the next morning.

"Colleen said her friend came to visit her, and she didn't want to see him, so she told him to go," Janice explained to me.

"But he wouldn't go, so then Daddy made him," Glen said.

"Will he come back?" Janice was thinking ahead.

"No," Carl said as he fetched the coffee pot and topped up my cup and his own.

That satisfied Janice.

Janice was such a mixture of old soul and child. I'd wanted to keep her with her class through grade school; my sister had skipped a year; my younger brother had skipped two years; and it had been hard for them socially. But the school had moved Janice into grade four language and math when she was in grade three. I hadn't known about it until she'd been there for three months. So she skipped a grade. Luckily, her birthday was in January, and she was tall, so it wasn't difficult for her, but she still had her problems. She and one girl in her class, Elizabeth, vied for top grades. Being academically gifted could cause jealousy.

"You know, Mom," she'd told me one day, "I either get good grades and have one friend, or I let my grades go down and have more friends."

That was the school culture; I wasn't going to be able to help her with that. "What do you think you'll choose?"

She thought about it. "One friend. The others wouldn't really be friends anyway."

So she had her one friend, Cindy, and seemed happy—usually.

Not this afternoon, though. She came home from school steaming with anger.

"That Eliz-a-beth!" She gave the name emphasis on every syllable. "She's a bully."

"What happened?"

Janice threw her boots into the mudroom, chucked her jacket after them, and stomped into the kitchen.

Glen headed for the fridge.

"One apple," I said to Glen. He took it and disappeared down to his bedroom.

"What happened?" I repeated.

Janice climbed onto a stool and put her chin in her hands. "Elizabeth got two boys to back her up and she crowded me into a corner."

"Where was the teacher?"

"It was lunch hour. There was no one else there. I went back for my jacket 'cause it was cold at lunch, and they caught me there."

I looked at her. I didn't see any bruises.

"What happened?"

"They crowded me, Elizabeth in front, and told me I wasn't as smart as I thought I was and they were going to beat me up."

"What did you say?"

"I didn't say anything. I just hauled back and thumped her right in the jaw. The boys disappeared. Elizabeth just lay on the floor."

I was shocked. "Was she conscious?" I'd better know how much of a problem this was going to be.

"Yes, she was conscious, moaning I'd killed her. I didn't hit her that hard. I didn't break her jaw or anything. There wasn't any blood."

I didn't know how to respond. Janice shouldn't hit anyone, but she also couldn't allow three kids to hit her. I settled for, "Good." No serious injury, then.

I didn't know what to say. Janice had faced a problem and dealt with it. She'd never been in a physical fight before. It wasn't her usual way of solving problems or the way I would have chosen, but I expect it was effective.

"Will she tell on you?"

"I don't care if she does."

Apparently, she didn't complain to the teacher as I didn't get a call from the principal or her parents. I asked, and Janice said Elizabeth left her alone now and the rest of the class seemed more friendly. Perhaps Janice wasn't the only one Elizabeth had bullied.

I WASN'T NEARLY AS EFFECTIVE when I had to handle bullying.

The BC Nurses' Union had been grumbling about wages and conditions. Public health nurses were in the same union as hospital nurses, so we needed to pay attention to their concerns. They had been threatening to strike, and Marlene, our union representative, kept us informed when a bulletin came to her.

"Will we strike?" Sophie asked her at coffee one morning.

"Hard to know," Marlene said. "But we'd better prepare for it."

Nurses weren't the only ones preparing for it. Paul came to my office with a letter in his hand.

"I'm going to need you to prepare a list of all the home care patients whose care is vital, and a list of all patients you won't visit while the strike is on. Victoria is asking us to justify how many nurses will be deemed essential and permitted to work during the strike."

"Has it been declared?"

"Not yet."

Paul was young and not used to his position, but you'd think he would have realized it was inappropriate to contact me about this.

"You need to give that request to Marlene," I said. "She's the union rep. She'll let us all know."

"I prefer to talk to you directly," he said.

I was surprised. Marlene was not going to like it. And why wouldn't he want to talk to Marlene? Did he see me as a social contact rather than a professional one and so easier to deal with?

"Such a twit sometimes," Marlene said when I reported to her. "Give your list to him and a copy to me."

I pondered over the list Paul had asked for. If we neglected to call in on a patient one week, they could be in trouble. Our visits were intended to prevent complications. If they didn't need us, they wouldn't be on our list. In the end, I took three patients off with a note that three weeks was as long as I trusted them to be left. Those three had caring families.

I went to Paul's office with my list a couple of days later.

He read it and, for the first time, I saw him angry.

"This is insulting. You've hardly scratched the list. I want it reduced so one nurse can handle it."

I watched him for a moment, puzzled by his reaction, then suddenly saw why he wanted the list cut. If he could use the strike as an excuse to reduce the number of nurses and their salaries, he could save money for the health unit. That would make him look efficient to head office in Victoria.

"This isn't about how many nurses' salaries you want to save," I said. "It's about how many patients need care."

"No matter. I want that list reduced. See to it." He threw the list across the desk.

He was acting like a bully. I thought of Janice's expeditious method of dealing with bullying. That wouldn't work here. Did he really think that he could tell the nurses what to do? That wasn't in his job description. He didn't supervise the nurses. The community could do without him a lot more easily than it could do without nurses.

I raised my voice and called, "Marlene. Get in here."

Her office was next to Paul's and she was with me in seconds.

"What's up?"

"As my union rep," I said, looking straight at Paul and not Marlene, "I want you to tell Paul he can't dictate who goes on my home care list."

Paul snapped. "This has nothing to do with you, Marlene."

"As the union rep, I'm afraid it does, Paul. You and I will discuss it."

I stood and left the office. I was too angry to talk to him, and Marlene would do a better job.

I sat at my desk and fumed. I never expected Paul to be so dictatorial. He'd never paid much attention to what the nurses did before. I went out on a baby visit and left the mess to Marlene.

She came to my office later in the afternoon.

"Sorted?" I asked.

"He's sorry."

"I see that." I stared at the single red rose on my desk.

"He sent that?" Marlene was incredulous.

"Highly inappropriate, wouldn't you say?"

"I would. Cowardly, too. He could have come and said sorry in person."

"Or written a note. This makes me sick."

"What are you going to do?"

I stared at the offensive rose. "I can't educate him on the creepiness of sending me a rose." Roses, even a single rose, were a romantic gesture, not one appropriate to a professional relationship. It sent all the wrong signals. Not that I thought he was being romantic, just clumsy. "So, I'm going to ignore it and be very polite to him."

"What are you going to do with the rose?"

"Give it to Mrs. Michelson. She'll like it."

She did.

I worried about the strike for about two weeks. We had directives from Victoria about what we were to do to keep the health unit running and what we couldn't do. The public health nurses had meetings with Marlene that didn't include Paul, and I had meetings with the home care staff. They trusted me to deal with the problem; I trusted Marlene to do the same.

There would be great pressure on us to conform to the plan of the Registered Nurses' Association. It would be difficult as we couldn't refuse to strike with them, and we did want to support them. But after two weeks, we stopped getting missives from Victoria. Marlene was on the phone to the Registered Nurses' Association daily, and one morning she announced that there would not be a strike. The Nurses' Association had negotiated a contract. We would all get an increase in wages. I'm not sure it was worth the worry, but I didn't know all the issues at stake. I was just relieved it was over.

CHAPTER TWENTY

MEDDLING
IN THE HOSPITAL

VICTORIA STILL HAD NOT sent a nursing supervisor. The nurses remained adamant they would not take on the position, so on the first of December, Paul took on signing all the forms, ordering supplies, and supervising nursing schedules. I expect his bosses in Victoria insisted on it. Marlene said she hadn't told Paul that he had to do it; she'd just suggested that to the head office. Smart woman. Before everything else, forms and statistics mattered. He complained at the staff meeting.

"I shouldn't have to do this. It's not part of my responsibilities."

"Not ours either," Marlene said. "We aren't being paid for it and, as long as one of us takes it on, Victoria is in no hurry to replace Angela." Marlene had more contact with the supervisors at head office than the rest of us. She was likely right about this.

Paul agreed. "They don't seem to be. I guess they're saving the cost of her wages. That will make this health unit look more efficient."

No one spoke. Would Paul see that as positive? Finally, Marlene said, "If that's your goal, you should be happy to take on the supervisory role."

"Well, it's not my main goal, and I'm not happy."

"Let's talk about this privately after the meeting."

We relied on Marlene to represent us in any talks with Paul. I definitely didn't want to talk to him. His efforts to bully me when he thought a nursing strike was imminent still rankled. I said "good morning" and was carefully polite, but he had revealed himself to be obnoxious, and I didn't want a repeat of that. He and Tansey were leaving for a three-week holiday over Christmas, so I would only have to deal with him for a short time. Time away from him might make me more tolerant.

JANICE INFORMED US one morning that we had to deliver Cleo to the boar within twenty-four hours.

"There's not much time," she pointed out with a clear directive in her tone.

Carl looked at me in consternation. "The truck's not functional; I'm bleeding the brake lines. I was going to finish it tonight."

"I can't help you with either project." I had no idea how to bleed brake lines, and I was not going to try and wrangle a five-hundred-pound sow.

"We can use your car, Dad," Janice said.

Carl, noticing Janice's use of "we," looked dismayed. He kept his car scrupulously clean. I could imagine what Cleo could do to it. Eat the upholstery? Pigs were fussy about where they defecated, so she likely wouldn't do that, but pee? Perhaps.

"You can't come with me. You have to go to school."

"But Dad!"

"School," he said.

She grabbed her lunch bag and left. Glen followed her. Carl called the Blenkinsops to let them know when he'd be there, then headed back to the bedroom to change out of his suit and into jeans and a shirt.

"Phone the office, will you?" he asked me as he was leaving. "Tell them I'll be in at ten. Then come and help me load Cleo."

"Do you want to cover the seats with a tarp?"

He thought for a moment. "She'd only pull it off and try to eat it."

Cleo was not difficult to load, but she was peculiar. She would only load if you put a bucket on her head, aimed her backwards, and banged on the bucket. Carl had a makeshift ramp from the ground to the back seat of his Buick. I stood to one side, ready to push Cleo through the door, or rather guide her if she allowed me to. A five-hundred-pound pig was not easy to shove. Other ranchers seemed to load their pigs with taps on the pig's haunches, but Cleo ignored that, so we had devised a unique system. Annoyed by the noisy bucket, she tried to move away from it and backed into the car. Carl slammed the door shut.

"I'll deliver her, come back for a shower, and get to work."

It was quite a sight. Cleo's body occupied the whole back seat area, crosswise, while her broad head hung over Carl's shoulder. She drooled.

Last year, when Cleo needed to go to the boar, Carl and Janice took her to Mr. Sorenson's farm, north of Williams Lake about fifteen miles. Janice had watched the process of mating and had been disturbed by the corkscrew, two-foot-long penis the boar presented.

"My poor Cleo," she'd said to me when she had arrived home. They left Cleo with the boar for more mating over the next few days to be sure it was effective.

Mr. Sorenson had called then and said we should come and get Cleo. Carl was engrossed in an important hockey game on television; I had just finished dinner preparations, as friends were coming, and had put the turkey in the oven.

"Take the truck," Carl said. "Janice can load Cleo. Sorenson will help."

Carl had built wooden sides and a back around the tail section of the truck so Cleo would be safely enclosed. I drove north on the highway to the Sorensons' farm. Janice sat on the bench seat beside me. We managed the loading without incident. I think Janice thought she was rescuing Cleo from abuse. On the way home, it started to snow, at first just light flakes but soon a thick blast driving at us. The tires on the truck were good but not studded. I was managing the road and the snow when Cleo shifted her weight to one side and the truck skidded.

Janice shot me a wide-eyed look.

"We are going to be fine," I said, grimly struggling with the steering wheel and heading straight again. I fought that truck every time Cleo moved to one side or the other all the way home. It was like having a five-hundred-pound ball rolling around the back. Once we were on the gravel road, it was easier as there was more traction for the tires. I drove into our yard with some relief. We unloaded Cleo, who grunted her pleasure at being home. I had a fellow feeling. I felt lucky not to have landed us in the ditch or spun into the wrong lane. I left Janice sitting beside Cleo in her pen, making comforting noises and talking to her, then went to complain to Carl about the drive. He wasn't impressed.

"You made it, didn't you? Besides, you're a good driver."

I still resented having to make that trip. Was a hockey game more important than my safety? I supposed that was a bit melodramatic.

Now, Carl taking Cleo to the Blenkinsops' in his Buick was payback for last year's miserable trip.

I was in the yard after feeding the hens when Carl returned.

"She slobbered all over me. I really need a shower," he said through the open window of his Buick. He did need a shower. The smell of a pig in close quarters drifted through the open window and no doubt penetrated his pores.

I kept a straight face. I imagined Carl hated driving Cleo through town. He'd loathe the ludicrous picture he must have made. I must be truly petty because *I* enjoyed it.

"Your turn, my love. I had the snow and the treacherous driving last year."

He looked straight at me. "You resented that all year?"

I nodded.

He shook his head. "I guess it *was* my turn."

"You're a good dad."

He smiled. "Flattery will get you everywhere." He gave me a quick kiss and dashed off to shower, dress, and make his ten o'clock appointment.

THE NEXT MORNING, I drove to the hospital to do my bi-weekly round as liaison nurse for the community. As usual, I interviewed the patients who lived out of town and had vague addresses, like "four miles past the turnoff to Horsefly." A nurse could spend an afternoon wandering around the country with those directions. I needed a more precise description.

I wrote down everything they told me. "Go along the Likely Road until you come to the tree that's been struck by lightning."

"On the right or left?"

"On the right. Then you'll cross a little bridge. Turn right on the first road, well, a trail really, past the bridge and go about a mile. The road ends in our yard."

"How do I know if I've missed the turnoff?"

"If the Likely Road starts going downhill, you've gone too far."

I wrote that down. Details like these were invaluable.

I collected four rural addresses and would ask Ellie to type out the directions and add them to the chart when I got back to the office. The maternity ward was busy, so I didn't stop to chat, but headed up the stairs to the pediatric ward. The nurses there occasionally gave me referrals to families where they thought the child might need help at home. We hadn't yet put any children on our home care list, but we could.

The head nurse, Luella, who was young, energetic, and cheerful, knew her patients well. She was single and, as far as I know, didn't have any family here as she was from the Philippines. She had British Columbian qualifications.

"Anything for me, Luella?"

"I want to talk to you, but first I have to order more Kwellada from the pharmacy. We just admitted two Indian kids, and we need to treat them."

She reached for the phone.

"Do they have lice?"

"I don't think so."

"So why are you treating them for lice?"

"They're Indian."

My stomach clenched.

"Kwellada can cause convulsions in some cases. If you administer it when there is no reason to do so, you might be disciplined by the RNABC." She let the phone drop back on its cradle. The Nurses' Association had the power to suspend licences.

"I hadn't thought of that. It's hospital policy."

"You aren't required to carry out an incorrect policy. And I tell you, Luella, if my kid comes in here and you wash his head with Kwellada, I'll sue you." I smiled.

She stared at me, processing the facts. I was a nurse. I had an Indigenous child. My husband was a lawyer. I would sue.

"I hadn't thought of it like that. It's prejudice. Right?"

I agreed. "It's prejudice."

"Funny. It's clear when you explain it, but I just hadn't thought about it that way." She nodded briskly. "I'll change things."

So many people don't think about practices that are racist. Education is a slow process. "Okay." I was sure she *would* make changes. "Now, what did you want to talk to me about?"

"I've got a boy in 302. He's twelve and broke his leg riding calves at home."

"Practising," I said. "Wanting to be a rodeo cowboy."

"Probably. Anyway, he's got a cast on and he could go home, but Dr. Craisson wants to keep him here over Christmas."

We looked at each other.

"The good doctor's beds are down, right?" I was sure that was the explanation.

Doctors were allotted so many beds for their patients. If they didn't use them one month, their beds could be allotted to another doctor the next. Dr. Craisson wanted his patient to take up bed space so he could qualify for next month's quota. He would also get paid for the daily, unnecessary hospital visit.

"Are you going to talk to him?" I asked.

"I tried. He just ignores me."

I thought about it. "Let's see the boy's chart."

She passed it to me and I read his name—Corey Whitman—
and his parents' names. His address was Alexis Creek. I handed
the chart back to Luella and headed down the corridor. I walked
into 302 and found Corey sitting on a chair with a bedside table in
front of him, gluing together a model of a sportscar.

"A Porsche?" I asked. Glen had educated me on a few of the
popular car models.

"Yeah. Neat, eh?" He bent his head over his model.

I admired it.

"I'm Mrs. Crook, the public health nurse. How are you getting
on?"

"Okay. I can use the crutches." He gestured to the pair beside
him. "I can get to the bathroom, and I can go up and down stairs.
So why can't I go home?" His face was serious, even sullen, his
jaw muscles tight.

"Good question. I'll see what I can do."

He grinned. The transformation was amazing. I'd given him
hope. I'd better follow through.

I went back to the nurses' station and reached for the phone to
call the administrator, Tony Heathman.

"Marion Crook here," I said.

"Oh, hello, Marion." We knew each other, having met through
work and socially over the years. "What can I do for you?"

"There's a boy, Corey Whitman, on pediatrics. His parents are concerned he is not being discharged." I assumed they were concerned.

"I know," Tony said. "He's Dr. Craisson's patient. That man can
cause so much trouble; I hate to cross him on this."

"Because the child won't complain and the family is Indian."

"Well, yes. They don't usually complain."

"I think I can help you out with Dr. Craisson."

"You can?"

"Tell him the family has asked a lawyer to look into whether the
hospital can keep him when it isn't necessary."

"What lawyer?"

"Carl Crook," I lied.

"Your husband?"

"Yes."

I added pressure. "The boy has an uncle who works at *The Tri-bune*. You don't want the press involved." I was lying again and exerting a kind of blackmail on Tony. I thought about Corey and the hope in his eyes.

"I'd better tell Craisson he has to discharge him, then. We'd both get into a pile of trouble."

"You want to avoid that."

"Thanks, Marion. I appreciate the heads up."

"No problem. But Tony, you will keep this information confidential, won't you? I shouldn't really have told you."

"Certainly." I could count on that. He wouldn't want anyone to know he'd been aiding Craisson.

"I'll hold Carl off for a day," I promised.

"The boy will be discharged today," he promised in return.

"All right. Good."

I hung up the phone and smiled at Luella.

"He's going home?" she asked, with doubt in her voice.

"Today," I said. I felt a little guilty about lying to Tony—but only a little.

"I'll send a message to his parents. I can catch the noon broadcast." His parents or their friends and relatives would hear about Corey's discharge on the regular Message Time on the local radio. Everyone listened to it and passed on the information. You could follow dramas such as a death in a family, then the arrangements for rides to the funeral, then the arrangements for rides home. Wedding anniversary parties were announced. Job opportunities. Employers looking for absent workers. Delays in deliveries. All kinds of details of life far away from regular telephone service.

"Did you check to see if they have a phone?" There were phones out in the Chilcotin.

She looked at me. "Prejudice again? Because he's Indian and lives in the country, I assume they don't have a phone?"

"They might not." I wouldn't accuse her of prejudice because she thought they might not have a phone. Many people lived far from the phone lines. It was interesting, though, that she was questioning herself and wondering if prejudice was dictating her assumptions.

She checked the chart. "They do." She shook her head. "I am going to have to be more aware of what I'm doing."

"You're fabulous at the bedside," I reassured her.

I left her happily getting the patient ready. I hoped Dr. Craisson would sign the discharge order and not force Tony to override him. I hoped I wouldn't have to get Carl involved.

When I was back the next week, just days before Christmas, I popped up to the third floor after my rounds on the maternity ward to wish Luella a Merry Christmas. Luella told me Dr. Craisson had signed the order and Corey had gone home in time for Christmas. We smiled at each other, satisfied with the results of our efforts. I'd just turned to leave when June Lake, a regular ward nurse, ran into me. She grabbed me by the shoulders.

"Marion, go stay with the ICU patients. I have to catch a patient who eloped."

A patient had escaped? "Eloped" always made me think of romantic couples, but it was a common term applied to a patient who ran off. Where would he go? It was cold outside.

Obediently, I went down the hall to the Intensive Care Unit. I hoped there was no one who was in crisis as I was almost useless there. June was not supposed to leave the patients unattended, so it was reasonable to ask me to stand in, but having me in charge was not going to be adequate supervision. I *could* call for help—and I would, if necessary.

I walked into the ICU. There was an empty bed and two occupied ones. Both patients were sleeping. I'd better read the charts in case one or both woke up and needed something. There was one chart open on the desk. *Phillip McIntyre, age 26, acute pancre-atitis* identified the man and his problem. That must be the patient who had run off. Pancreatitis can cause delirium; he wouldn't be thinking straight. I checked the charts to inform myself of what conditions the remaining patients had and prayed fervently they would remain stable. I understood June's predicament. She couldn't leave her ICU patients, and she couldn't let a confused patient loose in the hospital. I would have to stay here until they found him or until someone came to relieve me.

The phone rang.

"ICU, Marion Crook speaking."

"Marion." It was Nan Morrice, the nursing supervisor. "Are the police there yet?"

I assumed she'd called the police to help find the patient in case they had to subdue him or had to expand the search to outside the hospital. Pancreatitis can create bizarre behaviour.

At that moment, I caught a movement at the edge of my vision. I turned my head and watched an RCMP regulation stetson sail through the air and land on the desk in front of me. I didn't see the Mountie. Where there was an RCMP stetson, there was an officer.

"Yes, they're here." I could only imagine that the officer had run past the ICU and chucked the hat.

"Good." She hung up.

They did find the patient. When they brought him back and got him into bed, I left. The Intensive Care Unit was not a work environment where I shone.

CHRISTMAS WAS ONLY a week away. I had cross-country skis for all of us, even a short pair for David. I stashed most of the presents in a storage bin under the hall closet, a place I hoped the kids wouldn't find. I'd planned a party between Christmas and New Year's. Christmas was on a Thursday this year, so I set the party for the twenty-seventh. Work schedules were relaxed. Many shops and businesses closed during that week. We had Christmas Day,

Boxing Day, and New Year's Day as official federal holidays, but Williams Lake added Wrestling Day, on the second of January, so everyone closed that day except for essential services. I supposed some town official thought Boxing Day referred to the sport and not the exchange of gifts, or perhaps they thought Wrestling Day a good joke.

Carl took the week off before Christmas. I went to work but managed to do all the grocery shopping during my work hours. I baked every evening. The kids helped and made a joyous mess with icing sugar, food colouring, and cookies. They used bright colours and garish decorations, but the cookies were crisp and crunchy and looked festive. I stacked the freezer with brownies and butter tarts. I had tins of shortbread already made and two Christmas cakes. I was the only one in the family who liked it, but some of my guests would. I had a big ham in the cooler, and I'd make the German potato salad the night before. I'd bought buns and frozen them because my breadmaking was unreliable. As well, I had the Christmas turkey in the cooler, and the ingredients for the steamed carrot pudding. The guests never came empty-handed, so we would have lots of food. Carl had a stash of beer, scotch, rye, and gin for those who wanted them as well as several sweet liqueurs. We were ready.

Christmas day was exciting as the kids got up early.

"Stockings only before breakfast," I decreed. They took their stockings, which were filled with small toys, puzzles, an orange, and some candy, back to their rooms. I think they all went to Janice's room. When they emerged an hour later, I started breakfast: bacon, scrambled eggs with whipped cream, and stollen. That Christmas bread was the one bread I could make.

"Hey, David," Janice said. "Look. There's Santa's sleigh tracks in the snow." Janice had cracked the myth of Santa Claus but was eager to perpetuate it for David's sake.

On Christmas Eve, Carl had waited until all the kids were asleep then, with a combination of a sled, hockey sticks turned upside-down and poked in the snow for deer tracks, a chewed carrot at the side of those tracks, and an hour of work, he'd managed credible evidence of Santa's visit. When they went outside, the kids would see sleigh tracks on the roof.

"So?" David said. "He came, didn't he? Look at the tree! Presents."

There was an impressive stack of presents crowded under the tree and spilling into the living room.

Janice looked at me, disappointed in David's casual acceptance of Santa's sleigh.

I laughed. "The tracks are convincing," I said. After all, if you believed in Santa Claus, you'd take the sleigh tracks for granted.

"Guess so."

Santa had presents for everyone. I had started shopping in September and collected them over the months. Carl had a gift for me, a pretty little opal ring with diamonds, and two from Santa, ski gloves and flashy, dangly earrings. We opened gifts after breakfast, one at a time so the gift exchange took all morning. Then I set the turkey in the oven and we went out into the winter day to try our new skis. We had all skied before on old second-hand skis. The new ones had quick-release bindings that made getting into them a simple matter of shoving your foot in and pressing the clamp tight, and getting out by pressing on the release button.

Carl went first and broke a trail for us. He carried the lunch in a backpack. We swished through the flat trail following him—Janice, Glen, David, and me at the rear. We weren't going to go far as David wouldn't be able to keep up for long.

We headed off toward the far meadow. The air was a crisp ten degrees below freezing. The sun lit the ice crystals, making the snow a sparkling carpet and the firs glint like Christmas trees full of stars. There was no birdsong, although some birds did stay all winter. All was quiet. Everyone had parkas, wool socks, ski pants, toques, and gloves, so we were warm enough. We only travelled the trail for about twenty minutes when Carl stepped off the path into the trees. He stamped the snow down to create a clearing and pulled some newspaper from his backpack.

"Dry wood," he instructed the kids. "Take it from the underside of the trees. There should be some dead wood there."

The kids reached up into the fir trees and collected tinder. Carl found some bigger logs—I think he knew they were there—and started a fire. We warmed our sandwiches on the fire: shrimp sandwiches, a treat we didn't have often, and black olives. For dessert, we had butter tarts. We didn't linger. Even with the fire it was cold when we weren't moving. We doused the fire with snow, although no fire would travel far in this weather. We slid back home more quickly as we went over our tracks and arrived rosy-cheeked and happy. The kids went to their rooms to play with their presents.

Christmas when I was young was full of relatives and food. Here, I couldn't supply the relatives. My parents were in the Fraser Valley but didn't communicate much, in any case. We did have the polite Christmas phone call, so stayed in touch. Carl's parents now spent the winter months in Arizona. We'd call them later when we could exchange thanks for the gifts they'd sent. But I could supply the food for our Christmas celebration. It would be quieter but satisfying in its own way. Carl set out a new jigsaw puzzle in the TV room and put some Christmas music on the stereo. I started the Christmas dinner. The cold settled around the house and into the land around us, but inside we were warm and happy. I was content.

CHAPTER TWENTY-ONE

SEARCHING
FOR A LOST CHILD

ON BOXING DAY, we got up late and had waffles and bacon. We went for another ski, but again Carl, David, and I didn't stay out long. Janice and Glen left us for an extra loop around the ranch. They were quick and wanted to skim away with some speed without being held back by David.

"Keep your ears covered. Frostbite hurts."

"Okay."

They came in for lunch and we grazed on leftovers. I had just cleaned up the leavings from lunch when I got a call from our neighbour Katie. She and her family lived on one of the lots we'd cut out from the ranch and sold a few years ago. Their road did not connect with ours, so we didn't see them, although I had met them. They'd built on their lot the previous year and moved in. I knew they had children who took the school bus with Janice and Glen, but they were too far away to be playmates. Their house was about a mile from us across the bull pasture and the woods beyond.

"Merry Christmas, Marion."

"The same to you."

"Is it okay if we cross-country ski on your ranch?"

"Sure," I said. "We have a few trails groomed but you can make your own, if you like."

"Thanks."

It was a lovely day for skiing, sunny and about five degrees below freezing. If I wasn't so busy, I'd go out again, but I was cooking for tomorrow's party. Carl was preparing for it by clearing the roads and the parking area with the blade on the tractor. About two o'clock, Katie called again.

"Could you watch out for Amy? She's eight and was skiing with us and decided to go back by herself. She hasn't come home. I'm sure she'll come soon, but we want to let you know she might be still on your ranch."

I looked out the window. The light was bright, but it would only last another two hours.

"We'll look for her. Where were you skiing?"

She told me.

"I'll phone some neighbours."

"Thanks." I could hear the relief in her voice.

I called my family together. "Janice and Glen, you ski between here and the far meadow. Stay together and be back here in an hour. If you find her, one of you stay with her or lead her here, and one of you ski home quickly and tell us."

They immediately put on their gear.

"Carl? What will you do?"

"I'll ski closer to where they live, on the far side of the bull pasture, and follow the tracks. Either she's on the tracks or I'll see where she left the trail and can follow her."

"Okay. I'm going to phone the Fords. I'll send them to the far meadow on their snowmobiles. They'll pass you two," I said to Janice and Glen, "but they'll go farther and faster than you can. Then David and I will go to Katie's and see if we can help there."

Carl and Glen left the room, but Janice lingered. "Mom, we saw wolf tracks this morning."

They hadn't told me that. I expect they didn't want me to forbid them to ski while the wolf was around. I'd never seen a wolf on the ranch. They were rare in this part of the country. They could take a calf down. Probably not a full-grown cow, but certainly a calf—or a child. I'd heard a cougar once and kept the kids close to the house until we no longer heard it. But I'd never even heard a wolf. I imagined an eight-year-old girl lost in the woods with a wolf waiting for her to sit down with exhaustion. I shivered.

"Where?" I asked her.

"On the way to the far meadow. We turned around when we saw them."

"I don't think she could have gone that far," I reassured her. "You'd better stay away from that trail. We'll let the Fords do that one. Check the woods around the corrals. We'll find her," I said.

I wasn't as confident as I sounded. This was a big ranch, and we bordered on five hundred acres of uninhabited crown land on one side and about four hundred acres on the other.

After calling the Fords and setting them out on the search, I pulled into Katie's yard. David and I got out and approached the house. I carried a plate of brownies for the searchers and handed them to the man who answered the door. He invited us in.

"Where's Katie?" I asked him.

"She's out searching. I'm her cousin, Gord. I don't ski. And they thought someone should be in the house in case she comes back."

"Good plan." I introduced myself and David and told Gord what I'd done.

"Oh, she'll be all right. It's a lot of fuss. She can ski. She'll come home."

It was now three-thirty and starting to get dark. The sun set around four. Obviously, this man didn't understand the danger to Amy from the cold—and possibly from the wolf.

"Did you phone the police?"

"Oh, no. I wouldn't do that."

"Where's your phone?"

There was no point in spending time trying to educate this man from the city on the way cold and darkness could kill. As soon as it was dark, Amy would be almost impossible to find. There were no streetlights or lights of any kind to help us, and even the moon was on the wane.

I outlined the problem to the police. Then I spoke with the cousin, trying to find out where Katie and her family were searching. The police arrived while I was on the phone checking with my family. Carl and the kids had just walked in without finding Amy.

"I'm going to rig up some lights so we can go back out and search in the dark," Carl said.

Then I again used Katie's phone while I had the chance and phoned the Fords.

"We found her!" Doreen Ford was ecstatic. "I was just going to phone your place."

"Thank God." I breathed out a long sigh of relief. "Where?"

"On the trail to the far meadow. Tom took the snowmobile down there and first he found her skis. She'd kicked them off. Then he saw her. She was still walking but very tired."

"And heading for the crown land."

"Not only that. There were wolf tracks following her."

"Oh, my God. Thank Tom for me. I'll send the parents for her when they get back to the house."

"We wrapped her in a sleeping bag, but I don't think she's hypothermic. She was dressed well."

"Thanks, Doreen."

I disconnected and phoned Carl.

"Thank God." He echoed my relief.

David put his hand on my leg. "Mommy."

I crouched down and looked at him. "The little girl has been found, Davie. She's fine."

He patted my leg, then grabbed my hand. He didn't understand why I was worried, but he knew I was.

I bade the cousin goodbye and went out to the yard to talk to the police officer who had just arrived. I kept hold of David's hand. At some recess of my mind, I think I was reassuring myself that my child was safe. I told the officer a searcher on a snowmobile had found her, and thanked him for coming.

"No problem. Glad she's okay."

We both looked at the darkening sky. Shadows were lengthening under the fir trees in the yard. The snow took on a grey hue. There was wilderness all around us, miles of trees and meadows with no roads or even trails. Little Amy would have been in deep trouble . . .

"Where was she?" the officer asked as he got back into his car.

"Two miles from here." I pointed.

"Nothing but bush there."

"That's right."

He shook his head. "She's lucky."

Katie skied into the yard just then. She looked tired and pale. I expect she now realized how dangerous Amy's disappearance was. I was quick to tell her the good news.

"Oh, Jesus Christ." I think that was a fervent prayer of thanks.

I told her how to drive to Fords' place, and told her where they'd found her.

"She skied exactly 180 degrees the wrong way," I said.

"She is not going skiing out there ever again."

"She can go again," I said, "but ski with her many times until she knows the trails well."

Katie shook her head. "Not on your life."

She was the parent. It was her choice. At least she understood how dangerous it was to leave a child on their own in the woods. I thought about it as I drove home. I let Janice and Glen wander about the woods, but they were unlikely to get lost. They had been walking, riding, and skiing the trails for years.

We ate more leftovers that night, and the kids made inroads on the sugar cookies.

"She was lucky," Glen said, echoing the officer's comment.

"You'd better stay off the far meadow trail until the wolf leaves," I told them.

"He'll be gone after tomorrow," Carl said. "All the noise from the party will scare him back into the bush."

He was likely right about that.

OUR FRIENDS DID MAKE a lot of noise swooping down the hill on sleds outside our yard gate, and skiing around the corrals and the pond. We didn't skate on the pond as it wasn't yet frozen solid, but the snowshoe race, where proficient snowshoers were handicapped by cans tied on the backs of their broad, bear-paw snowshoes, made enough noise to scare all the nearby animals farther into the woods. The cans rattled, the onlookers cheered, the contestants yelled at each other. Wolves wouldn't like it and would abandon this area.

When it started to get dark at three-thirty, people came into the house and began to sample the food. Peggy MacFarlane, the psychologist from the Mental Health office, asked me over the canapés if I would teach parenting classes. I was astounded.

"Why me?"

"You're a parent and you teach all the time."

Both were true, but I didn't consider myself any expert in parenting.

"I have a syllabus and a course outline," she offered as an incentive.

"I'd need that. I'll consider it." Peggy was an asset to the community. She was overworked because we had no other psychologist in town. Now, she was enjoying her holiday time and had brought along her husband, her mother, and her brother, Bill Reid. Her mother was Haida. I hadn't known Peggy had that heritage. Her brother was an artist in Vancouver, a sculptor and a carver. I didn't have time to talk to him, but he and his family seemed to be enjoying themselves. At one point during the evening, I saw Bill towing one of David's old toys, a duck that made a noise when you pulled it. He looked delighted.

"Isn't that something?" He grinned at me.

I chuckled at the sight of this tall man towing the toy and agreed it was entertaining.

Like any good party, there was noise, laughter, good food and drinks, and snatches of conversation with many people. I was proud of Janice and Glen, who made themselves useful by serving food and supplying napkins. Then they gave up helping to play games after supper with the many kids who were part of the party.

THE WORK WEEK between Christmas and New Year's had been slack. Half the nurses had taken the week off, and few people dropped into the health unit. The people of the town and the surrounding area stepped away from regular life and had a holiday.

In January, we were back to our usual pace of work. Paul returned, although he told us at our first staff meeting he was leaving at the end of February. That would be a relief, although I could have continued working with him if I had had to. Victoria told Marlene they had hired a nursing supervisor who was arriving the first of February. There was no talk of a replacement for Paul. Either the Ministry of Health couldn't find an appropriate person or they were saving salaries again.

I DROVE OUT past 150 Mile House to a well-baby visit with Mrs. Fraser and family. I'd read the chart before I left: this baby was her fourth child. I had received directions to her home from Ann Fraser when she was in the hospital:

"Go about twenty miles south on the highway, then turn left at the 141. Then go until you see a snake fence on the right. Follow the snake fence until it stops. Turn right there and go about a half mile."

I'd never travelled down the 141 Mile House Road. Its name suggested there had been a lodge or some kind of stopping house on the highway for the stage and mule trains that came up this way during the Cariboo Gold Rush. There was nothing left of it now. I looked around at the snow-covered pastures before I turned onto the gravel road.

It felt good to be out on the road after a few weeks of office work through the end of December and early January. The temperature had dipped to twenty degrees below freezing. If my car broke down, I would feel the cold quickly. I had a candle packed in the glove compartment and a blanket in the back seat, but I trusted nothing would go wrong with my Suburban.

I listened to the radio as I drove. The Williams Lake station, CKWL, had a talk show every afternoon. A woman came on decrying abortion. I was surprised. No one usually talked about it. It was legal if a committee of doctors approved your application. Getting permission was a cumbersome and capricious process that made access difficult, but at least abortion was possible for some. I listened carefully. She was the president of the Catholic Women's League and she was single-minded about her views. I wondered if this meant more Catholic women would go underground looking for abortions. They had certainly embraced birth control as soon as it became legal, but abortion was not as accessible.

I concentrated on my driving. I was grateful for the big tires of this Suburban. I still had to drive carefully as it tended to slide on the corners, but it was much heavier than the old Chevy II I used to drive, and it felt safer. The gravel road had been plowed, so it was easy to navigate. I drove about ten minutes before I saw the snake fence. Snow glittered along the top of every dark rail, looking like an art installation of intentional geometrical design, but fences were expressions of practicality and only incidentally of beauty. Snake fences were constructed by placing a rail between two others at each end. The rails were kept stable by angling the rails at about forty-five degrees where they met. That meant they changed direction at every corner by forty-five degrees, so they "snaked' back and forth, zigzagging across the fields. Other types of fences were bound with leather lacing at the corners; still others had tripods of stakes stabilizing the joins.

I'd sent a message on the radio Message Time telling Mrs. Fraser when I would arrive. They had cleared the yard; I didn't have to slide through the snow. Two border collies dashed out to investigate me. I didn't think they'd be loose if they were dangerous, so, trusting the Frasers, I got out. The dogs sniffed me then darted back to the house.

I unloaded the scale and grabbed my black bag. I could see the house had been set in a clearing at the top of a small rise. There were trees, mostly fir, all around. A slight breeze intensified the cold and I felt the nip of it on my ears and nose.

The door opened as I approached.

"Good of you to come!" Mrs. Fraser called.

I hurried to get through the door before cold got into the house.

"It's lovely out here. Nice to get out of the office."

I followed her into the boot room of a large log cabin. She took my scale while I divested myself of boots, scarf, parka, and gloves.

The main room contained the kitchen, living, and dining area, with several doors leading into other rooms. A bathroom and bedrooms, I assumed.

Ann Fraser had a husband and three older children, none of whom seemed to be around.

"Everyone's gone to the neighbour's," she said. "They've got a new bull Mike is thinking about using, and the kids can play with the neighbour's kids. It gives me a breather."

She had one child in school but the other two were still small.

"Let's get this little one weighed."

It was what every mother wanted me to do first, as weight gain usually meant a healthy baby.

"What's her name?" I asked.

"Cindy," she said.

I'd have to tell Sophie. We had a competition on how many times we found the same name. So far, I'd found one more Cindy than she had, although her district was ahead on Stephanies.

This little girl was gaining well. She was pink, plump, and alert. After I'd done the usual physical exam measuring height, weight, head circumference, chest circumference, startle reflex, and all the ways I had to find any problems, Ann re-dressed Cindy and put her back into the cradle nearby while I brought out the chart and recorded everything as quickly as I could.

We talked about her concerns—not many, as she was an experienced mother. Still, she was glad to accept my approval of her care. She must have known she was competent, but it was reassuring to have someone else notice that. We talked about her other children, and I went over each child's immunization status. She said she'd come to the Williams Lake clinic for Cindy's two-month shot as it made a great excuse to get to town. She poured me coffee and offered a just-made bun. Delicious.

"I'm not good at breadmaking," I confessed. That was true. Breads and buns were a hit-and-miss endeavour, except for stollen.

"It seems to be a gift. You have it or you don't. When you live this far from a store, it becomes a necessity."

"What are you making over there?" I pointed to a bucket near the stove, which had some kind of mixture in it.

"Oh, that's the muck I make to stuff cracks in the logs."

I showed my curiosity.

"Flour, salt, sawdust, and manure," she said.

"Really?"

"The house is pretty tight and warm, but sometimes the chinking falls out, or parts of it do, so I watch in the morning to see if there's any frost anywhere, then bung in some more chinking to stop the air coming in."

"Seems to be working. It's warm."

"The baby needs it warm."

Ann Fraser was about the same age as me. Both our lives had changed greatly in the last ten years. She was probably as energetic and wide-eyed as I was back in those days when we were probably both dating different men and looking at life as a huge adventure. Marriage and children disrupted everything, although I still saw life as an adventure. I wondered if she did too. I thought about the amount of work it took to keep her children warm and safe this far from town. I'd seen the wood stacked by the stove; she'd stoke it all day to keep the fire going. That meant fetching wood and lifting and shoving it into the heater. She had electricity, so I assumed she had an electric heater to augment the stove. Still, she'd be busy all day long. I had a fireplace, but I also had an oil furnace, so heat came on with the touch of a dial; I didn't have to spend all day looking after a fire.

I'd heard one of the nurses in the staff room wonder why people wanted to live way out in the bush. "They're trying to prove they can live the way their grandparents did. Why do that?" No doubt for some, there would be great satisfaction in it. Some did live the way their grandparents did, but Ann's family had modern electricity and running water. There had been an up-to-date washing machine in the boot room where I'd entered. In the big room, there were children's books on a shelf and a television. No doubt they had an oversized truck, a modern tractor, and haying equipment. Many ranchers had huge balers that made the gigantic round bales, containing about six hundred pounds of hay that was resistant to mould and rot when rolled that way. They were moved only with machinery and required none of the hard work of lifting and stacking we had to do with our small rectangular bales. And of course, the machinery needed to be tinkered with to keep running, which would gratify the ranchers. It was an axiom of ranching that machinery always broke down just when it was needed. Scratch a rancher, find a mechanic. I know Carl was always happy to take something apart. Glen was going to be the same.

I drove back to the office on clear, dry roads. There was snow piled up at the sides of the highway, and we would get more for the next three months. As usual, I made it back to the office without a broken gas line or axle, or any other part of my vehicle damaged. When I walked into the office, I found Ellie surrounded by paper. She looked up as I came in and glanced at her watch. I did the same. It was almost three o'clock, quitting time for me.

"Can you sign some of these tomorrow?" She was sorting and allocating the piles of paperwork she needed to send to Victoria.

"Where's Paul?"

"Gone to Quesnel. He's staying there the rest of the week."

Paul did need to go there routinely. Perhaps he wasn't hiding from the paperwork.

"All right. I'll sign them tomorrow. I'd better pick up David and get on home." Since the Ministry had hired a new supervisor, I didn't need to refuse.

I definitely did not want to be an administrator. I got more satisfaction from driving into the country to visit the Ann Frasers in my district than I would sorting through papers.

CHAPTER TWENTY-TWO

DEALING WITH
A GIFT HORSE

T HE WEATHER WAS COLD enough by the first of February to freeze Williams Lake and the pond on the ranch. The pond was shallow and usually froze quickly. When we saw the cattle walking on the ice, we knew it was safe for us. To be sure, Carl drilled a hole and measured it. It was almost two feet thick. Carl drove the tractor with the blade onto the ice and cleared the snow off a big section of it so the kids could skate.

The neighbour kids came over, and soon there were impromptu hockey games on the weekends. David and I joined them for a short while. The previous year, David had skated with double-bladed skates strapped onto his boots, but this year he had real skates. He spent more time on his knees chasing the puck than he did standing up, but he tried. I enjoyed skating a circular route around the outside of the rink, dodging the errant hockey puck. The beaver dam at the end was bigger this year and doing a good job of holding the water in the pond. Carl broke the ice near the dam every day on his way to work so the cattle could drink. Four cows were gathered around it, their red-brown coats the only bit of colour in the landscape. The ice rumbled and boomed. The hockey game stopped for a moment. We all froze in place like a tableau. We knew the ice was safe and the booming was the ice underneath shifting with the change of temperature, but it startled us all the same. The ice quieted and the game continued.

I'd started the parenting classes Peggy MacFarlane had convinced me to teach. I studied madly for days before each class, following the curriculum guideline Peggy had supplied. I learned about win-win discussions, "I" messages, and active listening. I applied what I learned to my own kids. I hoped it was a better way to parent, but parenting is not an exact science and I often didn't know what to do. Maybe most parents don't have so many dilemmas. Carl said I tended to overthink the situation and the kids would be fine no matter what I said or did. I didn't agree.

MY DAD DECIDED to pay us a visit.

"I'll bring Frisky, Henessey, and the sleigh. You can have them all," he told me when he phoned.

My dad had a mare, Frisky, and a young gelding, Henessey. I expected he was cutting down on his farm in the Fraser Valley, preparing for retirement.

"Ron has a truck and he'll haul all this."

Ron was my brother, older by a year and a half. We didn't see much of each other as he was a busy lawyer in our hometown of Cloverdale, about an eight-hour drive from the Cariboo, and he was kept occupied with a young family. It was good of him to take the time to drive Dad and his horse and sleigh. My dad's eyesight was fading, so it would be dangerous for him to drive. They arrived and unloaded Frisky, a handsome, four-year-old bay. Dad told me he had Frisky's mother and had raised her from a filly. He also brought a beautiful, romantic-looking cutter, a sleigh with curved runners and a velvet padded front seat. There was room behind the seat for kids to ride.

We put the horses in the yard near the barn with Flip, our calm, reliable pony. We wouldn't let the new horses out to graze on the ranch because they might get lost or beset by coyotes. In the barnyard, they would have Flip's company and stay close. I didn't trust the horses to be loose on a thousand acres, and I didn't want to try to find them when the kids wanted to ride. Ron left in the morning, but not before he noticed our chicken house.

"Do your chickens ski?"

It was a fair comment. Our chicken coop looked like a chalet. Carl, Janice, Glen, and I (before David was born) had sat down around the dining room table and designed a log chicken coop about six feet high on the sides with a conventional roof. Then we started to peel the logs. We managed to get logs three high on four sides—that's twelve logs—before we were fed up with the tedious work. That was when we redesigned the building with its steep, sloping roof. It worked well as the nest boxes were on the short sides. It was a distinctive-looking chicken coop.

Dad stayed for a few days and taught me how to harness Frisky and hook her to the cutter. He supervised me driving the sleigh around the ranch. It wasn't difficult; I just had to pay attention. Frisky responded well to my direction. Dad also chopped firewood, cleaned the chicken coop, rearranged the bales in the barn for more efficient access, and checked the feet of all the sheep. He had grown up on his dad's dairy farm with twelve siblings. I had grown up on a smaller farm with five siblings. I had been the one most interested in the animals and had looked after the stock when Dad was away. When I came back from driving Dad to the airport, Carl was sitting in the living room.

"I'm exhausted," he said. "I can't keep up with your dad."

It was a good thing Dad didn't come often as he was constantly moving. He got a lot done, but he was more active than even I was.

As I hugged Dad goodbye, I thanked him for bringing the horses and the sleigh.

"You'll be fine. Just don't let Frisky get away with anything."

"I won't," I promised, but I didn't know what he meant.

I found out.

I had the sleigh loaded with all three kids and had just shaken the reins to encourage Frisky over the plywood I'd laid over the cattle-guard, and out onto the ranch proper. The kids were excited, and I was concentrating on holding the reins correctly. Frisky stopped.

"Walk on," I encouraged her with a flick of the reins.

She stood perfectly still then lowered her head. I realized her intention.

"Everyone out. Jump!" I grabbed David, and we all jumped before Frisky knuckled her front legs, lowered her hind legs, and rolled, overturning the sleigh.

I had never heard of a horse deliberately overturning a cart or a sleigh. It was bizarre. It took an hour to disentangle Frisky from the traces, right the sleigh, and get the horse, sleigh, and kids back to the barn.

"Frisky doesn't like the wagon thing, Mom," Glen said.

"The cutter," I said. "I got that."

I had a long talk with my dad that night on the phone. The upshot was I sold the sleigh to Walt Cobb, who lived out Miocene way, and sent the money to my dad. We kept the horses as they were fine when under a saddle.

The other animal on the ranch who was giving us trouble was Sylvester, the rooster. He had started to fly at David whenever David went into the chicken coop to collect the eggs. I told David not to go without one of the older kids. Then Glen complained that Sylvester was going after him. The next week it was Janice, which meant I had to collect the eggs. I wondered what was going on in Sylvester's brain that he decided to challenge taller and taller humans. This Wednesday morning I took David with me, but my presence wasn't enough to deter Sylvester. He came flying at David, feet straight out and curved and his beak ready to attack. I didn't think. I just hauled back and drop-kicked Sylvester across the coop. He tumbled over and over but shook himself and stood up. At least I hadn't killed him. I felt guilty for kicking him, but I wasn't going to let him attack David. I waited for him to launch another attack, but he slunk over to the door and hopped out. That cured him. He no longer tried to intimidate the kids, and allowed them to collect the eggs unmolested. I didn't feel as badly as I probably should have.

AT WORK ON MONDAY, I was reading over the items in my pending box when Ellie called.

"There's a young woman here who wants to see a nurse."

"I'll come for her."

I didn't know if I got more walk-in patients than other nurses, but I suspected so. My office was the closest one to the reception area.

The girl was about seventeen, thin, blond, with a freckled face and huge brown eyes. She smiled.

"Hi. I'm Stacy White. Can I talk to you?"

"Sure. Follow me."

I settled her in a chair then turned my chair so we were facing each other.

"How can I help?"

"It's like this," she said. "Josh, my boyfriend, got sent to jail. He'll be there six months, and I need a place to stay."

Life would be difficult for her. I assumed she couldn't go home, but why come here? "Tell me more."

"Well, I'm five months pregnant, and I need to look after myself until Josh can come back and look after us."

"I see."

"I can get Welfare to pay for food, but they won't pay for a place to stay. They want to send me to a home for unwed mothers 'cause Josh and I haven't got around to getting married yet. I won't go there, because they'll take our baby. I know they will. I've heard about those places, and I won't go. So can you find me a place where I can look after myself and wait?"

In some ways, Stacy seemed incredibly naïve. Did she think a public health nurse could magically produce what she needed? In other ways, she was wise. She was trying to control what happened to her and her baby.

"What's your doctor's name?"

She looked worried. "I suppose I should have a doctor soon, but I don't have one yet."

Yikes. You definitely should have a doctor. I didn't say that aloud. Mothers this young could have a difficult birth.

"If you will wait in the clinic room while I make some phone calls, I'll see what I can do. I'd better have your full name and present address."

She gave it to me and I started a chart for her.

"I have to leave there at the end of the month, though, because Josh only paid a month ahead."

At least that gave me two weeks to find something. I started to think more charitably of the absent Josh.

I escorted her to the clinic room. "There are several prenatal pamphlets and books here," I said. "Help yourself."

I went back to my office and thought. The president of the Catholic Women's League would be a good place to start. I'd heard her on the radio decrying abortion. Here was a young girl who, when pregnant, opted to keep the baby.

I called the president and put the problem to her. She didn't share my point of view.

"I can't be concerned about her. My concern is to stamp out abortions."

My mind blanked for a moment. Then I said, "But isn't your aim to allow children to be born? That's what this young woman is trying to do."

"She shouldn't have slept with anyone."

"Had sex, you mean?"

"She caused her own misfortune. She's not my problem."

I hung up before I became unprofessional and swore at her. What hypocrisy!

I went back to Stacy and told her it might take some time for me to find her a place, but I'd try. I asked her to come see me in a week.

I didn't know if anything would come up, but I asked the other nurses to spread the word and see what happened. I was handicapped by Stacy's insistence that I not talk to the Welfare workers.

I got a call a few days later from Aileen Darcy. She was a former nurse and wife of Dr. Darcy. She was also a member of the Catholic Women's League.

"Do you still have a young, pregnant girl who needs a place to stay?" she asked in her soft voice.

"I do."

"Ian and I would like to take her."

"That's incredibly generous of you, Aileen. It will really help."

"What's she like?"

"A little naïve, but determined. I can't know how she'll fit into your home, but she's afraid Social Welfare will take her baby from her. If you could set yourself up as her protector, she'll probably cooperate with you."

"It will be nice for us to have a young girl around. I have three boys. It will be good for us all."

I fervently hoped so.

Aileen came to the health unit a few days later and met Stacy.

"I hope you'll be happy with us," Aileen said.

I hoped so too because from my point of view it was ideal. Stacy had a place to stay with a kind, gentle, and knowledgeable nurse, and her doctor husband could oversee Stacy's prenatal care. If only Stacy appreciated it. She seemed to.

I turned to her. "Are you happy with this home?"

"I think so," she said. "It's been lonely since Josh went away."

"Do you want me to get your things now, or would you like a few days to get organized?" Aileen asked.

"How about you come for me . . . ?" She paused. "You *can* come for me?"

"Yes," Aileen said. "I can."

"Okay. How about you come on Saturday at noon. Would that be okay? I'll be all packed up then."

Aileen smiled. "That would be fine. I'll get your room ready. I have a cradle you can use. We can decorate it."

This time, Stacy beamed. "That's so nice of you."

It looked like a good start.

JUST AFTER THREE, Carl joined me at Cataline school, where we were scheduled to see the teachers for a semi-annual report. Glen's teacher reported he was superb in some areas and inattentive in others, which was standard for him. Janice's teacher, Chris Spence, had quite a lot to say.

"She's accomplished, as you know," he concluded. "You need to consider sending her to a more competitive school than our high school."

I stared at him. "Send her away?"

"There are good boarding schools where she will have classes with students who are even brighter than she is. She needs that."

I was appalled. "What's the problem with our high school here?"

"We have good teachers," Chris said carefully, "but she is already somewhat isolated because she is so quick at grasping concepts. She has one friend."

"Cindy," I said.

"Yes. Cindy. She'll find it more difficult to succeed in high school because she'll get more social pressure to fail. She won't be happy. She really needs to get to a more challenging school—in grade eight."

Carl and I thanked him, then stood outside by our vehicles talking.

I did not like the idea of sending her away to boarding school. "She could get her social acceptance from the 4-H group. She's happy with them."

"True, but what about her studies?" Carl asked.

"Grade eight is two years from now. She'll be twelve. I can't do it," I wailed. I hated the idea of sending her to Vancouver or Victoria. And then what about the boys? We couldn't send Janice for a good education and then tell the boys they couldn't have that opportunity.

"I hate it too," Carl said. "She's my right hand on the ranch. I'd miss her."

"I'd feel like my heart was broken."

"How would she feel?" he asked me.

I thought about it and sighed. "I think she'd love it."

We'd talk about it more. We wouldn't talk to Janice until we had investigated her options. I still hated the idea.

ON THE WEEKEND, Glen and I went out the back door for a ski. Carl had David with him, and Janice was fussing around Cleo. Mr. Blenkinsop had assured Carl that Cleo had mated, so piglets were expected in March.

Glen and I skied out to the far meadow. The wolf had left us. We checked for tracks when we skied. Nothing. Carl had been right about the noise from the Christmas party. The weather had warmed a little and it was only about five degrees below freezing— just cold enough so our skis didn't stick. Icicles hung along bare branches where the sun had melted the snow during the day and frozen the droplets at night. The sunlight played among the icicles, creating a sparkling vision.

"Look, Glen. Pretty, isn't it?"

"Uh huh."

We skied a circle around the far meadow, back through the old mill site and home. When we were kicking off our skis at the back door, I asked, "Did you tell your friends about your new skis?"

He turned to me and stared. "Nobody waits for me to tell them anything."

Then he went into the house, leaving me stunned at the door. I was aware Glen had trouble saying what he was thinking. He took time to find the words he needed. I tried to give him time so he could talk, but I hadn't realized how it was affecting his friendships.

I SPOKE TO THE SPEECH THERAPIST, Laura Pascott, at coffee that week. She had come in January to fill the vacant therapist job.

"Glen's bright," I told her. "He just can't find the words he needs fast enough to hold his own in a conversation."

"How does he go about looking for the words he wants?"

"He thinks about it for a time, then sometimes he just describes the word. Like he'll say, 'Those things on the car that go round and round' when he wants 'wheels.'"

She was quiet for a moment, then said, "That's called Johnson Syndrome. I can fix that. I had a similar patient when I was at Oregon State. No problem."

I stared at her. "Really?"

"Yes. Schedule him in to see me once a week for eight weeks. That should do it."

All my kids had been in and out of the health unit for years and made friends with the staff. Glen was happy to meet with a friend of mine and not the least bit nervous about it. I picked him up after school and left him with Laura.

I TOLD MY FRIEND CYNTHIA about it when next I met her. We met at the Cariboo Friendship Centre Café, The Hearth, where we usually got a coffee and a pastry. We tried to meet about once a month.

"Nice she diagnosed him, and nice you could get him in for treatment."

"Well," I said, feeling only slightly guilty, "she's not supposed to take school-aged children. They are supposed to be seen by the school district's therapist."

"And I suppose that therapist has the whole of the Cariboo to care for."

"She does."

"Go for it," Cynthia advised. "Besides, you break the rules for other people. Might as well do it for your own kid."

I smiled. "I'm not losing sleep over sneaking him in to see her."

"Good." She gestured with her coffee cup at the walls around us. "What do you think of this place?"

"It seems to be working okay. It's got a few rooms for people who need shelter, right?"

"Yes, but we have in mind to increase that to permanent housing. You know, a place for people who have no other place."

I imagined it. "Maybe build up vertically? And have a couple of floors of apartments?"

She had more plans. "That, and we really need a nursery school. A place where kids can get a head start."

I'd heard of the Head Start Program. It had started in the United States and was established across the country.

"That would be a great way to get kids ready for school."

"Then we should hire our own Native counsellors so our people wouldn't have to do without help, because either they can't pay for the counsellors or the counsellors come with so much prejudice they're useless."

"Offices," I said. "A whole bank of offices."

"Yeah." She sighed. Her vision hung in my imagination.

"Maybe a bookstore," I suggested. "I can't find any books where the kids have brown skin. All the characters are white."

"There aren't any brown dolls either."

"I know. When David was two, I tried to find a brown doll. Even a Black one would have been better than a white one. There were those Indian princesses who looked white and had a lot of inauthentic regalia, but I couldn't bring myself to get one. I wanted a cuddly brown baby doll."

"Did you find one?"

"I found a Black doll in Vancouver. But it wasn't right. I mean, Black is not Native."

"I know. None of my kids had a Native doll."

"If seventy percent of the parents want a white doll, that means thirty percent want a brown one or a Black one."

"Where did you get those numbers?"

"Census." All kinds of information came across my desk from Victoria.

"Do dolls matter?"

"They matter to me. I get that the whole idea of separate races was invented to create imaginary boundaries. At one point the Irish were considered a separate race. It's a convenient way to keep some people away from prosperity and resources. It's hugely political, but our kids have to feel their skin is just fine."

We sat in silence for a moment. I was thinking about the many ways the idea of separate races divided us. "Maybe we should make some brown dolls?"

"Can you sew?" she asked me.

"Not well enough for that."

"Me either."

That project died a quick death, but I hoped Cynthia's other visions for the Friendship Centre would be realized.

CHAPTER TWENTY-THREE

TAKING ON
DR. CRAISSON—AGAIN

"I PUT A SURPRISE in your office," Ellie said when I returned just before noon on Thursday after two baby visits. She came out from behind the counter and followed me. The door was closed.

I turned to her and raised my eyebrows, my hand on the doorknob.

"Just look," she said.

I opened the door to find a small dog, a long-haired dachshund, brindle-coloured and very fat, waddling toward me. Ellie had provided the dog with a blanket and a dish of water.

"Whose dog? And why in my office?"

Ellie stood at the door. I crouched down and petted the dog. I could see she wasn't fat; she was pregnant.

"She was outside, scratching at the door when I came to work this morning. I couldn't leave her there. It was cold."

"Of course not."

"I brought her in and got her warmed up, then I called around to the vets' offices and left a 'found' message at the radio station and at the paper. She's a cute dog. Someone will be missing her."

"If they didn't dump her because she's going to have puppies."

I ran my hands over the dog's back and palpated her abdomen. She had several puppies in there.

"Hello, Pickles," I said.

"Pickles?" Ellie repeated.

"I have no idea why *Pickles*. It just popped into my head."

"She's cute," Ellie said again.

Pickles raised her head and stared at me with her huge brown eyes. I wouldn't say she was cute; I'd say she was dignified.

"Why my office?" I asked again and stood. Pickles went back to her blanket and curled into a circle with her head on her paws. She still looked at me.

"We talked it over and thought you'd be the best one to take her until her owners came for her. On a ranch and all that."

This was the second dog I would be bringing home. The first one was a Pekinese who had been hit by a car. I'd found her in the ditch and taken her to the vet for treatment. I thought about keeping her, but she didn't fit into the household. Carl had forgotten about her injured leg and picked her up. Her leg had pained her and she'd snapped. From the dog's point of view it was understandable, but Carl wasn't happy. So I found a home for her.

There was no response to Ellie's search for an owner, so I brought Pickles home with me and deposited her in the kitchen. The kids were enraptured with Pickles. Carl was tolerant.

"Pretty cute," he said. She was obviously not a ranch dog.

Again, I didn't think *cute* fit her. She was more self-contained and dignified than cute to me.

No one claimed her. She was definitely my dog. She sat at my feet when I was sitting and followed me around the house when I moved. At night, she took turns sleeping in the kids' rooms. I was smitten. I'd loved our old dog Keo and missed him when he left us, and Ben, Glen's dog, was sweet, but Pickles had bonded to me in a way I'd never experienced before. She was a darling. I loved her straight away. She helped me to better understand Janice's relationship with Cleo.

About a week after she arrived, Glen came up to breakfast full of news.

"Pickles had babies. They're under my bed."

We all trooped down the stairs to his room and lay on the floor peering at Pickles. She came out to greet me, licked my hand, then turned her head toward the puppies as if to say, *There. Look at those.*

"Very well done, Pickles." I petted her.

Glen squirmed under the bed and handed out the puppies one by one. There were six of them.

"They're adorable," Janice said.

"Soft," David pronounced.

Carl smiled at the tiny puppies. "Really, really cute."

I agreed with that. These were the epitome of cute. "Put them back, Glen."

"Can they stay under my bed? Ben's really good with them. He just sniffs them; he doesn't hurt them."

"If Pickles doesn't move them."

Pickles left them under the bed for a week then transferred them to a box near the wood stove in the rec room. She was the most undemonstrative mother I've ever seen, and some of my sheep, Number Forty-Nine, for instance, could run a competition for neglect. Pickles trotted down to feed her pups when she needed to but otherwise ignored them. It was as if she was saying, *Pregnancy and motherhood were not my choice. I'm doing my duty here, but that's all I'll do.* With that obvious independent spirit her devotion to me was a valued gift.

I found homes for all the puppies at six weeks. The health unit staff searched for people to adopt them as they felt guilty for foisting Pickles on me. The puppies were going to be small dogs, and that helped to place them as there weren't many small dogs in Williams Lake. The kids were sad to see them leave our house; they'd spent hours playing with them. I enjoyed them, but six puppies made a lot of work with newspaper training and introducing them to dog food. I was quite happy to place the last one in the hands of Amy MacDonald.

After the puppies left, I took Pickles to the vet to have her spayed. I'm sure she was grateful.

AT WORK, it was easier to get out into the country at this time of year than it had been in the deep winter when I had the constant concern that I might slide off the road. But it did take planning. Black ice was still a problem as the sun melted the snow during the day and the drop in temperature at night froze that melted snow. I waited until about ten in the morning to leave the health unit as the highway wasn't sanded or salted, and I wanted that thin covering of ice to melt away before I drove on it.

The snow had disappeared from pastures near the road and on some of the hillsides. We would probably get more, at least flurries, but today made me hope for spring. South of Williams Lake, near 141 Mile, I spotted buffalo in a pasture to the east. I'd heard a rancher was trying to raise buffalo for meat. I pulled over and took five minutes to look at them. Huge beasts, almost prehistoric looking. I wondered how hard they'd be to manage. Cattle could be a handful at times but buffalo were much bigger and heavier. A truck slowed down and stopped. The driver looked at me. I waved and turned on my signal, indicating I was going to pull back onto the highway. He honked and moved past. While it seemed I was alone on the road and isolated in these little-populated places, there were people like that truck driver who were looking out for me. No wonder I felt so at home in the country.

I thought about my children. I had expected to bring them up in the Cariboo, but it looked like I was going to have to send Janice south to boarding school. Would Glen and David follow? Would that mean I was not going to have my family close around me for long? That was not what I had expected, not what I had planned. It was two years into the future. I wasn't going to think about it now.

My visit was to a ranch family who lived about five miles east off the highway. Mrs. Rutherford was worried about her mother, who was getting more and more forgetful. Mrs. Rutherford anticipated a time when it wouldn't be possible to keep her at home. She needed to find a care home for her.

"I hate to do it, Mrs. Crook, but she's going to be a danger to herself. I can't be with her every minute. I'm often out of the house because I'm needed on the ranch." Most ranchers were a couple who both worked with the stock and with the crops.

"At least we have a care home in Williams Lake now." I gave her a brochure and told her how to contact the social worker to help with the process of admission.

"Once you apply for the home, a long-term care nurse assessor will come out and visit you and assess your mother for her need for care."

"We have to pass a test?"

"Just to see what level of care she needs."

"Okay. I don't want to send her to Kamloops or Prince George."

"You might want to make sure she doesn't have too many assets when she applies for admission."

Mrs. Rutherford looked at me, her eyes sharp with intelligence.

"Government takes their cut, do they?"

"They do." Sally had taught me that applicants needed to give their families their inheritance before they applied for government housing. That wasn't something social workers mentioned.

"If she doesn't like it there, or you find a private home who can take her, you will have the money to help her move."

I WAS BACK AT THE OFFICE after lunch. Kate arrived, slung her black bag on my counter, shut the door, and flopped into a chair, facing me. Her red hair curled around her face, her eyes huge and full of worry.

"What's up?" I asked her. Something certainly was.

"Everything's gone arseways." She looked straight at me. "Dr. Craisson says he's going to complain to the RNABC and get them to take away my nursing licence."

That was a serious threat. She couldn't work without a licence; it would be a life-changing catastrophe. I knew Dr. Craisson was a troublemaker, and the Registered Nurses' Association of BC wasn't going to act on his orders, but they would investigate an official complaint. He could cause Kate some sleepless nights. I'd better find out how bad the problem was.

"What happened?"

"You know I've been going to see Mr. Babcock?"

"Yes." I mentally reviewed Mr. Babcock's diagnosis and treatment. He had been going to Dr. Craisson for treatment of a stomach ulcer.

"You know Bev, his wife, asked me if I thought she should ask *her* doctor see him because he was not doing so well. And I said yes because it was obvious the man had more than a stomach ulcer. He was cachexic and in pain."

I hadn't seen Mr. Babcock but Kate had described his loss of muscle mass to me.

"The two of them went to her doctor, the new doctor, and he diagnosed Stage 4 cancer. Now Mr. B. is on big doses of pain medication while they wait for him to die."

That was sad. I didn't know how long he had been receiving the wrong treatment or what difference it would have made if Dr. Craisson had diagnosed it correctly. It would be impossible to prove negligence even if the family had the money and the energy to start a case against him.

"What's Dr Craisson's beef?" After all, he was the one in the wrong here.

"The sleeven says I advised them to go to a different doctor, which is unethical, and he's going to get my licence taken away." There had to be Irish in Kate's background. "Sleeven," a sneaky toad of a man, perfectly described Craisson.

We stared at each other. It was unethical for a nurse to criticize a doctor. That was going to have to change one day, but today it was a problem.

"Did you?"

"I didn't. When Bev suggested she take her husband to her doctor, I just agreed with her."

"Good," I said. The suggestion had not come from her, although I was reasonably sure Kate had hinted and nudged until Mrs. Babcock had come up with the idea.

"I was careful," she reassured me, reading my mind, "so I know I'm okay, but he can still give me grief, that pitiful excuse for a doctor."

I picked up the phone and got through to Dr. Craisson. I was almost looking forward to the encounter; I felt energized.

"Dr. Craisson. Marion Crook here from the health unit. I understand you threatened one of my nurses." I'd been dealing with Dr. Craisson and his mistakes for years. Attack was always the best negotiating tactic with him.

He sputtered. "I didn't threaten her. I told her I was going to get her licence taken away. She can't counsel my patients to leave my practice."

"She didn't."

"He's going to another doctor."

"His wife said she wanted him to see her doctor, and my nurse said of course she had a right to do that. And she has."

"She should have told him to stay with me."

"Now *that* would be unethical."

"I don't like it. She's wrong."

"I will consult my husband about this, but I am quite sure my nurse is correct, and I am quite sure that any more threats to her would constitute harassment."

There was silence. This had nothing to do with what was best for the patient. It was all about Dr. Craisson's need to control. He hung up.

"Well?" Kate asked.

"I don't think he'll bother you anymore."

"He didn't admit he'd misdiagnosed, did he?"

"I didn't mention that because I knew he wouldn't admit it. He never does."

"Do you think you wound his neck in?"

I stared at her, trying to work out what she meant.

"Got him to keep quiet?" she explained.

"Probably."

"Is he afraid of you?" She was curious.

"Not me. I think he remembered my husband's a lawyer."

"Oh. Right. Handy, that." She got up, picked up her bag, and started out the door. She turned. "Thanks. It was a distinct pleasure to listen to you."

I grinned. "I have to admit, I enjoyed it."

We heard no more from Dr. Craisson on the subject.

JANICE WAS WORRIED about the chickens. We had purchased twenty-five chicks a month earlier, and they now had the body size of a man's fist and were scurrying around the chicken coop, avoiding the big hens and Sylvester, the rooster. They were no trouble to feed as Carl had constructed a fence of chicken wire that allowed them to go under it but prevented the large birds from doing the same. We threw the chicks' food into their small pen where they were able to eat unmolested.

"What's the matter?" I asked.

"They're cold. They don't have enough feathers yet and it's chilly at night."

"What do you think they need besides the heat lamp in the coop?"

"Coats."

"Coats?" I looked at her blankly. There was a certain logic in her answer. Their feather coats had not grown sufficiently to keep them warm; therefore, they needed other coats.

I gave that some thought. After rummaging through the stored baby clothes I'd been meaning to donate, I found infant T-shirts. Most of them were white with yellow or green stripes and snaps at the shoulder.

"What do you think?" I asked as I displayed them to her.

"Perfect."

We took the tiny T-shirts to the chicken yard and proceeded to dress the chicks. They were a colourful sight. The T-shirts fitted them quite well, with their necks emerging from the neck holes and their feet from the arm holes.

"That's better," Janice said with satisfaction.

When Carl came home, he took one look at the chicks in shirts, leaned on the fender of his car, and laughed and laughed until tears ran down his cheeks. "Only at my house," he said.

"Are you implying we are all a little nuts?"

"Well . . ." He grinned.

This from the man who transported a five-hundred-pound pig in his car like a royal dignitary.

CHAPTER TWENTY-FOUR

ASSESSING
MY LIFE

ARCH WAS A COOL MONTH, with temperatures still plunging below freezing every night. There wasn't a chance of anything growing here for another month— no crocus, daffodils, or tulips. At least it was usually sunny. Driving down the highway toward Williams Lake, I appreciated the sun streaming through the windshield, giving the illusion of warmth and spring. I hoped I wouldn't have to travel on dirt tracks during the coming season of spring mud.

I was surprised to see Sally heading into the office as I pulled in.

"What are you doing here so early?" I asked her. The home care meeting was at ten, and she rarely started work before that. I had long ago accepted that she worked when the hours suited her and her patients. She never left work undone, and she often worked late or on her unpaid hours. I didn't complain.

"I haven't been to bed yet."

"Is someone sick in your house?"

She followed me into the office, shucked her parka, and headed for the staff room and coffee. I followed her.

"I was playing poker with the guys." She poured herself the first of many coffees and sat at the small table.

"Poker? What guys?" I got my own coffee and joined her. Sally had a hard-working husband and three almost-grown-up children.

She was a well-respected nurse. Playing poker all night somehow didn't fit with my vision of her. She named three businessmen.

"Don't worry. I never gamble the grocery money. I have a separate account for my gambling, and I use that. I buy stocks as well. Another gamble." She took another sip of coffee and let out a satisfied sigh.

I was quiet for a moment, absorbing this new image of Sally. "How did you make out last night?"

"Up five thousand. Down three. So I did all right."

I blinked. She'd won almost a month's wages in one night. I was curious.

"Do you usually win?"

She grinned. "Not always. Sometimes I have to stop playing for a few months until I can accumulate enough to play again."

Up five thousand and down three? That would be scary. I wouldn't have the nerve to do that, but I could see that playing for those stakes might be exhilarating. I was impressed that the three businessmen accepted her as a poker partner. Sally must have been the only woman in town to play in that league.

At ten, the other nurses arrived for our weekly planning and we went through our patient list.

"Mrs. Michelson has a bed in the assisted living home," I told them. That information had just come through from the home.

"That's fabulous," Jane said. "She'll like it there."

"Bound to be happier," Sally agreed.

"So what happens to Mrs. Barnston?" Violet asked. She was studying the chart.

"She might just acidify in her own bile," Pam said. Then, just when I was thinking that was harsh, she added, "And that would be disastrous for her."

Some people withdraw from emotional contact with others after a tragedy, but Pam seemed to be more empathetic, more bonded to her patients since her son died.

"It might be a salutary experience for her," Kate suggested. "But she's going be lonely and bad-tempered with it."

We were quiet for a moment thinking about it.

"Bound to be even unhappier," Pam agreed.

"She'll be calling us over every day," Sally prophesied.

"You know," Kate said, "I haven't a baldy notion what to do about it." The other nurses were silent. No one had a solution.

I'd been thinking about the problem since I'd got the news of the freed bed this morning. "Why don't I suggest to Social Welfare that the family hire a live-in companion? It wouldn't cost them much and, as they don't want Mrs. Barnston living with them, they'll be motivated."

"Someone who is amazingly tolerant," Pam suggested, "who won't get upset by Mrs. Barnston's nasty comments."

"Someone deaf," Sally said.

I MANAGED A BABY VISIT in the morning after the home care meeting and before the public health nurses' staff meeting. I was looking forward to this meeting. We had a new nursing supervisor, Madeleine Atley, who had her master's degree. I hoped she'd provide leadership, but the first thing she did was move her office desk so she sat behind it. That indicated she wanted distance from whomever was sitting opposite her. Most nurses put their desk against the wall so they could turn their chair and listen without a desk between them and the person consulting them. Still, she might have felt intimidated by the competency of the staff nurses. Marlene was an intelligent, efficient, and highly educated nurse. Cathy and Sophie ran their districts with impressive efficiency. Madeleine couldn't know the outlying communities yet and would have to rely on us to inform her of what was needed and what problems might be pending. The Cariboo Health Unit might be a difficult first appointment. I was happy to have someone who would take care of the paperwork and, now Paul had left us, deal with the local doctors.

She seemed polite, interested, and non-intrusive, but that's not how Sylvia saw her.

One morning Sylvia walked into my office, shut my door, and sat down.

"Marion, I don't know what to do."

"What's the matter?"

Sylvia was a little older than me, an RN with years of experience. Her husband had left her with four young kids last year. They were all in school, so that made it a little easier to manage, but it was a hard job. She'd said at coffee that she was negotiating a divorce.

"Kids giving you trouble?" I asked.

"No. Not more than usual, although there are some days when I take out the garbage I want to keep on walking, just wander away."

"They're teenagers now, I guess."

"Not quite. I'm sure worse is yet to come. No, it's not the kids. It's Madeleine."

I'd noticed Madeleine had criticized Sylvia a few times. I suspected she was trying to bring Sylvia's work up to Marlene's standards. But that wasn't fair or necessary.

"The Cariboo is Madeleine's first supervisory job," I said. "She's bound to be a bit awkward at first."

"I know. I've tried to be patient, and I know some of the things she says are right. I should do more, but, you know, I just can't right now."

"Are you getting behind? Do you need a hand?"

"No, I don't think so. Although if I do, I'll call you."

"We'll all help."

"Thanks, but she'd just see that as evidence of my incompetence—and it would be."

"Everyone has down times, Sylvia. We'll help, and we won't mention it to Madeleine."

"Thanks."

"What are you going to do?" It was bad timing for Madeleine to be leaning on Sylvia when she was worried about her personal life. That's when she needed support.

"More of the same, I guess. But I feel better for having talked to you."

I hadn't really helped her much. I needed to do more. "What do you say about coming to the ranch on Saturday night? I'll throw together some pizza and we can have a nurses' night."

She smiled. "That would be great."

It would at least let her feel that we cared about her. I thought Madeleine would make a good supervisor in time. She had vision, an idea of how she wanted the health unit to work, and she was much more practical than Paul had been. But she needed to refine her style a little.

I invited the public health nurses to the ranch for Saturday, and they all agreed.

Marlene asked me, "Did you invite Madeleine?"

If I invited Madeleine, Sylvia wouldn't come, and the whole purpose of the party was to comfort Sylvia. Sylvia had told me about her troubles with Madeleine in confidence, and I wasn't about to betray her to Marlene.

"No," I said. "This is just a staff nurse party."

"She's going to be hurt."

"I'm sorry if that happens, but this party is only for staff nurses."

"I think you should include her."

"You can set up a staff lunch and invite her to that, but she's not coming on Saturday. This is my house, my party, and I'm not going to invite her."

"I think that's hurtful." Marlene was determined to make her point.

It might be hurtful to Madeleine, but I was determined to support Sylvia. If Madeleine was hurt, she might get the point that we supported one another and she could be more generous in her approach to Sylvia. I was *not* going to invite Madeleine.

CARL TOOK THE KIDS to a movie on Saturday night, so we had the house to ourselves. The nurses arrived and seemed happy to be there. They loved my kitchen.

"You put your spices in alphabetical order?" Sophie peered into my cupboards.

"I have a lot of spices and it's easier to find them that way."

"Compulsive?" Sophie asked.

I thought about it. "Only around spices."

Marlene hadn't arrived when I served the pizza. I was upset because I really cared about her, and in supporting Sylvia I hoped I hadn't alienated Marlene. She burst in just as I lifted the last pizza out of the oven.

"I'm sorry, I'm sorry," she said, "for being late and for being such a grump." She shoved a bag into my hand. "I'm late because I was making you an apology present."

I looked into the bag and discovered a hand-sewn pot holder.

"Am I forgiven?" she asked.

I hugged her. "Absolutely."

We had a loud and wonderful time with beer and pizza. It was only after they left that I found Sophie had systematically rearranged my spice cabinet so *nothing* was in alphabetical order.

AT THE END OF MARCH, Janice started spending more time with Cleo. On this Sunday afternoon, she'd taken her books out there, arranged a heat lamp to keep her and Cleo warm, and sat in the straw, reading to her. The sow was getting extremely large. I hoped there were no more than twelve piglets in there, because that was the number of teats she had.

Janice had some advance orders for her pigs when they reached eight weeks. She kept track of who had asked her for one in her 4-H booklet. She would call all her customers a week before the piglets were ready to go and arrange for delivery.

Glen had not taken another calf for a 4-H project. We all agreed he wasn't interested. He liked the social aspect of the club but not the animal care. David was a pre-member of 4-H and just attended meetings. He was going to take one of Janice's piglets next year. He would be five in August and off to kindergarten. The children were growing and changing so quickly.

Janice wasn't happy with one of the changes.

"You know, Mom, I wish you'd never got Glen those lessons."

"Why?" Glen had made amazing progress under the speech pathologist's direction. She'd been right. She could "fix" Glen's problem. He was so fluent in speech now that he gave a puppet show at David's nursery school and managed the speech parts for all the characters. Watching him speak so easily, I had to talk to myself so I didn't cry.

"Why, Jan, what's the problem?"

"He talks all the time now."

"He has some catching up to do."

"Well, it's annoying."

"It's the nature of younger brothers to be annoying."

She raised her eyebrows.

"Sorry. That's the way he is now. You'll have to accept it."

I wondered if she missed her position of chief interpreter for Glen. She used to speak for both of them at home, and I suspected she had often been his emissary at school.

I looked around the yard. The snow had melted off the board-walk to the back door but was still piled up against the cotoneaster hedge. The bushes looked dead, with tiny dark branches inter-twined into a dense thicket, but there was hidden life there. It would start pushing out green leaves at the end of May and be full of foliage and yellow flowers by July. Summer would eventually rush in after a cold and muddy spring.

I knocked mud off my boots on the stairs, walked into the house, and shucked my coat and boots. I peeked into David's room. He was sitting on his bed with several trucks, two books, and the cat Missy beside him. He smiled at me. I sat beside him and hugged him.

"Tell me about your trucks."

He explained the elaborate scenario he was imagining that required trucks. His speech was clear now and, although he didn't talk a lot, he said what he wanted to say and everyone understood him.

I found Glen on the lower floor in the rec room. He and Carl had built a sturdy platform that held a train set. Glen had climbed up onto it and was sitting in the middle, directing traffic. His dog Ben was sitting on the floor below him, patiently waiting. The sun streamed in the big window behind him, illuminating the tracks and the tiny houses and stores he'd arranged.

"Watch this, Mom." He demonstrated a signal arm and a train running along the outside track.

"Very cool," I said.

Carl was taking a nap on the living room floor. I don't know how he could trust that no one would pounce on him, but he dropped off to sleep there without any difficulty. Dogs could walk over him, the cat could snuggle in beside him, and the kids could run by, but he slept on.

I poured myself a coffee and sat by the window, looking down the valley. I was happy with my place in life, with my husband, my children, and my work. I worried about high school for my children, but that was more than a year in the future. I thought about my own education. I still wanted a master's degree, but there wasn't a hope I could get it. I would have to go to Vancouver to attend classes, and I couldn't leave everything here to do that. I'd taken a university English course by correspondence, but I missed the seminars, the discussions over coffee, the ideas of others. A master's degree wasn't available by correspondence, in any case. Still, I wanted to learn more. Perhaps I should take a break from public health and work in the hospital for a time. That would be stimulating. I'd learn new skills, see a different aspect of nursing. There were choices here in the Cariboo for family, work, and social life. There was lots to do and much that was important. It was all one giant, complicated, satisfying, balancing act. It was enough. I was content—for now.

ACKNOWLEDGEMENTS

MANY PEOPLE HELPED ME research this book. I am grateful to Casey Bennett and Katie Edinger of the Museum of the Cariboo Chilcotin, who spent a considerable amount of time pulling up old pictures and articles that helped enormously. I am also grateful to Monica Lamb-Yorski and the staff of *The Tribune*, who pulled those heavy albums of newspapers off the shelves so I could read through them. Sage Birchwater checked my facts on an incident I reported from those days and set me straight. I am also grateful to the contributors of the Facebook group "Williams Lake and Cariboo-Chilcotin History," who posted pictures and answered my questions. Patricia Finley, who appears as a home care nurse in the book, added memories and opinions to the book. Reconnecting with her and other nurses from those times—Carol, Arlene, Maureen, and Lorraine—was heartwarming. They stimulated more memories. I enjoyed the many people in Williams Lake and area who came to celebrate my first book, *Always Pack a Candle: A Nurse in the Cariboo-Chilcotin*, and the generous hospitality of Joanne and Angela Laird of The Open Book, a marvelous bookstore in downtown Williams Lake. You all enriched my memories and this book.

READ ABOUT MARION MCKINNON
CROOK'S EARLY YEARS AS A NURSE
IN THE CARIBOO–CHILCOTIN

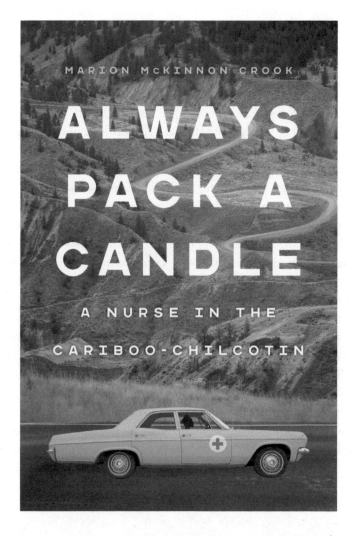

MARION McKINNON CROOK

ALWAYS
PACK A
CANDLE

A NURSE IN THE

CARIBOO-CHILCOTIN

Winner, 2021 BC Historical Federation's
Community History Book Award

Always Pack a Candle
A Nurse in the Cariboo-Chilcotin

ISBN 978-1-77203-362-5 | $26.95

The true story of an adventurous young nurse who provided much-needed health care to the rural communities of the Cariboo-Chilcotin in the 1960s.

In 1963, newly minted public health nurse Marion McKinnon arrived in the small community of Williams Lake in BC's Cariboo region. Armed with more confidence than experience, she got into her government-issued Chevy—packed with immunization supplies, baby scales, and emergency drugs—and headed out into her 9,300-square-kilometre territory, inhabited by ranchers; mill workers; and many vulnerable men, women, and children who were at risk of falling through the cracks of Canada's social welfare system.

At twenty-two, a naïve yet enthusiastic Marion relied entirely on her academic knowledge and her common sense. She doled out birth control and parenting advice to women who had far more life experience than she. She routinely dealt with condescending doctors and dismissive or openly belligerent patients. She immunized school children en masse and made home visits to impoverished communities. She drove out into the vast countryside in freezing temperatures, with only a candle, antifreeze, chains, and chocolate bars as emergency equipment.

In one year, Marion received a more rigorous education in the field than she had at university. She helped countless people, made many mistakes, learned to recognize systemic injustice, and even managed to get into a couple of romantic entanglements. *Always Pack a Candle* is an unforgettable and eye-opening memoir of one frontline worker's courage, humility, and compassion.

For more information, visit heritagehouse.ca

MARION MCKINNON CROOK is a nurse, an educator, and the author of more than fifteen books, including the bestselling *Always Pack a Candle*, which won the BC Historical Federation's Community History Book Award. In addition to her nursing degree, McKinnon Crook holds a master's in liberal studies and a PhD in education. Now a full-time writer, she lives on BC's Sunshine Coast with her dog and cat, who hate each other. For more information, visit marioncrookauthor.com.